Questions to Ask a Bulldog Breeder

When looking for a Bulldog puppy, and so you know that your puppy is off to a good start, get a healthy, well-bred, and well-adjusted pup from a reputable breeder. Chapter 4 contains information to help you find a breeder. Keep this list of questions handy when talking to breeders, to help you find the right one:

- **How long have you been breeding? Is breeding a business or a hobby for you? How often do your dogs produce a litter?** Done right, no breeder is going to be able to make a living breeding Bulldogs. If she says that breeding is a business, look for another breeder.

- **Is this breed right for me?** A good breeder wants all her puppies to go to permanent homes. Asking this question gives her a chance to ask a few of her own and to talk about the negative aspects of owning a Bulldog.

- **May I meet the parents or at least the mother of the puppies?** Any adult dog you meet should be friendly, not shy or fearful. Most breeders should be willing to grant your request.

- **Where do you raise the puppies?** Have the breeder show you the kennel area when she shows you the puppies. If the breeder brings out individual puppies and won't show you where they live, find another breeder.

- **May I see the pedigree and registration form?** If you're thinking of showing your Bully, a pedigree ensures that you are getting a purebred Bulldog.

- **Will I receive a health record?** Your breeder provides a health record with each puppy, showing what vaccinations have been given, and the dates the puppies were wormed.

- **How old are the puppies?** A puppy needs to stay with his mother and siblings until he is *at least* seven weeks old. If the breeder is selling younger puppies, find another breeder.

- **What happens if I can't keep the dog?** Most reputable breeders will take back any dog of their breeding at any time.

For Dummies: Bestselling Book Series for Beginners

Bulldogs For Dummies®

Knowing about Poisonous Household Stuff

Many common household items are poisonous to Bulldogs. You may think that your Bulldog can't reach or find these items, but check your cupboards to make sure. It's amazing what Bulldogs can get into, and what they find they tend to eat. Keep your Bulldog safe! Remember, if it's bad for you, it's bad for your dog.

Drugs and supplements

- Acetaminophen
- Amphetamine
- Antihistamines and decongestants
- Aspirin
- Iron
- Nonsteroidal Anti-Inflammatory Drugs (NSAIDs)
- Sodium phosphate enemas
- Tricyclic antidepressants
- Zinc

Food

- Chocolate and caffeine
- Grapes/Raisins
- Macadamia nuts
- Mushrooms
- Onions and garlic

For a complete list of foods to avoid and the reasoning, visit www.peteducation.com/article.cfm?cls=2&cat=1939&articleid=1030.

Household chemicals

- Acids
- Alkalis (corrosives)
- Antifreeze
- Arsenic
- Borate
- Bleach
- Batteries
- Citrus oils
- Detergents
- Ethylene glycol
- Isopropanol
- Kerosene and gasoline
- Lead
- Mercury
- Metaldehyde
- Moth balls
- Phenol and phenolic compounds
- Pine oils and cleaners
- Tobacco

Insecticides, pesticides, and rodenticides

- Amitraz
- Anticoagulants
- Borate
- Bromethalin
- Cholecalciferol or Vitamin D Rodenticides
- DEET
- Ivermectin (Avermectins)
- Organophosphates and Carbamates
- Pyrethrin
- Rodenticides
- Rotenone
- Strychnine

Plants

The list of plants is too long to show here. For a list of poisonous plants, visit www.peteducation.com/article.cfm?cls=2&cat=1684&articleid=1553.

For Dummies: Bestselling Book Series for Beginners

Bulldogs

FOR

DUMMIES®

by Susan M. Ewing

WILEY

Wiley Publishing, Inc.

Bulldogs For Dummies®

Published by
Wiley Publishing, Inc.
111 River St.
Hoboken, NJ 07030-5774
www.wiley.com

WILEY

About the Author

Susan Ewing has been "in dogs" since 1977 and enjoys showing and trying various performance events, with the emphasis on "trying."

She holds a Master's degree in Television/Radio from Syracuse University and has attended canine seminars at Cornell University. She is a member of the Dog Writers Association of America and of the Cat Writers' Association and is listed in the 2005 edition of *Who's Who in America*.

Ewing has been writing professionally since she was 16 and is the author of several books: *The Pembroke Welsh Corgi: Family Friend and Farmhand; The New Owner's Guide to Pembroke Welsh Corgis; The Pug;* and *The Dachshund*. Her column, "The Pet Pen," is in *The Post-Journal* (Jamestown, NY) every Saturday. One of her essays is a part of the book, *Cats Do It Better Than People*.

Her articles have appeared in *AKC Gazette, Family Dog, Bloodlines, German Shepherd Dog Review, Good Dog!, Pet Odyssey, Dog Fancy, Dog World, Puppies USA,* the national Schipperke Club newsletter, *ASPCA's Animal Watch,* and *Bird Talk*.

She has been a radio copywriter, owned and operated a boarding kennel, and served as the director of the Lucy-Desi Museum in Jamestown, NY.

Ewing currently lives in Mesa, Arizona, with her husband Jim and two dogs, Griffin and Rhiannon.

Dedication

For Jim, who is the "purple bead."

For my mother, Joyce Morris, and my brother, Greg Morris.

For John Monroe-Cassel. I raise a wee dram to toast minister, counselor, friend. Iechyd da.

And to the memory of Robert Morris, Gladys Taylor, and Walton Strahl.

Author's Acknowledgments

When I was young (okay, not so young) and foolish, I thought writing a book was a solo act. Now that I've written a few, I know writing is the work of an ensemble.

Special thanks to everyone at Wiley, with huge thanks to Acquisitions Editor Stacy Kennedy, Project Editor Natalie Harris, and Copy Editor Carrie Burchfield. You are all fantastic. Another huge thank you goes to Jennifer Joseph, health chair of the Bulldog Club of America, whose technical advice was invaluable.

More thanks go to Glenn and Kathy Rea, Bulldog people extraordinaire. Glenn was always available to "talk Bulldogs" and let me sift through hundreds of photographs, so I could pick my favorites for this book.

Thanks also to Lon DiSunno, Anthony Ficarotta, Dorothy Wysaski, DVM, and Christine Dresser, DVM, for their help. I'd like also like to say thank you to Amy Munion, DVM, and the staff at Pet Haven Animal Hospital.

Thanks and cyber hugs to those on the Dog Writers Association of America e-mail list for general advice, answers to specific questions, and moral support.

Thanks to all the breeders, judges, handlers, and exhibitors over the years who generously shared what they knew, all for the love of dogs.

Publisher's Acknowledgments

We're proud of this book; please send us your comments through our Dummies online registration form located at www.dummies.com/register/.

Some of the people who helped bring this book to market include the following:

Acquisitions, Editorial, and Media Development

Project Editor: Natalie Faye Harris

Acquisitions Editor: Stacy Kennedy

Copy Editors: Carrie A. Burchfield, Jennifer Bingham

Editorial Program Assistant: Courtney Allen

General Reviewer: Jennifer Joseph

Editorial Managers: Christy Beck, Michelle Hacker

Editorial Assistants: Hanna Scott, David Lutton, Nadine Bell

Cover Photo: © Terry Husebye/ Getty Images/Stone

Cartoons: Rich Tennant (www.the5thwave.com)

Composition Services

Project Coordinator: Maridee Ennis

Layout and Graphics: Andrea Dahl, Stephanie D. Jumper, Barry Offringa, Melanee Prendergast, Julie Trippetti

Proofreaders: Jessica Kramer, TECHBOOKS Production Services

Indexer: TECHBOOKS Production Services

Publishing and Editorial for Consumer Dummies

Diane Graves Steele, Vice President and Publisher, Consumer Dummies

Joyce Pepple, Acquisitions Director, Consumer Dummies

Kristin A. Cocks, Product Development Director, Consumer Dummies

Michael Spring, Vice President and Publisher, Travel

Kelly Regan, Editorial Director, Travel

Publishing for Technology Dummies

Andy Cummings, Vice President and Publisher, Dummies Technology/General User

Composition Services

Gerry Fahey, Vice President of Production Services

Debbie Stailey, Director of Composition Services

Contents at a Glance

Table of Contents

Introduction

*T*he title pretty much tells you what this book is about: Bulldogs. My instructions for writing this introduction include the phrase "what the topic is all about." That phrase reminds me of the wonderful BBC series *As Time Goes By.* One of the characters on the show wrote a book titled *My Life in Kenya,* and people constantly asked him what the book was about, to which he replied, "My life in Kenya." So the answer to what this book is about is Bulldogs.

I suppose that the next question is *how* is the book about Bulldogs. Well, you won't find a how-to manual, with step-by-step training instructions within these pages, but you get a good overview of the Bulldog — history, development, and temperament.

Why may be the next inquiry. Why write this book? That question can be summed up in one word: Roscoe. Roscoe, as a stocky red and white Bulldog puppy, captured my heart. All puppies are usually adorable, so the allure wasn't that, although Roscoe certainly was adorable. He reminded me of an animated parson's table — short, stocky, and squarely built. Roscoe didn't belong to me but to a neighbor, but he seemed to like me or at least to find me an interesting person worthy of examination.

The neighbors had an older Labrador Retriever as well as Roscoe, and he soon established the boundaries with Roscoe. The dogs stayed in their own yard with their owners with no fence. (They weren't allowed outdoors unsupervised.)

Anyway, whenever I came home from the grocery store, the minute I pulled into my garage, Roscoe would trot over, oblivious to the commands from his owner to return. Bulldogs are very single minded, and Roscoe seemed to feel that it was his duty to accompany me as I walked from the car to the house with bags of groceries —back and forth, three or four round trips, until all the groceries were inside. Roscoe never wandered off to explore the yard, and he never went home until I was finished. After the groceries were inside my house, Roscoe and I walked over to his house together. I said goodbye and went home, and Roscoe stayed where he belonged. How can you not love a dog like that?

More about why. My friend was shopping at a flea market and bought me a small book: *The Complete Bulldog: A complete book of guidance and authoritative information regarding the Bulldog,* by Walter E. Simmonds, written in 1926. The book is less than one hundred pages but seems to capture the essence of this stocky, wrinkly breed. I hope I've captured some of that same essence in this book.

About This Book

Anthony Ficarotta, a Bulldog lover, once said to me, "Anyone who knows everything is stupid." So keeping that in mind, I won't say that this book tells you *everything* you ever wanted to know about Bulldogs, but I think that it comes very, very close. I tell you about personality and temperament, about history and health. I give you suggestions about finding a Bulldog to join your family and ways to train and feed your Bulldog. I describe ways to keep your Bulldog safe and happy.

If you're thinking about getting a Bulldog, this book helps you choose a puppy, and if you already have a Bulldog, *Bulldogs For Dummies* helps you and your pet live happily ever after.

Conventions Used in This Book

In terms of conventional usage, nothing too unusual stands out. Organizations that are commonly abbreviated are also spelled out the first time I use them.

I use *italics* for emphasis and for key terms.

Boldfaced words highlight the key words in bulleted lists.

`Monofont` is used for Web addresses.

Another point about Web addresses: When this book was printed, some Web addresses may have extended to two lines of text. If that's the case, no extra characters were added (such as a hyphen or spaces) to indicate the break. So if you use one of these addresses, just type the address exactly as you see it in the book, pretending that the line break doesn't exist.

What You're Not to Read

I hope you read every single word in this book, but it's not absolutely necessary. You can get lots of basic information and never read any text preceded by the Technical Stuff icon. Some of the Technical Stuff isn't that technical, and some of it is interesting, but none of it is a must. Sidebars are another part of the book you don't have to read. Sidebars aren't critical to the text. They contain bits of trivia and other nonessential text. They may also contain odd scraps of information that I've discovered after 30 years with dogs. I think that a lot of good reading resides in the sidebars, but you can skip them and not miss anything essential to your Bully's welfare. Sometimes you may even want to skip complete chapters that aren't relevant to you.

Foolish Assumptions

Making assumptions is almost always foolish, and I haven't made many except to assume that you, the reader, are interested in Bulldogs. You may have your first puppy, or you may have had Bulldogs for years. You may not even have a Bulldog yet but are reading this book to discover all you can before you bring home your first Bully puppy.

I have not assumed much, but I have pretended a lot. When writing about how to choose a puppy, I've pretended that you don't have one and have never gone through the selection process. Later, I pretend that you have small children. I pretend that you have other pets and that you don't have a veterinarian yet. Even in non-fiction, I can use make-believe.

For my final assumption, I am going to assume that by pretending, I've covered the topic of Bulldogs thoroughly for you.

How This Book Is Organized

Bulldogs For Dummies has five parts, and each stands alone, so you can quickly find the section that interests you right now. You don't have to read this book in order. Within each part, chapters deal with different aspects of that "part."

Part 1: A Bully for You

In this part, I discuss the Bulldog breed and how it developed over the years. I describe the original function of the Bully and what Bulldogs are like today. I also compare the different origins of the breed, from the English Bulldog (the one covered in this book) to the French and American Bulldogs. You also find the standard for the breed. Then I talk about getting a puppy versus an older dog and where to find the Bully of your dreams: a breeder, a pet store, or a rescue organization.

Part II: Living with Your Bulldog

Before you bring your puppy home, do some shopping. Nothing is more fun than picking out those special food and water dishes, the perfect bed, the collar, and the lead. I give you suggestions to help you with your selections and also information on introducing your puppy to your home, family, and other pets. I also provide both indoor and outdoor safety tips for your pup.

One chapter is strictly about food, and if your Bully spoke, he'd tell you to start with that chapter. Dog food has come a long way from the days when dogs were fed table scraps. The food chapter may help you decide on the best nutrition for your dog.

Another chapter deals with grooming information. You may think that grooming isn't needed with your short-haired Bully, and coat care is minimal, but those lovely Bulldog wrinkles need attention, as well as nails, ears, and tail.

Part III: Training, Working, and Traveling: The Busy Bulldog

Bulldogs are pretty mellow dogs, but even the calmest dog still needs training. In this chapter, you find information on housetraining your Bulldog, including crate training, paper training, and litter training. Then I go over the basics like walking on a lead, sitting, and staying. If you want to do additional training, you can read about showing your dog, competing in obedience or agility, or visiting hospitals and schools with your Bully. You may read the advice on how to enjoy travel with your dog and what to do if the unthinkable happens and your dog is lost.

Part IV: Keeping Your Bulldog Healthy

This part deals with the best ways to give your Bulldog a long and healthy life. I provide pointers on choosing a veterinarian and discuss various vaccinations and common diseases. You can also find information on acupuncture, holistic medicine, homeopathic care, and chiropractic care.

Common Bulldog health problems are covered in this part, and a chapter on first aid for dogs may be helpful for you too.

Finally, a special-care chapter for your older Bulldog is included. Your Bully may need a little more TLC as he ages. You may need a box of tissues.

Part V: The Part of Tens

This part is included in every *For Dummies* book, and this section is the part that I always read first. Bulldog resources, ten reasons not to breed your Bully, and ten of the most important things to do for your dog are right at your fingertips.

Icons Used in This Book

Icons are the cute little graphics you find in the left margin. When a paragraph has something special to say, the icons alert you to the paragraph. Icons indicate special tips, potentially dangerous items or information for your Bulldog, items to remember, and technical information.

This little icon lets you know that a shortcut or an easier or better way to do something may exist.

Just what it says. These paragraphs are bits of information to remember to help keep your Bully happy and healthy.

If you don't read anything else, read these warnings! This icon alerts you to potential threats to your dog's health and safety.

You can skip these sections if you want to. Technical stuff can be very interesting, but you don't need to know it to raise, and live with, your Bulldog successfully.

Where to Go from Here

Remember the joke about the two-ton gorilla? The question is "Where does a two-ton gorilla sleep?", and the answer is "Anywhere he wants!" Reading this book is like that. Where do you go from here? Anywhere you want to! That's the beauty of the parts of a *For Dummies* book: You don't need to start with Part 1, Chapter 1, and go straight through to the end. You can read that way, of course, but you can also skip around. If you're trying to decide whether a Bulldog is the right dog for you, start with Chapters 1, 2, and 3. If you already have your puppy and need information on housetraining, turn to Chapter 9. If you're concerned about health issues, read Chapters 13 and 14. Want to read the official American Kennel Club (AKC) standard? Start with Chapter 2. More interested in what and how to feed your Bully? Read Chapter 7.

Or if you're like me, look at all the pictures first and then read all the cartoons!

Wherever you start, you're going to start appreciating the wonderful Bulldog in all his wrinkly glory. I enjoyed writing the book; I hope you enjoy reading it.

Part I
A Bully for You

The 5th Wave   By Rich Tennant

In this part . . .

What makes the Bulldog the way he is? What don't you know about the breed that you would like to know? Is a Bulldog right for you? In this part, I ask you to consider your lifestyle and help you determine whether the Bulldog is the breed for you. Discover the Bulldog's history and read about his physical build and temperament. If you decide that it's a Bully and nothing else for you and your family, I give you ideas on where to find your puppy and how to choose the one who's right for you.

Chapter 1

Bulldog: A Tough Name for a Big Softy

* *

In This Chapter

▶ Getting to know your Bulldog

▶ Caring for and feeding your Bulldog

▶ Being active with your Bulldog

* *

*J*ust the name "Bulldog" conjures up an image of a real tough guy, and when you put a picture of the dog with the name, you get an image of a real tough dog. Bulldogs are stocky, sturdy dogs with a solid, foursquare stance and a face that says, "Bring it on; I can take it." All those wrinkles and that pushed-in nose give an impression of gruffness and a ready-to-fight attitude. No wonder the Bulldog is the mascot of the United States Marines!

The English Bulldog was unofficially adopted as the Marine Corps mascot during World War I, when the German army reportedly nicknamed the attacking Marines *Teufelhunden,* meaning "Devil Dogs."

Yet in spite of that face and sturdy body, today's Bulldog is a sweetie — a real softie with no hard feelings toward anyone.

Transitioning from the Bull Baiter to Loving Companion

Bulldogs weren't always big softies. Originally, the Bulldog was bred for the sport of bull-baiting in England. The fanciers of the sport molded a Bulldog to perform specifically for bull-baiting.

The Bulldog who fought a bull in the ring needed to be a certain build and to have fighting qualities. Breeders worked diligently to mold the fighter that became the bull baiter. The fanciers wanted a dog built low to the ground to make it harder for the bull to get his horns underneath the dog. If the bull lifted the Bulldog on his horns, the dog would be thrown across the stadium.

Plus the dog needed to be sturdy and well muscled to withstand the occasional toss. Many early Bulldogs were smaller and lighter than the Bullies of today. The nose needed to be set back from the front of the muzzle and needed to turn up, so that when the dog had a good grip on the bull's nose, the dog's nose wouldn't be buried in the bull's face. The dog would be able to breathe without ever letting go of the bull. The Bulldog's distinctive wrinkles were a sought-after feature because they channeled the bull's blood away from the dog's eyes and nose.

The breeders also wanted a dog who was determined and wouldn't quit. In bull-baiting, people placed bets on how long the dog would face the bull. Horrible stories circulated about handlers who maimed their dogs to show that the dogs, even on two or three legs, would keep going after the bull.

When bull-baiting was finally outlawed, the Bulldog's future looked grim. But fortunately, many people admired the Bulldog's temperament, and breeders set out to preserve and perfect the Bulldog by breeding out any viciousness but keeping the tenacious side of the dog's personality.

The result is today's Bulldog — fierce looking on the outside and a marshmallow on the inside. (See Figure 1-1.) But remember that your Bully's marshmallow interior can turn to granite if you ask him to do something he doesn't want to do. A Bulldog has retained his spirit of determination and steadfastness. You can't argue with a Bulldog. Read more about the transition of the Bulldog and bull-baiting in Chapter 2.

Figure 1-1: Recognizing the features of a typical adult Bulldog.

Getting to Know the Bulldog

The Bulldog is a member of the American Kennel Club's (AKC) Non-Sporting Group (see Chapter 2). The non-sporting group mostly includes dogs who may have had a specific job once upon a time but who are now considered great companion dogs. When you think about the Bully's role, that's not such a bad job description. Being a friend may be the most important job a dog can have.

So your Bully is a companion. Although plenty of Bulldogs compete in performance events (see Chapter 11), just as many are content to be low-maintenance buddies. Bullies are good with children and enjoy a walk with the family or a game of tag or hide-and-seek. They're not enthusiastic about playing fetch, but they certainly don't mind watching you get the ball.

Be aware of the fact that your Bulldog can't be your jogging companion. He isn't built for that, and his breathing (see Chapter 14) doesn't allow for wind sprints. The Bulldog is also highly susceptible to heat stroke, so beware of hot summer days.

Why non-sporting?

The Bulldog is too large for the toy group, and he definitely isn't a terrier — he'd never fit down the burrow of any small animal. The Bully isn't a sight or scent hound and doesn't have the endurance for chasing game, even if he wanted to. The Bulldog doesn't herd sheep or cattle, so that eliminates the herding group. He's not a sporting dog. He doesn't flush or point birds, and he can never retrieve a duck from a pond. He doesn't fill the bill as a dog to pull a cart or guard a flock or help fight crime as a policeman's pal. The non-sporting group categorizes all dogs that don't fit in any other class.

You can't force a Bulldog to do anything. He's bred to be single-minded and unyielding to rough handling. Also, fighting with your Bully can aggravate breathing problems, if they exist, and can lead to a serious emergency. Coax your Bully with kind words and tasty treats.

Caring for and Feeding Your Bulldog

A Bulldog isn't high maintenance, but she does need more care than you may think. The Bully doesn't have a lot of thick, fluffy undercoat to worry about, but Bulldogs do need care (see Chapter 8). Pay attention to particular parts of your Bully's body:

- ✔ **Hair:** Those tiny, short hairs shed, but the coat isn't the biggest concern with Bulldogs.

- ✔ **Wrinkles:** Wrinkles are the biggest issue concerning the Bulldog. Make sure your daily routine includes cleaning the wrinkles and drying them thoroughly to prevent rash, infection, or other skin problems.

- ✔ **Skin:** Bulldogs are prone to skin ailments and allergies. Check for hot spots and bald patches (see Chapter 14 for more information on Bully ailments).

- ✔ **Feet:** Trim your Bully's foot fur, and check between those toes for any sign of interdigital cysts. *Interdigital cysts* are pus-filled growths between the toes and are frequently caused by ingrown hairs. Check out Chapter 14 for information on dealing with these cysts.

✔ **Ears:** Keep the ears clean and dry.

✔ **Tail:** Don't forget your dog's tail. The base of some Bulldog tails fits into a sort of pocket of flesh, and that needs to be kept as clean and dry as the wrinkles. A dab of petroleum jelly in the pocket helps prevent irritation.

Bulldog care includes other functions, besides keeping the body groomed, that you need to perform to ensure a healthy pet:

✔ **Regularly visit your veterinarian.** Keep your vaccinations up to date, and consult your veterinarian if your dog is sick. Even if the sickness turns out to be something minor, it's always better to be safe than sorry. (See Chapter 13 for more on your vet.)

✔ **Make sure that your dog has identification.** Attach her license and rabies tags to a buckle collar. You may also want to include a tag with your name and phone number. Consider getting your Bully microchipped as another form of ID. (See Chapter 5 for more information on identifying your Bully.)

✔ **Watch what you feed your Bulldog.** Control her weight, and don't let her get too heavy. An overweight dog has even more trouble breathing and may develop hip problems and arthritis. Extra weight puts extra stress on her heart and lungs, too. Extra pounds can aggravate any existing problems and may cause others (see Chapter 7).

No matter what you feed your Bulldog, keep her fit and trim and healthy.

Keeping a Bulldog healthy can cost more than other dogs' health care. Surgery can be expensive because of certain procedures that are protocol for the Bulldog. Bullies may have small tracheas and elongated palates. When your dog has any kind of surgery, she may be in danger during the recovery period. At that time, she isn't fully awake, and the soft palate can fall over the opening of the trachea, cutting off the air supply. You pay extra for someone to sit with your dog, making sure that she can breathe.

Figure out your budget. Make sure that you can afford a Bulldog. The purchase price of the dog is just the beginning. Even if you don't include crates, beds, toys, baby gates, and fencing for the yard, you still have to buy food and pay for regular trips to the veterinarian, corrective surgeries, and emergencies.

Know that your Bulldog comes with a price tag. Don't be scared off by the costs; one dog costs a family roughly $6,000 over the lifetime of the dog.

Showing Your Bulldog

No matter what you do together, remember that your Bully is a member of your family for life. The love and companionship make owning a Bully worth your time and money. Your Bulldog may be your child's best friend, your special cuddle buddy, or the family trophy winner — or even all three!

If you decide that you want to experience the excitement of showing your dog, you can choose among some of the following activities:

- ✔ **Conformation:** You may want to show your dog in *conformation,* which some people describe as a beauty contest for dogs. The Westminster Kennel Club Dog Show is an example of a conformation show.

- ✔ **Obedience:** You can try obedience. In *obedience,* at the basic level, your dog is judged on how well he walks by your side (heels), sits, downs, and comes when called. At advanced levels, your dog must also retrieve and jump high and broad jumps.

 No matter what you decide to try with your dog, teach him some basic commands. Even if you never go beyond Sit, Down, and Stay, these commands can help make daily living more enjoyable. Chapter 10 tells you how to train and work with your Bulldog to help him become a perfect gentleman.

- ✔ **Rally:** The relatively new sport of rally may attract you. *Rally* judges the same behaviors as obedience, but in rally (see Chapter 11) you perform the behavior posted on each sign on the course, not the commands of a judge.

- ✔ **Agility:** If your Bully is athletic, agility may be just the activity you're looking for. An *agility* course consists of several jumps, a teeter-totter, a tunnel, an elevated dog walk, and an A-frame, and your dog must run the course in a specific amount of time.

- ✔ **Tracking:** Last, you can compete in *tracking* — it's just what it sounds like. Your dog follows a track with a specified number of turns and must find one or more specific articles on the track.

For more information on showing your Bully, see Chapters 2 and 11.

Chapter 2

Acquainting Yourself with the Bulldog Package

In This Chapter

▶ Knowing the origins of the Bulldog

▶ Seeing past the ugly mug — the picture of a Bulldog

▶ Looking at the American and French Bulldogs

▶ Showing Bulldogs

So you want to know a little more about Bulldogs? I'm glad you asked, because the Bully is an incredibly interesting dog, with an interesting history to match. In this chapter, I go over that history.

You may not realize that several different Bulldog breeds are available, which is a bit confusing for some people looking for their first Bulldog (see Figure 2-1). The Bulldog that is the subject of this book was once called the English Bulldog, and some people still refer to the Bulldog as the English Bulldog, even though the American Kennel Club (AKC) dropped the "English" part of the name over 80 years ago. The United Kennel Club (UKC) refers to the breed as the English Bulldog. A breed called the Olde English Bulldogge also exists. This breed is not the same as the Bulldog or as the UKC's English Bulldog. For purposes of recognition, when the Bulldog is referenced (without other origins) in this chapter, it is the English Bulldog. In this chapter, I acquaint you with the breed standards for the dog so you'll know one when you see one. I also give you a little information about showing your Bully. And finally, I give you a little more information on the French Bulldog and the American Bulldog, which you can also see in Figure 2-1.

Figure 2-1: Three different Bulldog breeds: Bulldog (A), French Bulldog (B), and American Bulldog (C).

Bull-Baiting to Bulldog Hugging

The origins of the Bulldog are vague. One source suggests that the Bulldog developed from a cross of three different breeds: the Pug, the Mastiff, and a breed of Spanish dog. Pugs were probably used, along with other breeds, to set the current Bulldog type after bull-baiting was banned. The screw-shaped tail of today's Bulldog probably came from the Pug.

What is known is that the butchers in the old days used dogs to manage the herds of cattle and to chase and worry specific animals before they were butchered. Besides being considered entertainment, bull-baiting before an animal was butchered was thought to make the meat more tender. A BBC radio report stated, "There was a widespread mistaken belief that torturing the bull before slaughtering it would make the meat tender. Butchers were sometimes required to have a bull baited before killing it. A refusal to do so could lead to the butcher being fined."

The sport of bull-baiting was brutal and cruel to both the bull and the dogs. But by the time the practice of bull-baiting was outlawed, it had produced a dog of such courage and determination that some people didn't want to see it disappear. For details on how breeders created Bulldogs to be perfect bull baiters, see Chapter 1.

In fact, the British thought so highly of the dog's personality that the dog has become the symbol of Britain. In 1875, the Bulldog Club was incorporated in England to promote and protect the breed, and the Bulldog Club of America was founded in 1890 and incorporated in 1904 for the same purpose.

Breeders worked to eliminate the ferocious side of the Bulldog's temperament while keeping his looks and his determination.

Picturing the Bulldog

The English Bulldog, also just called the Bulldog, is a heavy, low-built dog with lots of wrinkles on his face; a short, pushed-in nose; a gentle temperament; and plenty of determination.

Figure 2-2 shows the basic anatomy of a Bulldog, giving an idea of a Bulldog's proportions. Figure 2-3 shows how the Bulldog should appear from the front and back, and Figure 2-4 shows how the Bulldog shows the distinctive pear shape, easily seen from above.

Beyond the general appearance of the Bulldog, formal standards exist for the purpose of preserving the Bulldog breed. These standards, known as *breed standards,* serve as a blueprint for what features and characteristics the ideal dog should have.

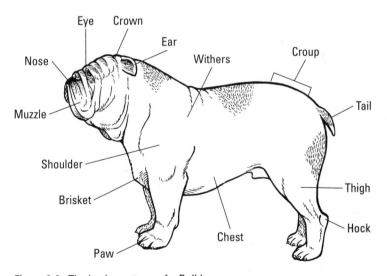

Figure 2-2: The basic anatomy of a Bulldog.

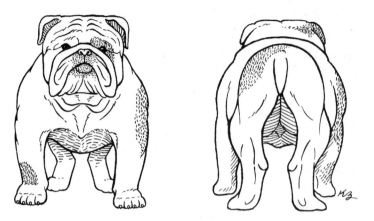

Figure 2-3: How the Bulldog should appear from the front and back.

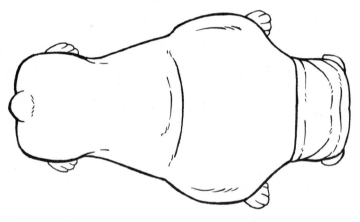

Figure 2-4: How the Bulldog shows the distinctive pear shape, easily seen from above.

These standards are promoted through breed and kennel clubs for the maintenance and welfare of the Bulldog breed. Three organizations oversee breed standards for the Bulldog: the American Kennel Club (AKC), the Kennel Club (UK), and the United Kennel Club (UKC). In the following sections, I go over the specific details of the Bulldog standard used by each group.

If a Bulldog breed club exists in your area, this group can also be an excellent source for information on Bulldogs, showers, and breeders.

Perusing the pedigree

A dog's *pedigree* is a family tree, telling you who his mother, father, grandmother, grandfather, and the rest of his ancestors were. Get a three-generation pedigree when you get your puppy.

The dogs listed on the top half of the pedigree are your puppy's father, grandfather, and great-grandfather. The dogs listed on the bottom half are the mother, grandmother, and great-grandmother. The pedigree also tells you which dogs are champions, indicated by the *ch* in front of their names. If a dog earned performance titles, he will be listed with initials after his name. An example is CD, which stands for Companion Dog. See Chapter 11 for the various championship titles.

Some pedigrees tell you what color each dog is. The pedigree may also note whether a dog is DNA tested. Many breeders submit proof of their dog's DNA to the AKC as a form of identification.

AKC Bulldog breed standard

Founded in 1884, the AKC is one of the nation's leading not-for-profit organizations devoted to the study, breeding, exhibiting, and advancement of purebred dogs. The AKC operates the world's largest purebred-dog registry and is a strong advocate and supporter of purebred dogs, responsible dog ownership, and canine health. The AKC advances the integrity of breeding and sport of purebred dogs.

The AKC's mission also includes

- ✔ Maintaining a registry for purebred dogs and preserving its integrity

- ✔ Sanctioning dog events that promote interest in breeding for type and function of purebred dogs and sustaining this process

- ✔ Taking necessary actions to protect and continue the sport of purebred dogs

In its operations, the AKC focuses on serving "The Fancy — the dedicated breeders, exhibitors, judges, handlers, and other participants and enthusiasts who make the sport of purebred dogs so rewarding and enjoyable." Visit the AKC at www.akc.org.

General appearance

The perfect Bulldog must be of medium size and smooth coat with heavy, thick-set, low-swung body, massive short-faced head, wide shoulders, and sturdy limbs.

The general appearance and attitude should suggest great stability, vigor, and strength.

The disposition should be equable and kind, resolute and courageous (not vicious or aggressive), and demeanor should be pacific and dignified. These attributes should be countenanced by the expression and behavior.

Size, proportion, symmetry

- ✔ **Size:** The size for mature dogs is about 50 pounds; for mature bitches, about 40 pounds.

- ✔ **Proportion:** The circumference of the skull in front of the ears should measure at least the height of the dog at the shoulders.

- ✔ **Symmetry:** The points should be well distributed and bear good relation one to the other, no feature being in such prominence from either excess or lack of quality that the animal appears deformed or ill-proportioned.

- ✔ **Influence of sex:** In comparison of specimens of different sex, due allowance should be made in favor of the bitches, which do not bear the characteristics of the breed to the same degree of perfection and grandeur as do the dogs.

Head

- ✔ **Eyes and eyelids:** The eyes, seen from the front, should be situated low down in the skull, as far from the ears as possible, and their corners should be in a straight line at right angles with the stop. They should be quite in front of the head, as wide apart as possible, provided their outer corners are within the outline of the cheeks when viewed from the front. They should be quite round in form, of moderate size, neither sunken nor bulging, and in color should be very dark. The lids should cover the white of the eyeball, when the dog is looking directly forward, and the lid should show no haw.

- ✔ **Ears:** The ears should be set high in the head, the front inner edge of each ear joining the outline of the skull at the top back corner of skull, so as to place them as wide apart, and as high, and as far from the eyes as possible. In size they should be small and thin. The shape termed "rose ear" is the most desirable. The rose ear folds inward at its back lower edge, the upper front edge curving over, outward and backward, showing part of the inside of the burr. (The ears should not be carried erect or prick-eared or buttoned and should never be cropped.)

✔ **Skull:** The skull should be very large, and in circumference, in front of the ears, should measure at least the height of the dog at the shoulders. Viewed from the front, it should appear very high from the corner of the lower jaw to the apex of the skull and also very broad and square. Viewed at the side, the head should appear very high and very short from the point of the nose to occiput. The forehead should be flat (not rounded or domed), neither too prominent nor overhanging the face.

✔ **Cheeks:** The cheeks should be well rounded, protruding sideways and outward beyond the eyes.

✔ **Stop:** The temples or frontal bones should be very well defined, broad, square and high, causing a hollow or groove between the eyes. This indentation, or stop, should be both broad and deep and extend up the middle of the forehead, dividing the head vertically, being traceable to the top of the skull.

✔ **Face and muzzle:** The face, measured from the front of the cheekbone to the tip of the nose, should be extremely short, the muzzle being very short, broad, turned upward and very deep from the corner of the eye to the corner of the mouth.

✔ **Nose:** The nose should be large, broad and black, its tip set back deeply between the eyes. The distance from bottom of stop, between the eyes, to the tip of nose should be as short as possible and not exceed the length from the tip of nose to the edge of underlip. The nostrils should be wide, large and black, with a well-defined line between them. Any nose other than black is objectionable and a brown or liver-colored nose shall disqualify.

✔ **Lips:** The chops or "flews" should be thick, broad, pendant and very deep, completely overhanging the lower jaw at each side. They join the underlip in front and almost or quite cover the teeth, which should be scarcely noticeable when the mouth is closed.

✔ **Bite/jaws:** The jaws should be massive, very broad, square and undershot, the lower jaw projecting considerably in front of the upper jaw and turning up.

✔ **Teeth:** The teeth should be large and strong, with the canine teeth or tusks wide apart, and the six small teeth in front, between the canines, in an even, level row.

Neck, topline, and body

✓ **Neck:** The neck should be short, very thick, deep and strong and well arched at the back.

✓ **Topline:** There should be a slight fall in the back, close behind the shoulders (its lowest part), whence the spine should rise to the loins (the top of which should be higher than the top of the shoulders), thence curving again more suddenly to the tail, forming an arch (a very distinctive feature of the breed), termed "roach back" or, more correctly, "wheel-back."

✓ **Body:** The brisket and body should be very capacious, with full sides, well-rounded ribs and very deep from the shoulders down to its lowest part, where it joins the chest. It should be well let down between the shoulders and forelegs, giving the dog a broad, low, short-legged appearance.

✓ **Chest:** The chest should be very broad, deep and full.

✓ **Underline:** The body should be well ribbed up behind with the belly tucked up and not rotund.

✓ **Back and loin:** The back should be short and strong, very broad at the shoulders and comparatively narrow at the loins.

✓ **Tail:** The tail may be either straight or screwed (but never curved or curly), and in any case must be short, hung low, with decided downward carriage, thick root and fine tip. If straight, the tail should be cylindrical and of uniform taper. If screwed, the bends or kinks should be well defined, and they may be abrupt and even knotty, but no portion of the member should be elevated above the base or root.

Forequarters

✓ **Shoulders:** The shoulders should be muscular, very heavy, widespread and slanting outward, giving stability and great power.

✓ **Forelegs:** The forelegs should be short, very stout, straight and muscular, set wide apart, with well-developed calves, presenting a bowed outline, but the bones of the legs should not be curved or bandy, nor the feet brought too close together.

✓ **Elbows:** The elbows should be low and stand well out and loose from the body.

✓ **Feet:** The feet should be moderate in size, compact and firmly set. Toes compact, well split up, with high knuckles and very short stubby nails. The front feet may be straight or slightly out-turned.

Hindquarters

- ✔ **Legs:** The hind legs should be strong and muscular and longer than the forelegs, so as to elevate the loins above the shoulders. Hocks should be slightly bent and well let down, so as to give length and strength from the loins to hock. The lower leg should be short, straight and strong, with the stifles turned slightly outward and away from the body. The hocks are thereby made to approach each other, and the hind feet to turn outward.

- ✔ **Feet:** The feet should be moderate in size, compact and firmly set. Toes compact, well split up, with high knuckles and short stubby nails. The hind feet should be pointed well outward.

Coat and skin

- ✔ **Coat:** The coat should be straight, short, flat, close, of fine texture, smooth and glossy. (No fringe, feather, or curl.)

- ✔ **Skin:** The skin should be soft and loose, especially at the head, neck and shoulders.

- ✔ **Wrinkles and dewlap:** The head and face should be covered with heavy wrinkles, and at the throat, from jaw to chest, there should be two loose pendulous folds, forming the dewlap.

Color of coat

- ✔ The color of coat should be uniform, pure of its kind and brilliant.

- ✔ The various colors found in the breed are to be preferred in the following order:

   1. Red brindle

   2. All other brindles

   3. Solid white

   4. Solid red, fawn or fallow

   5. Piebald

   6. Inferior qualities of all the foregoing

- ✔ Note: A perfect piebald is preferable to a muddy brindle or defective solid color. Solid black is very undesirable, but not so objectionable if occurring to a moderate degree in piebald patches. The brindles to be perfect should have a fine, even, and equal distribution of the composite colors. In brindles and solid colors a small white patch on the chest is not considered detrimental. In piebalds the color patches should be well defined, of pure color, and symmetrically distributed.

Gait

- ✔ The style and carriage are peculiar, his gait being a loose-jointed, shuffling, sidewise motion, giving the characteristic roll.

- ✔ The action must, however, be unrestrained, free, and vigorous.

Temperament

- ✔ The disposition should be equable and kind, resolute and courageous (not vicious or aggressive), and demeanor should be pacific and dignified.

- ✔ These attributes should be countenanced by the expression and behavior.

UK Bulldog breed standard

The UK is committed to developing and supporting a nation of responsible dog owners. As well as organizing events and campaigns to help dog owners meet their responsibilities, the UK produces a range of literature to assist dog owners. Visit www.the-kennel-club.org.uk for more information.

The UK breed standards are drawn up through consultation between breed clubs and breed councils and the UK's Breed Standards and Stud Book Subcommittee. The standards below provide a picture in words of the ideal Bulldog.

General appearance

- ✔ Smooth-coated, thick set, rather low in stature, broad, powerful, and compact.

- ✔ Head, fairly large in proportion to size but no point so much in excess of others as to destroy the general symmetry, or make the dog appear deformed, or interfere with its powers of motion.

- ✔ Face short, muzzle broad, blunt, and inclined upwards.

- ✔ Dogs showing respiratory distress highly undesirable.

- ✔ Body short, well knit, limbs stout, well muscled, and in hard condition with no tendency toward obesity.

- ✔ Hindquarters high and strong but somewhat lighter in comparison with heavy foreparts.

- ✔ Bitches not so grand or well developed as dogs.

Characteristics

✔ Conveys impression of determination, strength, and activity.

Temperament

✔ Alert, bold, loyal, dependable, courageous.

✔ Fierce in appearance, but possessed of affectionate nature.

Head and skull

✔ Skull large in circumference. Viewed from front appears very high from corner of lower jaw to apex of skull; also very broad and square.

✔ Cheeks well rounded and extended sideways beyond eyes. Viewed from side, head appears very high and short from back to point of nose.

✔ Forehead flat with skin upon and about head, loose and wrinkled, neither prominent nor overhanging face. Projections of frontal bones prominent, broad, square and high; deep, wide indentation between eyes.

✔ From stop, a furrow, both broad and deep extending to middle of skull being traceable to apex.

✔ Face from front of cheek bone to nose, short, skin wrinkled.

✔ Muzzle short, broad, turned upwards and very deep from corner of eye to corner of mouth.

✔ Nose and nostrils large, broad and black, under no circumstances liver colour, red or brown; top set back toward eyes. Distance from inner corner of eye (or from centre of stop between eyes) to extreme tip of nose not exceeding length from tip of nose to edge of underlip. Nostrils large wide and open, with well defined vertical straight line between.

✔ Flews (chops) thick, broad, pendant and very deep, hanging completely over lower jaws at sides, not in front, joining underlip in front and quite covering teeth.

✔ Jaws broad, massive and square, lower jaw projecting in front of upper and turning up. Nose roll must not interfere with the line of layback. Viewed from front, the various properties of the face must be equally balanced on either side of an imaginary line down centre.

Eyes

✔ Seen from front, situated low down in skull, well away from ears.

✔ Eyes and stop in same straight line, at right angles to furrow. Wide apart, but outer corners within the outline of cheeks. Round in shape, of moderate size, neither sunken nor prominent, in colour very dark — almost black — showing no white when looking directly forward.

✔ Free from obvious eye problems.

Ears

✔ Set high — for example, the front edge of each ear (as viewed from front) joins outline of skull at top corner of such outline, so as to place them as wide apart, as high and as far from eyes as possible.

✔ Small and thin.

✔ Rose ear correct, for example, folding inwards back, upper or front inner edge curving outwards and backwards, showing part of inside of burr.

Mouth

✔ Jaws broad and square with six small front teeth between canines in an even row.

✔ Canines wide apart.

✔ Teeth large and strong, not seen when mouth closed. When viewed from front under jaw directly under upper jaw and parallel.

Neck

✔ Moderate in length, very thick, deep and strong.

✔ Well arched at back, with much loose, thick and wrinkled skin about throat, forming dewlap on each side, from lower jaw to chest.

Forequarters

✔ Shoulders broad, sloping and deep, very powerful and muscular giving appearance of being "tacked on" body.

✔ Brisket capacious, round and very deep from top of shoulders to lowest part where it joins chest. Well let down between forelegs. Large in diameter, round behind forelegs (not flat-sided, ribs well rounded).

✔ Forelegs very stout and strong, well developed, set wide apart, thick, muscular and straight, presenting rather bowed outline, but bones of legs large and straight, not bandy nor curved and short in proportion to hindlegs, but not so short as to make back appear long, or detract from dog's activity and so cripple him.

✔ Elbows low and standing well away from ribs. Pasterns short, straight and strong.

Body

✔ Chest wide, laterally round, prominent and deep.

✔ Back short, strong, broad at shoulders, comparatively narrower at loins. Slight fall to back close behind shoulders (lowest part) whence spine should rise to loins (top higher than top of shoulder), curving again more suddenly to tail, forming arch (termed roach back) — a distinctive characteristic of breed.

✔ Body well ribbed up behind with belly tucked up and not pendulous.

Hindquarters

✔ Legs large and muscular, longer in proportion than forelegs, so as to elevate loins.

✔ Hocks slightly bent, well let down; legs long and muscular from loins to hock; short, straight, strong lower part.

✔ Stifles round and turned slightly outwards away from body.

✔ Hocks thereby made to approach each other and hind feet to turn outwards.

Feet

✔ Fore, straight, and turning very slightly outward; of medium size and moderately round.

✔ Hind, round, and compact.

✔ Toes compact and thick, well split up, making knuckles prominent and high.

Tail

- ✔ Set on low, jutting out rather straight and then turning downwards.

- ✔ Round, smooth and devoid of fringe or coarse hair.

- ✔ Moderate in length — rather short than long — thick at root, tapering quickly to a fine point.

- ✔ Downward carriage (not having a decided upward curve at end) and never carried above back.

Gait/movement

- ✔ Peculiarly heavy and constrained, appearing to walk with short, quick steps on tips of toes, hind feet not lifted high, appearing to skim ground, running with one or other shoulder rather advanced.

- ✔ Soundness of movement of the utmost importance.

Coat

- ✔ Fine texture, short, close and smooth (hard only from shortness and closeness, not wiry).

Colour

- ✔ Whole or smut (i.e. whole colour with black mask or muzzle).

- ✔ Only whole colours (which should be brilliant and pure of their sort) viz., brindles, reds with their various shades, fawns, fallows etc., white and pied (i.e. combination of white with any of the foregoing colours).

- ✔ Dudley, black and black with tan highly undesirable.

Size

- ✔ Dogs: 25 kgs (55 lbs)
- ✔ Bitches: 23 kgs (50 lbs)

Faults

Any departure from the foregoing points should be considered a fault and the seriousness with which the fault should be regarded should be in exact proportion to its degree and its effect upon the health and welfare of the dog.

Note

Male animals should have two apparently normal testicles fully descended into the scrotum.

UKC Bulldog breed standard

With 250,000 registrations annually, the UKC is the second oldest and second largest all-breed dog registry in the United States. The UKC was founded in 1898 by Chauncey Z. Bennett, who wanted an emphasis on the total dog, meaning a dog that looks and performs equally well. Bennett encouraged breeders to breed for intelligence and working ability as well as good conformation. The UKC was conceived for the purpose of emphasizing each breed's individual working qualities and ensuring that those qualities continue to be linked with the breed's characteristic appearance.

The UKC recognized the English Bulldog in 1935. The Bulldog, as preferred by the UKC, is a shorter, squattier version of its progenitors. Regardless, the Bulldog has endeared itself to many because of its loving, gentle temperament. For further information, visit www.unitedkennelclub.com.

General appearance and characteristics

- ✔ The ideal English Bulldog is massive, of medium size and has a smooth coat, a heavy, thick-set, low-slung body, wide shoulders, sturdy limbs and a short-faced head.

- ✔ General appearance, coupled with attitude, suggests great stability, vigor and strength.

- ✔ The English Bulldog has an equable and kind disposition; and is resolute and courageous. The characteristic demeanor is one of peace and dignity. These attributes are evident in their expression and behavior.

- ✔ When comparing both sexes, due consideration is to be given to bitches, as they do not bear the breed characteristics to the same degree as the males.

- ✔ All points of the standard are well distributed and bear good relation one to the other. No feature is so prominent or so lacking that it makes the animal appear deformed out of proportion.

Head

✔ The skull is very large. The circumference, taken in front of the ears, measures at least the same as the height of the dog, measured from the shoulders to the ground. When viewed from the front, the head is very broad and square, and appears very high from the corner of the lower jaw to the apex of the skull.

✔ In profile, the head appears very high and very short from the occiput to the point of the nose. The forehead is flat, never rounded or domed; and never too prominent nor overhanging the face.

✔ The well-defined temples (frontal bones) are broad, square and high, causing the stop, a hollow, or groove, between the eyes.

✔ The broad, deep stop extends up the middle of the forehead, dividing the head vertically, being traceable to the top of the skull.

✔ The well-rounded cheeks protrude sideways and outward beyond the eyes.

✔ The extremely short face is measured from the front of the cheekbone to the tip of the nose.

✔ The very short muzzle is turned upward and is very deep from the corner of the eye to the corner of the mouth.

✔ The distance from the bottom of the stop (between the eyes) to the tip of the nose is to be as short as possible, and does not exceed the distance measured from the tip of the nose to the edge of the under lip.

✔ The massive jaws are broad and very square. The undershot lower jaw projects considerably in front of the upper jaw and turns up.

✔ The thick, broad, pendant flews, referred to as the "chops," are very deep. They completely overhang the lower jaw at each side. In front, they join the under lip, almost or quite covering the teeth, which are scarcely noticeable when the mouth is closed.

Teeth

✔ A full complement of large, strong, white teeth meet in an undershot bite.

✔ The canines are wide apart; and the incisors are in an even, level row.

Eyes

- ✔ The very dark eyes are quite round and moderate in size; never being sunken nor bulging. When the dog is looking directly forward, the lids cover the white of the eyeball. There is no haw showing.

- ✔ Viewed from the front, the eyes are situated low down in the skull, as far back from the ears as possible. They are quite in front of the head and as wide apart as possible, provided that their outer corners are within the outline of the cheek, when viewed from the front.

- ✔ The corners of the eyes are in a straight line at right angles with the stop.

Nose

- ✔ The large, broad nose is black in color. Its tip is set back deeply between the eyes.

- ✔ The wide, large nostrils are also black in color.

- ✔ Very serious fault — Nose color other than black.

- ✔ Disqualification — Brown or liver-colored nose.

Ears

- ✔ The small, thin rose ears are set high on the head.

- ✔ The front inner edge of each ear joins the outline of the skull at the top back corner of the skull, placing them wide apart and as far apart from the eyes as possible.

- ✔ Very serious faults — Erect ears; prick ears; button ears; cropped ears.

Neck

- ✔ The short, very thick neck is deep, strong, and well-arched.

Forequarters

- ✔ The very heavy, muscular shoulders are widespread and slant outward, providing stability and great power.

Forelegs

- ✔ The short, very stout forelegs are straight and muscular. They are set wide apart, their well-developed calves presenting a bowed outline.

✔ The legs themselves are not curved or bandy, nor are the feet brought too close together.

✔ The low elbows stand well out, and loose, from the body.

Body

✔ The brisket and body are very capacious, and very deep from the shoulders down to the lowest part.

✔ The very broad chest is deep and full.

✔ The brisket is well let down between the shoulders and the forelegs, causing a broad, low, short-legged appearance.

✔ The sides are full.

✔ The body is well-ribbed-up behind, and the ribs are well-rounded.

✔ The belly is tucked up; not rotund.

✔ The backline is short and strong. It is very broad at the shoulders and comparatively narrow at the loins. There is a slight fall in the back, its lowest part being close behind the shoulders. From there, the spine rises to the loins, then curves again more suddenly to the tail, to form the breed characteristic wheel back.

✔ The top of the loins is higher than the withers.

Hindquarters

✔ The strong, muscular hind legs are longer than the forelegs, contributing to the elevation of the loins above the level of the shoulders.

Hind legs

✔ The short lower legs are straight and strong.

✔ The stifles turn slightly outward and away from the body, causing the hocks to approach each other and the hind feet to turn outward.

✔ The slightly bent hocks are well let down, providing length and strength from the loins to the hock.

Feet

✔ The compact, firmly set feet are moderate in size.

✔ The compact toes are well split up and have high knuckles and short, stubby nails.

✔ The front feet may be straight or slightly turned out.

✔ The hind feet should be pointed well outward.

Tail

✔ The short tail is hung low, and has a thick root, a decided downward carriage and a fine tip. It may be straight or screwed, but never curved or curly.

✔ A straight tail is cylindrical and is tapered uniformly.

✔ A screw tail has well-defined bends or kinks that may be abrupt or even knotty, but no portion of the tail may be elevated above the base or root.

Skin

✔ The skin is soft and loose, especially at the head, neck and shoulders.

Wrinkles and dewlap

✔ The head and face are covered with heavy wrinkles.

✔ There should be two loose, pendulous folds forming the dewlap at the throat, from the jaw to the chest.

Coat

✔ The short, straight coat lies flat and close, and is smooth, glossy and of a fine texture.

✔ There are no fringes, feathers, or curls.

Color

✔ Coat color is uniform, pure, and brilliant.

✔ The various breed typical colors are to be preferred in the following order:

- Red brindle

- All other brindles (Note: To be considered perfect, brindles are to have a fine, even, and equal distribution of the composite colors.)

- Solid white

- Solid red

- Fawn or yellow

- Piebald
- Inferior specimens of all the foregoing (Note: A perfect piebald is preferable to a muddy brindle or a defective solid color. Solid black is very undesirable, but black is not so objectionable if occurring, to a moderate degree, in piebald patches.)

✔ Note: A small white patch on the chest is acceptable in brindles and solid-colored dogs. Color patches on piebalds are expected to be well-defined, of pure color, and symmetrically distributed.

Weight

✔ Weight for mature dogs is approximately 50 pounds.

✔ Weight for mature bitches is approximately 40 pounds.

Gait

✔ Movement style and carriage are distinctive to the breed. It is a loose-jointed, shuffling, sideways motion, causing the characteristic roll.

✔ However, action is free, vigorous, and unrestricted.

Disqualifications

✔ Unilateral or bilateral cryptorchid

✔ Viciousness or extreme shyness

✔ Brown or liver-colored nose

✔ Albinism

The French and American Bulldogs

Though similar to the more common English Bulldog, the French and American versions do display some important points of difference. Refer back to Figure 2-1 to see how the various Bulldog breeds differ in appearance.

The French Bulldog

The French Bulldog looks like a miniature Bulldog with bat ears. The English produced some toy Bulldogs in the mid-1800s, but they didn't become popular, and many were sent to France. In

France, they were crossed with other breeds and called French Bulldogs. The breed was a popular pet of Parisian prostitutes and then became popular with fashionable ladies who considered it daring to have a prostitute's dog.

At first, the French Bulldog had two ear types: the rose ear and the bat ear. American breeders championed the bat ear, and the French Bulldog Club of America was founded in 1898 to further the breed.

The French Bulldog and the Bulldog are two separate and distinct breeds, but the standard for the French Bulldog is similar to that of the English Bulldog. According to the standard, the Bulldog's chest should be "very broad, deep, and full." In the French Bulldog standard, the chest "is broad, deep, and full." Tail, topline, and permissible colors are also similar.

The American Bulldog

The American Bulldog is recognized by the UKC but not by the AKC. The American Bulldog — used as a cattle and hog dog — is a more athletic version of the Bulldog. The American version is a great companion as well. As far as body type, the American Bulldog still has a large head but a well-defined stop and more muzzle than a Bulldog. Ears may be drop, semi-prick, rose, or cropped.

 American Bulldogs range in height from 20 to 27 inches, depending on whether the dog is male or female. A male weighs 75 to 125 pounds, a female 60 to 100 pounds. A Bulldog male weighs about 50 pounds, a female 40 pounds. The American Bulldog has a topline that slopes slightly from the withers to the tail; a Bulldog has the distinctive roach or wheel back.

The American Bulldog is protective and may be used as a guard dog, whereas the Bulldog prefers a snooze on the couch.

Chapter 3

Deciding on a Bulldog

In This Chapter

▶ Discovering the ins and outs of Bullies

▶ Owning a Bulldog: What does it really cost?

*B*ulldog puppies are adorable, and adult Bullies have an engaging seriousness in their wrinkled faces, but looks alone aren't reason enough to run right out and purchase a Bulldog. Before you commit to ten years of Bulldog care, take a minute to consider whether a Bulldog is what you really want. This chapter provides key facts to keep in mind before taking the step of getting a Bully of your own.

The Bulldog Point of View

Bulldogs possess behavioral quirks specific to their breed that require you to take some time to think about how good the match would be before you get one. If any of the traits mentioned in this chapter doesn't fit in with your lifestyle or with what you expect from your dog, consider getting a different breed. However, a Bulldog may be perfect for you if the following list represents your behaviors and the kind of dog you want:

- ✔ *Couch Potato* is your middle name.

- ✔ Grooming isn't on your list of fun things to do.

- ✔ You leave for much of the day.

- ✔ You want a companion to hang out with after a hard day's work.

Bulldogs love to be with their families, but they also like to snooze the day away. You can go off to work and know that your Bully isn't desperate for an afternoon game of fetch. And when you return home, your pal will be waiting for a snuggle on the couch.

When you come home and plop down on the couch, you may notice that your Bully has left behind a present for you. You have dog hair all over your black pants! A Bulldog's short and smooth coat sheds much more hair than you may imagine, and your Bulldog sheds year round, but you won't have the hours of combing, brushing, and trimming maintenance that you would with many longer-coated breeds. Do pay attention to his wrinkles, though; you can easily manage a little touch up during your evening TV time on the couch. See Chapter 8 for tips on grooming your Bulldog.

Recognizing that Bullies aren't athletes

You must realize that your Bulldog is your companion; she isn't an athlete. In fact, Bulldogs are predisposed for lounging around.

If you want a dog to keep you company in your active lifestyle, consider a different breed. The Bulldog isn't built for speed, and even if she wanted to run, jump, and play for extended periods of time, she just can't. Her short, pushed-in nose doesn't allow airflow like active dogs, and an elongated soft palate and small trachea further hamper a Bully's breathing. High heat and humidity also make Bulldogs unhappy, and hot conditions can affect their health. Overheating poses a real danger for a Bulldog.

If you expect to spend a day paddling around the lake with your Bully, you may need to reconsider. Drowning is a major cause of death in Bulldogs. As one breeder says, "They swim like a rock."

A Bulldog's temperament slows her down, too. Bulldogs want to please themselves. They aren't driven to work, and they don't act on command to please their owners.

Integrating Bullies with children and animals

If you have children, trust that your sturdy Bulldog can take a bit of rough play and is gentle enough in nature not to snap at your kids. With that said, supervise your child and dog at all times. You don't want either to get too rough. Teach your children to be gentle with any dog. Be aware that the Bulldog is powerful, and small children may get knocked over during playtime.

Never leave any dog unattended with a baby. Babies make fast, jerky movements and high-pitched noises. Instinctively, dogs like to catch and kill critters that make these movements and sounds.

If your Bulldog joins other pets in the family, he tends to fit in just fine. Bulldogs generally get along with other dogs, but to be on the safe side, choose a dog of the opposite sex to the one in residence. Same-sex dogs may get along at first, but after the puppy reaches sexual maturity, jealousy and territorialism can present trouble. Same-sex dog fights can be very serious, and once the dogs have decided they don't like each other, they'll always need to be separated. Spaying and neutering your Bulldog often eliminates some of this behavior (see Chapter 14).

Bulldogs adjust appropriately to cats if raised with them. Perform introductions gradually, and don't leave the pets alone together until you're sure that everyone gets along.

Rabbits, gerbils, hamsters, guinea pigs, and other small pets top the list of prey for a Bulldog. Use caution, because it's the Bulldog instinct to catch and kill these critters. Keep smaller pets out of harm's way when you can't supervise interactions.

Examining the Cost of Ownership

Bulldogs require investments of both time and money, so make sure you're vested in the process. The following list provides time and money issues to consider before getting your Bulldog. I don't give exact cost figures — cost can vary depending on where you live — but you'll get the general idea:

- A Bulldog puppy costs between $2,000 and $3,000.

- All dogs need regular veterinary checkups, and over the course of your dog's life, he'll need vaccinations, medicines, and possibly surgeries (see Part IV).

- Bulldogs love to chew and seem to have a preference for drywall. Their sturdy jaws can do serious damage to kitchen cabinets and furniture. If your adult Bully suffers from separation anxiety, the loneliness may manifest itself in destructive chewing. Consider crate training to alleviate some of these problems. (Head to Chapter 9 for crate training suggestions.)

- Surgical procedures may cost more for a Bulldog than for most other breeds. Bullies need constant supervision in recovery. Their elongated soft palates and enlarged tonsils may block airways and cause suffocation during recovery. During this period, some veterinarians charge extra for the time needed to sit with the Bulldog. Ask your veterinarian ahead of time whether there'll be an extra charge.

Careful breeding is reducing the incidence of some of the Bulldog's conditions. Most Bulldogs are sensitive to the pre-anesthetic acepromazine, and most vets familiar with the breed avoid this anesthetic. The largest issue is that Bulldogs take far less of most anesthesia than other dogs their weight. Finding a Bulldog-savvy vet can save both lives and pocketbooks.

✔ Your Bulldog requires time but not excessive amounts. Make sure you have the time to housetrain and walk and play with your Bulldog before you bring him home. Schedule time for cleaning face wrinkles and clipping nails, too.

✔ Don't forget the things that all dogs need: daily meals, dishes, toys, bedding, and other items that you think are essential for your Bulldog's well-being! (Check out Part II.)

Also understand the problems your Bulldog faces as a result of his build. Consider where he'll live. Be prepared to make adjustments and sacrifices to keep him happy and healthy. Do your homework, and run your budget, and then go find the Bulldog of your dreams.

Want ad: Bulldog for sale. Eats anything. Very fond of children.

Upon entering a small country store, a stranger noticed a sign stating, "DANGER! BEWARE OF DOG!" posted on the glass door. Inside, a Bulldog slept on the floor beside the cash register. The man asked the store manager, "Is that the dog folks are supposed to beware of?"

"Yep, that's him," came the reply.

The amused stranger inquired, "That certainly doesn't look like a dangerous dog to me. Why in the world would you post that sign?"

The owner responded, "Because before I posted that sign, people kept tripping over him."

Chapter 4

Finding the Best Bulldog for You

In This Chapter

▶ Getting a healthy dog

▶ Finding a Breeder

▶ Selecting a Bulldog

▶ Registering your dog

*A*re you looking for more than just a puppy? Do you need someone who is just a phone call away when you have a question or a problem? If you're looking for a support system, someone who helps you do your best for your Bully for his entire life, look for a reputable breeder.

In this chapter, I give you advice on finding a good Bulldog breeder. I also have some advice for you if you decide to go to a pet shop, and I let you in on some information about adopting older dogs, as well as hints for picking a healthy puppy. I also tell you a bit about registering your dog and making sure you get a pedigree.

Picking Your Pup

No matter where you get your Bulldog, finding a healthy one is important. Your dog is going to be part of your family for around eight to ten years. If you start with a sick puppy, he may never be healthy, and you'll incur veterinary bills right away and possibly for the dog's entire life. Ask about the parents of your dog and what their health is like. Meeting the parents or the mother gives you an idea of what your puppy may be like. Any adult you meet should be friendly, not shy or fearful.

A puppy needs to stay with his mother and siblings until he is at least 7 weeks old. If the breeder or pet store is selling younger puppies, find another place to get your dog. Some breeders feel that eight weeks is ideal; others like to keep the puppies for 12 weeks, making sure that the puppies have all their shots and starting them on crate training and housetraining.

Ask to see the puppy area. The surroundings should be clean, well lit, and near household activity. The puppies must be healthy. If the breeder brings out individual puppies and refuses to show you where the litter lives, find another breeder.

Here are some things to look for in a puppy:

- ✔ You want a healthy puppy. If the puppy is lethargic or has a running nose or gunk in his eyes, don't let your sympathy make your decision.

  If the puppy is dirty and has open sores, leave him behind.

- ✔ Choose an active puppy (see Figure 4-1) and one who has clear eyes and a healthy nose.

- ✔ Ask for the health records for the puppy. An updated shot record and worming history should be provided, as well as the pedigree. Ask whether the parents were tested for any health problems.

- ✔ Ask the age of the puppy. If he was taken from his mother and littermates too early, he may develop socialization problems later on.

Figure 4-1: This Bulldog puppy's play stance is typical behavior of a happy, healthy, and playful pup.

Finding a Bulldog Breeder

Serious, responsible breeders help you select just the right puppy for your family and always provide assistance for you and your dog. You can find a breeder in several different ways:

- ✔ Visit the Bulldog Club of America's Web site at `www.thebca.org`. You can locate breeders in your state or in nearby states. Be prepared to expand your search if you can't find a breeder close to you. Most breeders are also happy to recommend someone else if they're not expecting a litter soon or don't have puppies.

- ✔ If you're friend owns a Bulldog, ask him where he found his dog. Ask whether he's happy with his dog and the breeder. Your friend can make the introductions and recommend you to the breeder.

- ✔ Attend a dog show near you. Buy a catalog listing the owners of all the dogs entered at that show. Watch the Bulldog judging. Talk to some of the handlers about Bulldogs.

Talk to handlers *after* the dog show. Before the judging, limit your conversation. The handler may be too preoccupied to have a long conversation. She may be watching the judging pattern or trying to get her dog to be alert and happy before entering the ring. After the show, ask the handler whether you can speak with her. Most people are happy to answer questions about their favorite breed.

How do you know that breeders at shows or on Web sites are responsible? Well, you don't, but odds are that if they've joined the national club and shown their dogs, they take the time to do the job right. Unlike many breeds, where producing a litter is relatively easy, Bulldogs are all bred by using artificial insemination, and the puppies are delivered by C-section. A lot of thought and money go into every litter.

No matter where you find your breeder, be prepared to wait for your puppy. Producing a litter of Bulldog puppies is an expensive, time-consuming process, and the litters aren't very large. Breeders you talk to may already have a waiting list.

Even if you think that you've found a breeder, take the time to talk with him. If the breeder seems more interested in making a sale than in helping you understand and care for a Bulldog, maybe he isn't the right breeder after all. Take the time to find a breeder you like and trust. Believe me, your best friend for the life of your Bulldog is your breeder.

Facing the firing squad

After you've found your breeder, the questioning process begins. Whether the breeder has puppies at the moment, she'll still ask you questions — a lot of questions. You may want to reference Chapter 5 to prepare to answer some of the following questions.

A friend of mine is a breeder. Here are the questions she asks of potential Bulldog owners:

✔ **How did you hear about me?**

She wants to know whether someone she knows referred you to her. If she knows the person, she can ask opinions of you as a potential owner.

✔ **If you own or have owned a Bulldog, where did you get your dog?**

If you've owned a Bulldog previously, you know what you're getting into. If you rescued your dog, you may need more information from her about how to raise and train a puppy.

✔ **What books, if any, have you read about the breed?**

She doesn't want one of her puppies to go to someone who just wants a Bulldog on a whim, and she wants you to know what to expect if you own a Bulldog.

✔ **What are your expectations for your dog? Describe what you want in a dog.**

She wants to make sure that a Bulldog suits your lifestyle. She knows that a Bulldog can't keep up with a jogger, and you may be disappointed if you want a dog that's eager to play all day.

✔ **Do you prefer a male or a female puppy? Are you willing to take a puppy of the opposite sex? If not, what creates the preference?**

If you're not firm about your preference, the breeder may match you with the best puppy for your family, no matter what the sex.

✔ **Are you interested in an older puppy or an adult?**

Sometimes breeders keep puppies to see whether they display show potential. The puppies that don't make the grade are still good pets, and one of them may be perfect for you (if you aren't interested in showing your Bulldog).

✔ **Tell me about your household. Do you have a spouse, partner, or roommates? Children? Their ages?**

The breeder wants to make sure that everyone in the family welcomes the puppy. The breeder needs to feel that children are old enough to understand how to play properly with a puppy.

✔ **Do any family members suffer from allergies?**

The heartbreak from falling in love with a puppy and then having to give her up is overwhelming. The breeder wants to prevent this heartache if she can.

✔ **Who is responsible for the care and training of your pet?**

No breeder wants a puppy to be neglected. No matter how responsible your children are, an adult is ultimately responsible for the care of the puppy.

✔ **Would you characterize your family as the "outdoors type" or "homebodies"?**

Again, the breeder wants to make sure that the Bulldog is, in fact, the right breed for you.

✔ **Have you had a dog before? Do you have other pets (dogs, cats, birds, fish)? Please tell me about your pet-owning experience.**

She wants to hear that you're committed to spending the time and energy to care for a Bulldog.

✔ **Have you researched a veterinarian, or have you used a vet in the past? If so, please provide the name, address, and phone number.**

The breeder is concerned about her puppies and wants to make sure that you have a veterinarian lined up.

✔ **Do you live in a house, townhouse, condo, or apartment? How large is your yard, and what type of fencing do you have? Please describe, including height.**

Bulldogs can live happily in any style of home, but the breeder wants to know how you handle housetraining. If you have a yard where your Bully can run loose, make sure that the yard is secure and keeps your Bulldog safe.

✔ **Do you have a pool?**

Many breeders don't sell a Bulldog to a family with a pool. Bulldogs may love the water, but they're not good swimmers. Some Bullies can't swim at all.

✔ **If you rent, does your landlord allow you to have a dog? Please provide landlord contact information.**

Typically, a breeder doesn't let a dog go to a home where he's not allowed. She doesn't want one of her puppies returned or, worse, taken to a shelter.

✔ **In what rooms inside your home will your dog be permitted? How do you plan to keep your dog out of certain parts of your home if necessary?**

Making some rooms off limits is okay.

✔ **Have you thought about housetraining a puppy and handling an adult dog? Where will your dog go to eliminate? How will you clean up?**

More questions designed to make you think. A puppy isn't an impulse purchase. Think about what getting a puppy means in terms of time and effort.

✔ **How many hours each day will your dog be left alone? Do you have a secure place to leave your pet while you're away from home? Where will your pet sleep at night?**

Your breeder doesn't want your dog left out unattended all day or put in the basement or garage. Depending on the weather, certain ailments like heat stroke or frostbite can befall your dog. Leaving your dog out in the yard also provides an easy target for dognappers.

✔ **Can you devote the time needed during the critical first few months to teach manners and expose your puppy to many new experiences?**

Training and proper socialization are important elements in a puppy's development into a secure and happy adult companion.

✔ **Do you know where you can go for obedience training or socialization?**

Don't worry if you say no. Your breeder has suggestions if you want to take a class.

Don't be put off by the questions. The breeder wants to ensure that you know what you're getting into by choosing a Bulldog. The kind of home environment and the thought process put into purchasing a Bulldog are other factors that breeders want to know. She needs to be reassured that your home makes a great place for one of her beloved puppies.

Questioning the questioner

Prepare a list of questions for your Bulldog breeder, too. Below are some sample questions to ask. Any *reputable* breeder will be able to answer these questions. If you aren't satisfied with the answers or some questions can't be answered, tuck *your* tail and run:

✔ **How long have you been breeding? Is breeding a business or a hobby? How often do your dogs produce a litter?**

No breeder makes a living breeding Bulldogs if breeding is done correctly. If she says that breeding is her business, look for another breeder. If a breeder produces a few litters, she'll be able to tell you what to expect as your puppy grows.

✔ **Is a Bulldog right for me?**

The breeder wants all her puppies to go to permanent homes. Asking this question gives her a chance to ask a few questions of her own and to talk about the negative aspects of owning a Bulldog.

✔ **May I see the pedigree and registration form?**

You especially want to see the pedigree if you're thinking of showing. Pedigrees also ensure that you're getting a purebred Bulldog. A registration slip accompanies each puppy, so you can register your dog.

✔ **May I receive a health record?**

Your breeder provides a health record (or at least she should) with each puppy. The record shows what vaccinations your pup has received and the dates the puppies were wormed.

✔ **What happens if I can't keep the dog?**

Most reputable breeders can take back one of their dogs at any time, but the terms may vary from breeder to breeder. Read your contract. If you return a puppy within the time period allowed for a veterinary check, you may get a refund of the purchase price. If a problem such as temperament develops later, breeders frequently offer to replace the puppy with another one. If you've had your Bulldog for a few years and now circumstances prevent you from keeping her, your breeder may be able to take her, and you can have some peace of mind, knowing that your dog lives in a good home. But if this last scenario is your case, you don't get a refund. You may think that not getting your money back is unfair at first, but the breeder now has another dog to care for (and the costs incurred by that dog), and depending on the dog's age, your dog may not find a new home.

Surfing for Bulldogs

You may be tempted to look online for your Bulldog puppy. An online search may give you the names of breeders whether you look at the American Kennel Club (AKC) Web site or the Bulldog Club of America (BCA) site. You may even find individual breeders who aren't on either list. Some sites even sell puppies. You may get a good puppy online, but how do you know before it's too late? You're unable to see the parents; and even the puppy is a mystery until he arrives on your doorstep. Pictures can't tell you about the puppy's personality or whether he's healthy. Don't you want to know how your Bully was raised?

I trust certain breeders to send me a puppy sight unseen, but generally, I'd want to see the puppy and the mother before I'd buy a dog. Consider the money you may spend to purchase your dog. You want to go to a reputable breeder and visit your puppy before he comes home. You've invested in your Bully; now protect your investment.

Deciphering breeder contracts

After you've settled on a breeder, read the contract that the breeder has drawn up. Contracts can protect both you and the breeder, but make sure that you read the contract carefully before you sign. The contract may be as simple as a statement listing the dog, his pet or show quality, and instructions agreed on for care (such as agreeing to spay or neuter the puppy). Detailed contracts outline further evaluations of the dog to determine whether the Bully can be shown, the breeder can use a male as a stud, or the price was adjusted because the breeder wants a puppy back if you ever breed.

If you could turn back time

The contract may also state that if for any reason you can't keep the dog, the Bully returns to the breeder. Breeders do have this clause to prevent dogs they've bred from ending up in shelters or rescues. Don't be afraid to admit that you made a mistake or that you can't afford the dog. Breeders rather take the dog back than see him suffer in a shelter.

Registration stipulation

The contract may also state whether the puppy is under a limited registration. Breeders use *limited registration* to make sure that a pet isn't bred. Offspring from a limited-registration dog may not be registered with the American Kennel Club (AKC).

Health guarantees

The contract may include health information, or the health guarantee may be a separate document. The health guarantee gives you a specific amount of time — usually 48 hours — to take your puppy to a veterinarian for a health check. If a problem occurs within that time frame, the breeder may refund your purchase price. Breeders may also offer a replacement puppy if a major problem develops within the first year. Make sure that you understand the offerings in the contract before you take your puppy home.

Puppy co-ownership

Some breeders don't sell a puppy outright but insist on *co-ownership*. The breeder and you share custody of your Bulldog until one or more of the following events occur:

- ✓ **Your Bully earns a championship title.** Think about the time, the money, and the drive it takes to go to dog shows until your dog finishes. If you can't personally get the dog finished with his show circuit, is the breeder willing to show him? Who pays the expenses? Are you willing to be separated from your dog for six months to a year while he's being shown? Leaving your Bulldog with the breeder until your dog earns a title may be tough — it can mean months without seeing your dog!

- ✓ **Your Bully breeds, and the breeder gets a puppy.** If the breeder sells you a puppy at a reduced price and retains co-ownership until she gets a puppy back, make sure that you understand what is involved in breeding a Bulldog. That "bargain" puppy you got may cost you more in the long run than a puppy you pay full price for. See Chapter 18 for information and costs associated with breeding.

Co-ownerships can and do work, but know what you're getting into before you sign the papers. You may want that cute Bully puppy so much that you'll agree to anything right now, but you may be sorry a year from now.

Perusing Pet Shops

A cute Bulldog puppy and the instant gratification are hard to resist when you're able to scoop that puppy up and take him home, with no questions from a breeder and no waiting for a litter. Still, many of the same criteria apply no matter where your dog comes from.

You aren't able to meet either of the puppy's parents, which means that you don't have an idea of temperament or size. Generally, pet-shop Bulldogs are leggier and thinner than the Bulldogs that come from a breeder.

A puppy from a pet shop may cost more than a puppy from a breeder, and you lack the benefit of the breeder's experience. No one is available to call when you need advice. Whether your Bully has a major health problem or you can't keep your dog for any reason, the pet shop won't take him back.

Adopting an Older Bulldog

If you want an older dog, consider a dog from an animal shelter or from a Bulldog rescue group. The advantages to an adult dog seem endless:

- ✔ Your adult Bully may already be housetrained, and even if he isn't housetrained, he can train faster than a puppy and wait longer between trips outside.

- ✔ An older dog doesn't need the concentrated effort a puppy needs. Your dog still craves love and attention, but if you don't have the time or energy to deal with a puppy's training and socialization, an older Bulldog may be perfect for you.

- ✔ Older Bullies already "speak English." They understand the words you use, even if they don't always obey!

- ✔ Your dog is beyond the chewing stage. He is grateful for a soft bed and less likely to want to destroy it. He may not be as eager as a puppy to turn your good shoes into chew toys.

- ✔ Don't worry that an older dog won't bond with you. It's amazing how quickly that bond can form.

The disadvantage of getting an older dog is inheriting all his bad habits. You may not know what his life was like before you got him. The Bulldog Club of America (BCA) makes this statement about rescue on its Web site: "A majority of our rescues have social, emotional, behavioral, and health issues. If you aren't able or willing to deal with a not-so-perfect Bully, your wait may be a long one. Many rescued Bulldogs are dog aggressive and have trust issues. Some aren't suitable for placing with children. Rarely does a happy, well-adjusted Bulldog end up in our care. If you aren't committed to dealing with housebreaking issues in an adult dog or to provide obedience training, you may not really want to take on a rescued Bulldog."

You can still get a potentially wonderful dog from rescue, but you have to be willing to work to get that wonderful dog. The same determination to save a Bully by adopting from a shelter or applying to a rescue organization ought to be applied to turning your Bully into a cherished family member.

Take some extra time in training your dog new habits. An old dog *can* learn new tricks!

Considering shelter dogs

The Bulldog is a popular breed, so you may find one at your local shelter. Getting a dog from a shelter costs less than getting a puppy. Spay or neutering fees, along with up-to-date shots, are included in the adoption fee. Many shelters now foster their strays, sending them home with volunteers to monitor behavior around other dogs, cats, and children.

Some shelters keep a list of names of people who want a specific breed. See whether your shelter provides this service. Otherwise, call at least once a month. If possible, visit the shelter in person. Shelters rely on volunteer help, and frequent turnover may mean that the volunteer who said that she'd call you no longer works there.

Contacting Bully rescue groups

Dogs end up in rescue for a variety of reasons: owner death, family unwilling to care for pet, or serious health or behavior problems. Rescue workers work diligently to place Bulldogs in appropriate homes. Rescue personnel do everything possible to make a good match. They want the rescued dogs to go into permanent homes. Workers can usually tell you how the dog reacts to other animals and to children. Typically, dogs from rescue organizations are spayed or neutered and have all their shots. Many breed rescue groups have dogs available in each state. Vets, local animal shelters, and pet-supply stores often have information on how to contact these groups, and many can also be found on the Internet.

Registering Your Puppy

When your breeder registered the litter with the AKC (see Chapter 2), she received an individual registration form from the AKC for each puppy. You receive that form when you purchase your dog. Fill out the form, including your puppy's name, and send the form to the AKC with the registration fee.

You can also register online. Previously, the litter owner had to enter the dog's information before the new owner could register the dog online. Now the AKC registration forms include a PIN number that allows the new owner to register the dog quickly online.

Two types of registration are available: full and limited. A *full registration* indicates that the dog's offspring may be registered with the AKC. A *limited registration* renders any offspring ineligible for registration. Limited registration may be changed to full registration at any time, but only the breeder may make the change.

The purpose of limited registration prevents a fault from being passed on if the breeder doesn't feel that the dog meets the breed standard. A contract may call for the buyer to spay or neuter, but the limited registration ensures that owners aren't able to register the offspring of their dog.

Limited registration also means that the dog isn't eligible for AKC conformation events but is eligible for all other AKC sports, such as obedience and agility.

The AKC serves as the primary registry for Bulldogs in the United States. Pups sold with a Fédération Cynologique Internationale (FCI) registration are imports who may be eligible for AKC registration, but at a cost of around $100 extra. Many importers are profit driven, and the health and family history of the pup are often hard to verify. Also, many imported puppies are taken from their mothers too early, which may set the puppies up for behavioral problems. Unless you've visited the breeder and had a chance to inspect the breeding facilities and go through your checklist of breeder questions, buyer, beware.

You don't *have* to register your Bulldog, but I recommend it. If you decide to compete in any of the performance events, your dog needs to be registered. If you own an unregistered purebred Bully, submit a form and pictures of your dog to the AKC. If the AKC agrees that your dog is a purebred, the club assigns an Indefinite Listing Privilege (ILP) number that allows you and your Bully to compete in all performance events. You may not compete in conformation. Registering your puppy in the beginning is faster and easier, though.

Registries ensure that both a dog's parents are the same breed. Saying that a Bulldog is AKC registered isn't a guarantee of quality. You need to rely on the breeder for that.

Part II
Living with Your Bulldog

"Your loyalty and devotion are legendary. However, let me remind you that you are under oath."

In this part . . .

So you picked out your puppy . . . that was the easy part! Now you have to ensure his happiness and safety. Take the steps to puppy-proof your home and get ready to shop! Don't worry; I provide a list of all the items you need, as well as guide you in introducing your new puppy to the house, other family members, and other pets. And don't forget, after all these steps, you need to groom your Bully, and of course, feed him too.

Chapter 5

Preparing for Your Bulldog

. . . .

In This Chapter

▶ Fixing fences

▶ Dog-proofing your home

▶ Getting everything your Bulldog needs

▶ Getting proper ID

. . . .

*T*his chapter helps you prepare your home for the new arrival. Use the information contained here as a checklist to ensure that you have everything needed for your Bulldog *before* he sets foot in his new home. Having everything prepared in advance makes the transition less stressful for both you and your dog, so you can both enjoy your Bully's homecoming.

Making the Outdoors Safe for Your Bulldog

Before you bring your Bully home, take a look at your yard. If it's already fenced, you're a step ahead. Make sure that the fence you have can keep your Bully safe. You want to make sure that your puppy can't escape or get his head stuck in the fence. Fences with gaps large enough for a puppy to wiggle through need extra re-inforcement near the ground to cover the gaps.

Choosing traditional fencing

If you don't have a fence, think about your long-term needs. A chain-link fence is easier to care for than solid wood but doesn't give you or your property privacy. Sadly enough, you need to think about your community. People, including small children, and other dogs may tease or annoy your dog. A solid fence may also prevent your dog from being stolen because dognappers can't see what's behind the fence. Solid PVC fences are maintenance free and give you privacy. However, PVC fences are probably the most expensive of all the fence types.

Whatever kind of fencing you choose, make sure that it's high enough. Bulldogs aren't noted for a lot of fence jumping, but your fence needs to keep other dogs out as well as keep your Bully in. A fence height of 5 feet is the minimum I would consider, but assess your neighborhood. Just remember that your neighborhood can change. Having a higher fence installed initially is cheaper than paying for a total replacement later.

Opting for electronic fencing

Electronic fencing is an increasingly popular type of protection for your dog. Installation requires a buried wire around your property. The confining concept is simple: Your dog wears a collar, and when he nears the buried boundary, an audible tone warns him. If he continues to the border, he receives a mild shock from the collar. Because Bulldogs generally aren't crazy about mild shocks and noises they don't like, this routine of bells and shocks trains your dog to stay in his yard.

Have a reputable company install your electronic fencing. These companies don't just install the wire and give you a collar; they also work with you to train your dog properly, so he respects the boundaries.

Electronic fencing has its drawbacks. Although your dog is kept in his yard, other loose dogs can enter your property, as can people. Bulldogs maintain a sweet and even temperament, but that doesn't mean that they won't defend their territory from a stray dog or cat. You don't want strangers teasing or, worse, stealing your dog. You also run the risk of accidental pregnancy if your female Bully isn't spayed. Any male dog in the neighbor can access your female Bully. My vote is for a real fence.

Safeguarding Your Home

Puppies are like small children. They want to explore every inch of their world, and in the process, they want to taste everything. Like a small child, your Bully puppy puts everything in her mouth.

Protect your belongings and your dog with a little thought before the puppy arrives. Look around the rooms at puppy level. Remove or block off anything that poses a danger or can be destroyed.

Safety is your responsibility — put dangers out of your puppy's way. Don't let him sample anything that may cause harm or death. Here are some important safeguarding standards to consider:

- **Crate your puppy when you can't watch her or when you're going out.** If you do nothing else to puppyproof your house, do this.

- **Protect your dog from the electrical cords in the house.** Make cords as unreachable as possible. Tape down long cords that are reachable. A chewed lamp cord is a deadly hazard for your puppy.

- **Use childproof locks on cupboards in your kitchen or bathroom that have loose doors.** Especially consider locks for doors under sinks where cleaning supplies are stored.

No matter how well you puppy proof your house, your curious puppy will find and destroy something. You can have a perfect house, or you can have a puppy. There are some common-sense things you can do to protect your household items from your pup. Some examples are:

- If you own fragile collectibles, put them on high shelves on sturdy bookcases. Puppies can bump into tables and bookcases when they play. If the coffee table is covered with tempting items for your puppy, remove the temptations from sight.

- An oriental rug with tasty-looking fringe is a fun toy in the mind of your Bully, but don't leave her alone with the rug. I suggest rolling up the rug for a few months. Aside from ruining the look of that expensive rug, a puppy can swallow fringe and incur serious intestinal problems that require surgery.

- Got a priceless antique chair? Protect the rungs. Puppies love chair rungs. Chairs make wonderful teething toys. Puppies are also fast. I own a chair with rungs that is now decorated with teeth marks. I would have bet money that the most recent puppy was never alone with that chair.

- Make a spare room off limits to the puppy, and put rare furniture, special rugs, or other precious items in the room until the puppy is older. You can purchase baby gates to protect the closed-off rooms.

Examining Crates: All-Purpose Doggy Dens

Contrary to popular opinion, a crate isn't a jail cell. Some people see a crate and see bars. Dogs, on the other paw, see a crate as a den — a safe place to take a nap or get away for a while. If you've had a dog before, you know that dogs frequently hide under chairs, tables, or even beds for their naps. A dog may even squeeze between a sofa and the wall. Think *den* when you shop for a crate.

Most puppies adjust quickly to crates. Some crying and whining at night is normal, so grit your teeth, and remember that this, too, shall pass. As long as you're feeding your puppy well, keeping her warm and dry, and letting her out for potty breaks, let her cry. She'll stop eventually, honest.

Although most dogs quickly adjust to crates, occasionally a dog will not adapt to crating. I had a dog who seemed to have panic attacks when she was crated for long periods of time and another who didn't mind sleeping in a crate, but the door needed to be open. Fortunately, neither of these quirks started until after housetraining.

If you have a dog who objects to the crate after a reasonable try, don't force the issue. She can always hide under the bed for privacy or sleep with you in the bed, if that is acceptable. Remember that after you allow her to sleep with you, cuddling is a hard habit to break for your dog. See Chapter 9 for information on crate training.

Numbering the advantages

Purchasing a crate for your Bully provides him with a comfy den and also benefits you. Take a look at the following list, and see whether you can be persuaded to give crates a chance:

- ✔ **A crate gives your puppy a snug place of her own.**

- ✔ **Traveling is easier with a crate.** When you're visiting Aunt Betsy, your dog is safe and snug, and your aunt's furniture and rug are free from dog hair.

- ✔ **Crate training prepares a dog for any time when she may need to stay overnight at the veterinarian.** A vet visit can be stressful, but if your Bully's used to a crate, chances are she may relax and fall asleep, even in a strange place. When I board my dogs, I frequently request that their crates go in the indoor kennel run with them.

✔ **Crates are small, easy-to-clean areas.** If your puppy has an accident in the crate, the mess is a snap to clean. Wire crates frequently have a removable tray that makes cleanup even easier.

Deciding on the den

Crates are moderately expensive, but they can last a long time, depending on the aggressiveness and activity of your puppy when housed in the crate. Talk to your breeder about the right size of crate for your Bulldog. Here are a couple things to keep in mind about crate size:

✔ Your dog needs to be able to stand up in the crate, turn around easily, and lie down stretched out. Cramped crates can make your Bulldog uncomfortable and unhappy.

✔ On the other hand, a crate that is too large isn't the cozy den your dog wants, and the vastness may encourage him to sleep at one end and turn the other end into his bathroom.

You may even want two or three crates — one for the car, one for the family room, and one for the bedroom. Crates make wonderful bedside tables.

Plastic

Plastic crates or pet carriers provide more protection when traveling with or shipping your Bully. In the event of an accident, plastic crates play an even more important role in keeping your dog safe, as they're usually very durable and offer more impact resistance than other types of crates. Plastic crates also allow ventilation and function well at home in the air conditioning or heat (see Figure 5-1).

Wire

If you aren't much of a traveler or don't plan on shipping your Bulldog out of town, wire crates (my preference) are a good stay-at-home hostel for your puppy. In winter, cover the top and sides of the wire with a blanket or a custom-made cover to create a cozy den, and in warm weather, flip the sides up to provide air circulation.

Solid metal

Stay away from solid metal crates with your short-nosed pup. Solid metal crates tend to hold heat, and your Bulldog can become overheated.

Figure 5-1: The versatile pet carrier can be used as a dog bed, dog crate, and travel crate.

Buying Beds for Bulldogs

Beds come in wonderful colors and fabrics, and coordinating your dog's bed with your other household furnishings can be fun. Bed selections range from foam and beanbag beds all the way to real innerspring mattresses. Many beds are made specifically to fit crates. Look for a bed with protective covers that contain any doggy dribbles and accidents.

The main thing to keep in mind when selecting a bed is durability. Of course, your Bulldog's comfort is important, but you don't want to get him a bed that he can destroy in a matter of minutes. When shopping for a dog bed, no matter what kind you decide on, make sure it's tough enough to stand up to your Bully!

If you choose a foam bed, make sure that the cover surrounds the foam completely. If your Bully can reach the foam, he can eat it. Then it's goodbye bed, hello emergency surgery.

You may want to save the expensive mattress until your puppy is an adult. Many puppies chew on whatever is available, and I've seen beautiful wicker beds reduced to a pile of twigs.

Collars and Leads and Harnesses, Oh My!

Leads and collars help keep your puppy under control when you're out in public. Remember, not everyone loves dogs, so if you have control of your dog, you're less likely to scare other people. You can also keep your Bully from harm or pull him away from something he shouldn't be into when he's on a collar and lead.

Collars

Collars come in a wide assortment of colors with matching leads. A simple, flat nylon collar works well as a first collar. Adjustable collars are good investments because as your puppy grows into adulthood, he will need his collar let out; adjustable collars prevent multiple runs to the nearest pet store for a bigger collar.

If you want a permanent, more expensive collar for your Bully, wait until he's full grown.

Here are a few specialty collars you may see in the stores:

✔ **Buckle collar:** The buckle collar is often considered "daily wear" for dogs. It's a good bet for growing Bulldogs because it's easy to adjust the size of the collar as the dog grows. Buckle collars also stand up well to hard use and stay on Bulldogs well (see Figure 5-2A).

✔ **Slip collar:** The slip collar is a type of training collar designed to tighten around the dog's neck when the dog pulls too hard on the leash. Some dogs respond well to slip collars, although other dogs continue to pull so much that they are in danger of choking themselves (one of the reasons why these collars are also called choke collars). Consider using this type of collar when training your Bulldog (see Chapter 10), but don't use it for daily wear (see Figure 5-2B).

✔ **Prong collar:** There are a variety of training collars out there, depending on the dog and what he's being trained to do. For Bulldogs, the prong collar is fairly common, especially for Bullies that are stubborn and undisciplined on a lead (see Figure 5-2C). The prong collar looks a bit intimidating to some people, but properly fitted and used, it won't hurt your Bulldog and will help you better communicate to him what you'd like him to do. Work with a trainer to help get the right collar for your Bulldog and to learn how to use it (see Chapter 10).

✔ **Martingale collars.** These look a bit like a figure eight. The larger loop has a metal ring at each end, through which the smaller loop passes. The lead attaches to this smaller loop, and that loop draws the large loop closed. It prevents the collar from slipping over the dog's head but will close only to the size of the larger loop so that the dog can't be choked by the collar (see Figure 5-2D).

Slip collars, prong collars, Martingales, and other types of training collars should never be left on your Bulldog when he's not training. They can injure your Bulldog if he's unsupervised and gets into mischief while wearing them.

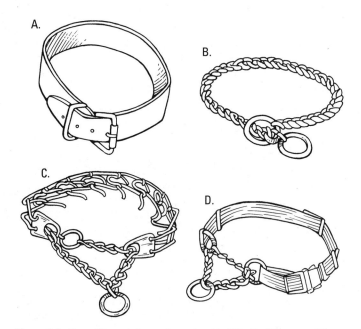

Figure 5-2: Four different dog collars: buckle (A), slip (B), prong (C), and martingale (D).

Leads

Leads come in various lengths, but for training and walking 6 feet is the most useful length. Purchase a practical nylon lead to match your puppy's collar (if you want) or a cotton lead if you can find one. Many times cotton leashes are 40 feet long and may not be the most sensible for training.

Leather leads

Leather leashes are a good choice. Leather is long lasting and looks good on your dog. After the leather is broken in, it will be supple and soft in your hand. Make sure to acquire the thinnest lead you can. The wider the lead, the less flexible it can be.

Chain leads

For some strange reason, chain leads are still on the market, and people buy them. You may think that a chain lead means your dog is strong and powerful and shows everyone that you need a heavy-duty leash to control your dog. In fact, chain leads are horrible to use. These leads come with a little plastic or leather loop for your hand, but the loop is just a handy way to make sure that you and your dog stay connected. Most of the time, whether walking your dog or training him, you need one hand on the actual lead — the chain.

Chains are hard, unyielding, and bulky, and if your puppy makes a sudden lunge forward, the chain may rip the skin off the palm of your hand.

Retractable leads

If you live near a wide-open field or park where you can walk your dog, you may want to use a retractable lead. Your dog may enjoy the extra 15 to 25 feet of wandering room. I find these leads awkward and annoying, but many people love the freedom for their dog. Remember to reel your dog in at the approach of other dogs or people.

Keep your dog close when you're crossing a street. If your dog gets too far ahead on a retractable lead, he may be in harm's way. I recently heard about a dog who was hit by a car and killed because the owner let her dog walk ahead on a retractable lead.

Harnesses

A harness is another option but not one I recommend. Bulldogs are strong, determined dogs, and a harness gives them a chance to pull you along wherever they want to go. You don't have the control over a dog in a harness — the dog controls you. A collar and lead are a better choice.

Toying Around

Toys are some of the most delightful items to shop for. You can spend all day looking at toys. The options are endless. Playful extras for your dog come in all shapes and sizes. And size is one of the first factors you need to think about. A toy that is too big is better than one that is too small. Amazingly enough, dogs consider swallowing just about anything, and you don't want playtime to end in tragedy. So when in doubt, go bigger.

Here are some facts on a few of the more popular dog toys:

- **Tug-of-war toys** are popular and teach your dog to grip, but be careful. Bulldogs are bred to hang on and never let go. Play at a level suitable to your puppy. Also, if you're considering advanced obedience with your Bully, don't play tug-of-war at all.

- **The Kong** is made of hard rubber and meant to keep your puppy occupied for hours. By stuffing cheese, peanut butter, or dog biscuits in the center of the Kong, you can amuse yourself while your Bully tries to extract the food from the Kong. If you're planning to be away from the house for a few hours, distract your puppy with a Kong. Kongs are also a great chewing workout for your puppy. Cubes and balls that release food when your dog knocks the toy around are alternatives to Kongs.

- **Plush toys** may have larger plastic noisemakers buried deep within their stuffing, but a determined dog can quickly disembowel a toy to reach the squeaker. The part of the toy that makes the noise is hard and may, if swallowed, become stuck in your dog's esophagus or block his intestine. Remember to supervise play with noisemaker toys until you know how your dog reacts to them.

Cutting out the squeaker in toys can prevent accidental swallowing. One of my dogs insisted on gutting his toys to reach the noisy part, so I finally starting cutting the squeakers out of toys before I gave them to him. I must admit that desqueaking ruins some of the fun but is much safer. You can also buy regular stuffed animals without the squeaker mechanism.

You don't have to buy all your dog's toys. Puppies play with almost anything. Here are some homemade toys your dog will love:

- Give your dog a plastic gallon milk jug, and watch him bat it around and bite it.

- A whole carrot provides some fun as well as chewing exercise.

✔ If your puppy is teething, sacrifice an old washcloth. Wet the cloth, put it in a plastic bag, and place it in the freezer. After the washcloth is frozen, take it out of the bag, and let your puppy gnaw on it.

✔ You can do the same thing with a tennis ball in an old sock. Put the tennis ball in the sock, knot the sock to keep the ball in place, wet the entire thing, and freeze.

✔ Knotted socks also make great toys for playing fetch. The socks are easy to throw and retrieve. Sock toys are also easy to wash and cheap to replace. The only problem may be that your puppy can't discern between your good socks and your bad socks. Look at the situation this way: Your puppy is going to chew, whether he's ever seen a sock before or not. I know, you're not supposed to turn items of clothing into dog toys because dogs don't know the difference between the play sock and your good socks. But *you* control the situation. Puppies can teach you to be neat and tidy. Don't leave your good socks or other unmentionables lying around to be chewed. Then use your old socks that would normally go in the trash as recycled puppy toys.

Gauging Grooming Tools

When you're on that shopping spree, remember to look for the grooming tools needed to keep your dog neat and tidy. Chapter 8 goes into more detail about how to groom your Bulldog and tells you exactly what you need.

Evaluating Food and Water Bowls

Choices abound in the area of doggy dishware. The following sections go over the three main types of dog bowls.

While you're shopping for your dog's dinnerware, consider a doggy placemat for the bowls. Mats wipe clean and prevent water and food from scattering all over your kitchen floor. Mats also come in all kinds of wonderful designs.

Stainless steel bowls

Stainless steel bowls are relatively inexpensive and indestructible dishware that can be thoroughly cleaned. Many stainless steel bowls also have rubber on the bottom to prevent skidding. Wash these bowls in the dishwasher regularly to ensure the cleanest dishes for your Bully.

Plastic dishes

Plastic dishes are cheaper than stainless steel but don't provide the durability of the stainless steel models. Plastic is also harder to clean and may retain stains and odors, and plastic may irritate your Bully's sensitive face and lips. Additionally, when your Bulldog has finished his dinner, he may decide to finish off his bowl, seeing that it is a dandy teething toy.

Ceramic bowls

Ceramic bowls may tempt you with the vast array of colors and sizes with wonderful designs and clever sayings. Ceramic is heavy enough to prevent spilling. It is breakable, so be careful. If you decide on ceramic bowls, make sure that the paint and glaze are lead free.

Preventing spills in the crate

Consider these for your dog's crate instead of a bowl:

- ✔ **Water bottles:** These bottles clip on the side of wire crates, and your dog licks the end of the tube to make the water flow. The benefits include spill prevention and cleanliness of the water. Water bottles are also great when traveling. Big dogs may have a hard time getting all the water they need with a water bottle, but for a short trip, the bottle is ideal. The bottle can also be perfect for your Bully puppy.

- ✔ **Stainless steel buckets:** If you want to help prevent spills when your dog grows up, attach a small stainless steel bucket to the side of the crate. Some bowls also fasten to crates, and plastic crates frequently come with small bowls attached to the door.

Chapter 6

Bringing Your Bulldog Home

. . . .

In This Chapter

▶ Picking up your Bulldog

▶ Showing your Bulldog the house

▶ Meeting other family members

▶ Setting up a schedule

▶ Detecting possible problems and sensible solutions

. . . .

*Y*ou chose the perfect Bulldog, and now the time has come to pick him up and bring him home. Remember, this process is new and strange for your Bully. Imagine how you'd feel if someone picked you up, took you away from your home and family, and set you down in a strange place where you didn't know the language. This chapter gives you the ins and outs of introducing your Bulldog into his new home and family and preparing yourself for things your Bulldog may do when he's exposed to his new life for the first time.

Bringing Home Bully

You don't want to be rushed, so plan to pick up your Bulldog on a weekend, when no one works or has school. If the timing is right, and you can pick your Bulldog up at the start of a vacation, that situation is even better. The exception to the vacation situation is Christmas. Many breeders won't even let people take puppies during the holidays. (See the sidebar "Christmas isn't the season for a new pet.")

Christmas isn't the season for a new pet

Christmas is the worst time to get a dog. Puppies make a great gift idea, and you can picture your children's faces when they open a box filled with the adorable puppy with a cute bow around his neck. Greeting cards and holiday commercials show puppies in stockings and under the tree, making the puppy seem like the ideal gift. Even though the family may be home, the trouble with the Christmas season is too much excitement and activity. The puppy may be overwhelmed and, in all the rush, ignored.

A housetraining schedule may be virtually impossible to establish, and your new dog may find it hard to adjust to his new place filled with friends and relatives. Your Bully needs a chance to be quietly introduced to the immediate family and to get to know the rooms of the house. Also, the chances of "excitement urination" increase with the addition of many people to meet and play with.

Besides not having an established schedule, the more people in your house, the more the chance exists that your puppy may be given "just a tiny piece" of cheese, turkey, or candy. A puppy's digestive system is sensitive, and with strange foods and strange people in a strange place, your puppy can have diarrhea or an upset stomach causing vomiting. The puppy doesn't need the added stress, and neither do you at this already-busy time of the year.

If you think that a dog is the perfect holiday surprise, take a picture of the dog for under the tree. Give a fancy gift certificate or a collar and lead. Wrap up a book on dog care, and plan to pick up the dog after the New Year. This presentation will make your entire family happier.

Whenever you pick up your Bulldog, take along a small crate (or size-appropriate carrier) or a cardboard box for the ride home. Line the carrier with newspapers or a towel or two. If you're bringing home a puppy, you should get the following from the breeder:

✔ Your puppy's three-generation pedigree

✔ A health record for your Bully

✔ Food for two or three days

✔ A toy or two (optional)

You should also expect that your breeder will give you support. Knowing that you can call your breeder whenever you have a question or problem is important. Support gives you peace of mind, as well as help when you need it.

Giving Your Bully the Guided House Tour

Note the word *guided* in the header above. Don't just open the door of the house and let your Bulldog roam unattended. Your pup will have plenty of time later to have a little adventure on his own. For now, remember that everything is totally new to him. He needs guidance:

1. **Give your puppy a "pit stop" in the yard before taking him into the house.**

   When you get your Bulldog home, make the first stop the yard. In a new or strange environment, even adult dogs may need to heed the call of nature. If you've chosen a specific area of the yard you want to use as a doggy bathroom, be sure that is where you set him down when you first come home.

2. **Take him in to his food and water dishes.**

   Have a bowl of water waiting for him. Show him the bowl, and give him a chance to have a drink. Put a few pieces of kibble or a small spoonful of canned food in his bowl. Don't worry if he doesn't eat it. Sometimes puppies won't eat at first. Remember, this time can be stressful. The bite of food is just to let him know that this spot is where he dines in the future.

3. **Take him to his crate, and put him inside.**

   If he's already used to a crate, you may want to shut the door for a few minutes and let your Bulldog relax. If you're not using a crate, put the puppy in the box or room where he'll be sleeping, and let him explore.

4. **Return the pup to the yard.**

   Although showing the dog around may not have taken long, now is a good time to take your dog back outside. Your puppy may have gone when you set him down in the yard before you brought him into the house, but puppies don't have control of their bladders yet, and excitement can make them have to go.

   If he relieved himself earlier, return to that spot in the yard. Returning to that spot helps your puppy smell where he went before and reminds him of what he's there to do. If he goes, tell your Bully how wonderful he is. If you have a treat in your pocket, give it to him. Then you can go back into the house for further introductions.

Getting to Know the Kids

If you have children, chances are you don't need to make formal introductions because they went with you when you picked up the puppy. Still, follow these basic rules for interaction between children and puppies:

- ✔ **Teach your children to approach any animal quietly and slowly.** No running and no grabbing.

- ✔ **Teach your children to be gentle.** A puppy isn't a toy. Children should gently stroke the puppy — soft pats, not hard thumps. Don't pull ears or tails or legs.

- ✔ **Supervise interactions with younger children at all times.** Young children may not understand about being gentle.

- ✔ **Never leave a baby alone with any dog.** Puppies can nip; nails can scratch; and a baby isn't a dog's toy any more than a puppy is a baby's toy.

- ✔ **Educate your children on how to pick up and hold a puppy.** Don't grab the dog around the middle and haul her around. Slip a hand under the puppy's chest and hold the hindquarters with the other hand. Hold the puppy gently but firmly against your chest. If a child is too small to hold the puppy, supervise a cuddle session with the child sitting down and the puppy in her lap.

- ✔ **Remember that puppies, like small children, need naps.** Your children may want to play with the puppy all the time. Make sure that you allow rest periods when your puppy can have an uninterrupted nap in his crate.

- ✔ **Depending on the age of your children, enlist them in the care of the puppy.** Kids can take the puppy out and give him his meals as part of their chores. Taking care of an animal is a good way to teach responsibility.

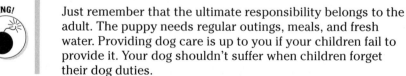

Just remember that the ultimate responsibility belongs to the adult. The puppy needs regular outings, meals, and fresh water. Providing dog care is up to you if your children fail to provide it. Your dog shouldn't suffer when children forget their dog duties.

Meeting the Other Pets

If you have other pets, make proper introductions. You want your puppy and your other pets to get to know one another with a minimum of stress for everyone involved, especially you!

Here are some tips for introducing your pup to other dogs:

- ✔ Supervise the meeting in the yard — not in the house. The yard is a bit more neutral.

- ✔ If you have multiple dogs, let them meet the new addition one at a time.

- ✔ Be careful and cautious in the beginning, but don't leash the resident dog. Sometimes a lead, especially if it gets pulled tight, can make the leashed dog more aggressive or protective than if he's left loose.

- ✔ Older dogs have different reactions to a puppy, and you need to know the personalities of your dogs. My male has always joyously greeted new puppies. One of my females considered all puppies hers to discipline as needed. Another of my girls just generally loved all other dogs, and still another was just amazed and bewildered at the small size of the newcomer.

If you have an adult cat or cats who aren't used to dogs, take the introductions slow, and be careful. You don't want your puppy's first experience with a cat to be a scratched nose.

One idea is to find a friend with a cat-friendly dog and invite your friend and dog over to the house before you bring home the puppy. Although the cat may hide, this process helps her get used to the idea of a dog.

When you finally bring your puppy home, put the cat in a room and close the door. Let the puppy and the cat get to know each other by sniffing at the crack under the door. When you let the cat out, make sure that the puppy is in his crate or in an exercise pen. Let the cat approach at her own pace, and encourage her to sniff around the crate. The cat shouldn't be threatened, therefore alleviating potential problems. The other advantage of crating your dog for the meeting is the cat won't run and the puppy won't be tempted to chase.

Don't rush things. When you finally let your animals meet without a barrier, keep the following tips in mind:

- ✔ Hold the puppy for the initial nose-to-nose hello.

- ✔ If everything seems friendly, put the puppy down, and let the animals interact. Continue to watch them.

- ✔ Don't let the puppy bother the cat when she's eating or in the litter box.

✔ Also, don't let the cat wander over to the puppy when he's eating. Keep them separate during meals so squabbling over food doesn't occur.

✔ Make sure that the cat always has a way to escape the attentions of the puppy. Cats can easily bound over a baby gate into a safe room or leap up to a kitchen counter if that's allowed. Eventually, your cat and dog may become best friends.

Your cats and dogs can become bosom buddies, but when it comes to smaller pets, hamsters and guinea pigs are likely to become lunch. Dogs are predators, and they look on small, rapidly moving, squeaky animals as prey. Occasionally, you may read of a dog and a guinea pig cuddling, but that situation is rare. Safeguard smaller pets and birds by putting their cages up high so your dog can't reach them. If relocating the cage isn't possible, make sure that your dog is never left alone in the same room as the smaller critters. If you let your bird or smaller pet out for playtime, put your dog in his crate, or shut him in another room. No reliable way exists to teach a dog not to chase (or kill) one of these smaller animals.

Setting Up Your Puppy's Schedule

Your puppy thrives on a schedule. Housetraining schedules are covered in Chapter 9, including suggested feeding and play times, as well as nap times. Play is vital but equally essential is rest. Help your children set a schedule for playing with the puppy and then putting the puppy in his bed or crate and letting him sleep. Post this schedule on the refrigerator door beside the housetraining schedule. With younger children, set a timer or alarm clock so playtime and naptime are observed.

Surviving the First Night

Although most puppies adjust quickly to a crate, your puppy may cry at bedtime the first few nights in his new home. Whining is understandable and natural. After all, you're new; the house is strange; and other, unfamiliar animals may be walking around. Your puppy is away from his mom and his littermates and the people he knew for the first eight weeks or so of his life. The surroundings even smell different to your dog.

Here are some tips on how to make the first night with your new dog a little more calm and stress free:

✔ **Make sure that your puppy is well fed.** Even a small meal before bedtime can help your dog fight the late-night tummy grumbles that may wake him and keep him from sleeping soundly.

✔ **Before bedtime, take your puppy outdoors.** A final pit stop ensures that your puppy isn't crying because he has to go.

✔ **Give your puppy a snuggly, soft dog toy to curl up with.** Remember your favorite stuffed toy when you were a child and how it comforted you? Your puppy can get comfort out of a toy as well.

✔ **Make sure that your puppy has soft bedding.** Provide enough padding to make a nest and to keep your dog warm. A warm environment is more conducive to dozing off than a cold, hard crate bottom.

✔ **Wrap an alarm clock that ticks in an old shirt or a towel.** Place the clock in the crate. The ticking sounds like a mother's heartbeat and can calm your jittery puppy.

After you've made sure that the puppy is well fed, dry, warm, and comfortable, if he is still crying, harden your heart, grit your teeth, and endure. Don't take your puppy out of the crate and into your bed unless that's where you intend to let your dog sleep for the rest of his life. I had a puppy once who was fine in his crate during the day, but at bedtime, his cries were pathetic and loud. Twenty minutes passed each night for about a week before he settled down, but it finally happened, and now he's very attached to his crate.

Tackling Problems before They Start

Have you heard the saying, "An ounce of prevention is worth a pound of cure?" It's a concise way of saying that sometimes it's easier to stop a problem before it starts. Try to think about what will happen in the future based on what's going on now. For example, the idea of sharing your bed with your adorable puppy may appeal to you. Before you invite him to share your pillow, think about what he'll be like full grown. If you'll want 60 pounds of dog snuggling next to you, fine. If not, don't start. The same goes for being on furniture or begging at the table. What you start now, be prepared to continue for the life of your dog.

Be firm and consistent in all your dealings with your puppy; call your breeder if you have specific questions about behavior or development; and memorize your veterinarian's phone number.

Follow those suggestions, and you should live through your Bully's puppyhood without acquiring too many gray hairs.

Examining the crate size

If, in spite of your closely followed housetraining schedule, your puppy consistently has accidents in his crate, consider whether his crate may be too big. Dogs generally don't want to go where they sleep, but if a crate is too big, a puppy can easily have a sleeping area at one end and a bathroom area at the other. Insert a divider into the carrier, or invest in or borrow a smaller crate so your puppy has enough room for sleeping but not enough room for a bathroom corner.

Throwing up

Is your puppy frequently regurgitating his food? He may be playing excessively too closely to feeding time. An excited, full puppy may need to empty his stomach. If your puppy is fine otherwise — active, playful, and with no temperature — the food he eats may be too rich for your puppy's stomach. Not every food is perfect for every puppy, and the food that his littermates thrive on may not be right for your pup. Gradually change over to another food, over the course of about a week. If problems persist, see your veterinarian.

Getting a grip

Nail clipping shouldn't be a problem yet, but start now to get your puppy used to having his nails clipped. Handle his feet every time you pick him up. Hold a paw for a few seconds. See Chapter 8 for more specific instructions on nail clipping.

Bulldogs are determined dogs, but they aren't built for struggles. Although you may be able eventually to get an adult of another breed to stop fighting you when you're cutting nails or holding a foot, a Bulldog won't stop. This struggle can lead to shortness of breath (for your dog and maybe you too) and threaten your dog's health. Use patience and perseverance, but never use force with your Bulldog, and don't fight with your Bulldog over something for so long that he is gasping for air.

Chapter 7

Feeding Your Bulldog

. . . .

In This Chapter

▶ Getting the dirt on dog food

▶ Deciding what to feed your Bully

▶ Selecting a mealtime

▶ Snacking on "people food"

▶ Dietary no-nos for Bulldogs

. . . .

*W*hen you first get your Bulldog, you may feed him whatever your breeder recommends or has been using. But you may consider another food as your puppy grows and his lifestyle changes. You may also find that your dog is allergic to ingredients in some food.

Cruise the pet food section of your local supermarket or pet superstore, and you quickly realize that feeding your dog can become complicated. The cuisine in these stores includes dozens of choices. Foods are divided into selections for puppies, adults, active dogs, and seniors. Overweight dogs can enjoy chow and treats especially for them, and even the dog with a little plaque problem has a meal to help clean his teeth.

Ultimately, you decide how and what to feed your Bulldog. This chapter helps you make an informed choice.

Reading the Label: Important Stuff about Your Dog's Food

It doesn't matter how expensive or inexpensive your dog food or what brand you go with; that's a matter of personal choice. Ultimately, what matters is knowing what is going in your dog. To get an idea of what's going into your dog, you need to pay careful attention to the label on the food that you buy. This section gives you some pointers on what to look for.

Listed in the first five ingredients of your dog's food should be an animal-based protein source: beef, chicken, or lamb. Ideally, one of those proteins should be in the first position, because this position generally indicates the main ingredient. Dogs eat just about anything, but they're primarily carnivores, so you want to make sure that your Bulldog's food consists mainly of meat.

Your dog's food may contain ingredients called meat byproducts. Meat byproducts may not sound appealing to us, but they're loaded with vitamins and minerals for your dog. These additives don't include hair, horn, teeth, hooves, feathers, or manure.

Another tip on discovering the right food for your dog includes understanding preservatives. *Preservatives,* chemical or natural, are substances added to foods to keep them from spoiling. You may want to avoid chemical preservatives in favor of natural preservatives, like vitamin E. But remember that natural preservatives don't last as long as chemical preservatives. They tend to break down when exposed to light and air. If you prefer a food with natural preservatives, buy smaller quantities, and store the food in a cool, dark place.

Dog food manufacturers don't have to list preservatives that are already in the products they purchase to make the dog food. A food that is called "preservative free" means that the manufacturer hasn't added a preservative. Preservatives may still be in the food.

The American Association of Feed Control Officials (AAFCO)

The American Association of Feed Control Officials (AAFCO) is the governing body for all animal feed products and sets guidelines and procedures for pet food manufacturers. This organization provides a system for developing laws, regulations, standards, and enforcement policies for the manufacture, labeling, distribution, and sale of animal feeds.

The Agriculture Department of all 50 states of the United States requires AAFCO compliance with regard to manufacture and labeling. This labeling compliance prevents false claims or statements, meaning that whatever is in your dog's food is on the label. A manufacturer must list the ingredients, in order, from the largest amount to the smallest. Preservatives, if any, must also be documented. Please remember, though, that the AAFCO regulations apply to quantity, not quality. You decide about the quality of the protein in your dog's food.

Another factor to consider when purchasing dog food is the filler, which is what the manufacturer uses to bulk up the food. Not only should the food be mostly meat instead of filler, but also some dogs are allergic to certain fillers because the fillers often consist of additives that dogs aren't designed to eat. Here are some common fillers:

✔ Corn is a cheap filler and frequently used in dog foods. I avoid corn because my male is allergic to it.

✔ Wheat and soy grains are also popular but may also cause problems due to allergies.

✔ Rice causes fewer allergic reactions and has become popular for that reason.

What you do depends on your dog's reaction to a particular food.

Making the Choice: Dry, Canned, or Semimoist

When I started sharing my home with dogs, the accepted wisdom was that after you found the right food, you should never, ever change — a good food was a good food and should never be switched for any other food. I know that this system still works for a lot of dog owners. For example, if you look at the University of Missouri's Web site, it states, "Dogs aren't people and are perfectly content to eat the same food every day." The Web site also states that you shouldn't change foods: "Pick one type and one brand and stick with it." If you buy into this philosophy, you can see that the food that your dog eats is going to be an important decision. In this section, I go over three of the basic categories that dog food falls into.

Dry food is a popular choice among dog owners. This selection is easy on your pocketbook, has a long shelf life, and gives your dog something to chew. If you decide to leave food out for your dog all day, dry food doesn't spoil in the bowl. Even if your Bulldog inhales his food with barely a thought for chewing, dry food is less apt to stick to teeth and cause dental problems.

But although dry foods are a popular purchase selection for humans, dogs love canned food. To your Bulldog, canned food smells good and tastes even better. This type of nourishment may have a larger proportion of meat than dry food, although canned food probably still contains fillers. Canned food generally sells at a higher price than dry. After opening a can, refrigerate the food, and use it within a day or two. Don't leave canned varieties out all day in your dog's bowl because the food spoils quickly. Canned food also sticks to the teeth more easily and can cause dental problems.

Mix canned and dry foods to stretch the canned food and give your dog a yummy meal. Canned food also gives you a method to hide any medication you may need to give your dog. Your Bully will enjoy the treat and have no idea he's being medicated at the same time.

The diet of variety

Some breeders, through general reading and online discussion, suggest that feeding the same food all the time isn't the best option for your dog. Feeding the same food all the time means that the digestive system produces the enzymes needed to process that one particular food. If another food is given, the system can't handle it. For example, wild deer can starve to death in a hard winter even if humans provide food because the food isn't what they're used to, and deer can't digest it.

Another argument is that longtime vegetarians may become ill if they eat meat, not because the meat is bad, but because their systems aren't used to dealing with meat. That's why if you need to switch dog foods, gradually mix the new food with the old. This mixture gives your dog's system time to adjust to the change.

Veterinarian Wendy Blount suggests feeding a variety of foods. Wendy practices in Nacogdoches, Texas, and is residency trained in Small Animal Internal Medicine. Her areas of interest in addition to internal medicine are nutrition and herbal medicine.

Dr. Blount combines dry and canned foods, never feeds the same food more than two days in a row, and frequently adds fresh food as well. She offers several reasons for this model: "The National Cancer Institute suggests that we [humans] need a varied diet of fresh (nonprocessed) foods to prevent cancer. Yet we recommend a steady diet of a single brand of processed foods for pets. And then we add to their diets minute amounts of carcinogens. And cancer is the number-one killer of dogs. How much sense does that make?"

Dr. Blount also notes, "Human medical research tells us that overexposure to certain antigens may precipitate food allergies in some predisposed individuals — many veterinary dermatologists agree and recommend rotating the diet for healthy dogs."

And finally, Blount says, "Feeding a variety of wholesome foods may compensate for individual variations in needs and/or unknown deficiencies in particular commercial foods."

The last option for dog food is the most expensive of the three choices: semimoist food. This food is frequently formed into attractive shapes for humans (because your dog doesn't care what it looks like), so it looks like ground beef or a hamburger patty. Food coloring gives the cuisine a meaty look. Read the label. Prominent animal proteins and vitamins may abound, but so do sugar and preservatives, and possibly flour, which all help the patty stay shaped. Avoid any food that doesn't look healthy for your Bully.

 With skin allergies being a common problem in Bulldogs, adding variety to your dog's diet may be the answer. Check with your veterinarian if you want to try diet variety with your Bully. For more on this option, see the sidebar "The diet of variety."

Cooking for Your Bulldog

The majority of dog owners make their food selection from the wide variety of prepared brands, but some people cook for their dogs, preparing their meals from scratch. If you decide that this option is best for you, remember that your dog's diet must still be balanced. Cooking up some chicken and rice may help your dog recover from an upset stomach, but the concoction isn't a balanced diet, and neither is a big, meaty bone, no matter how much your dog enjoys it. You have to make sure that any diet you feed your dog still contains the proper proportions of protein, fat, carbohydrates, vitamins, and minerals. Consult an animal nutritionist to make sure that the meals you cook for your dog supply the nourishment he needs.

Discover all that you can about this method of feeding. If you decide to cook for your dog, make sure that you have the time to commit. Cooking from scratch isn't a short-term project; your dog can live for the next ten years — are you going to cook the entire time? Think about storage space for ingredients and for prepared food. If you cook up a big batch of food, make sure that your freezer has room to hold the extras.

Many people who cook for their dogs use a meat base, such as ground beef or turkey. A pressure cooker reduces bones to mush, ensuring that your dog gets the calcium that bones supply. Add potatoes or oatmeal and vegetables of your choice. Add vitamin and mineral supplements after the food is cooked. An Internet search turns up dozens of books that contain specific recipes, and www.boxerlife.com/basics.htm lists cooking information and recipes.

Considering the BARF Diet (No, It's Not as Gross as It Sounds)

Some Bulldog owners prefer feeding raw-food diets, like the Bones and Raw Food or Biologically Appropriate Raw Foods (BARF) diet. Most people don't ride the fence when it comes to feeding raw. People are either totally against it or totally in favor of it. Proponents of raw food say that their dogs are healthier, with clean teeth and gleaming coats.

The presence of bacteria in uncooked food presents the most widely critiqued aspect of the raw method. Some people say that the dog's system takes care of these bacteria and that the dog's short digestive system doesn't let the "bad stuff" stay in the body long enough to do any harm.

If you decide to feed raw food, remember that your dog's diet must still be balanced. You may also add supplements. Suggestions vary as to types of supplements, but most raw diets include vitamin supplements and fish oil or flaxseed oil. *The Holistic Guide for a Healthy Dog,* (Howell Books) by Wendy Volhard and Kerry Brown, DVM, gives detailed information on proper foods and necessary supplements for a natural diet; and *Switching to Raw: A Fresh Food Diet For Dogs That Makes Sense,* by Susan K. Johnson (Birchrun Basics), is an easy-to-understand book about how to feed raw.

Feeding raw definitely takes more effort than opening a can or pouring some kibble from a bag. A general feeding pattern should include the following:

1. **Feed raw, meaty bones each morning.**

2. **Feed a variety of foods at night.**

3. **Alternate among organ meat, muscle meat, and vegetables.**

Vegetables need to be processed in a blender or food processor before you feed them to your dogs. The blending helps break up the cellulose. Dogs don't produce enzymes that digest cellulose, so unless you break the vegetables down, they pass through the dog's system untouched. If you decide to add grains, like rice or oatmeal, to your dog's diet, cook them first. Cooked potatoes may also be added for variety. You don't need to cook every day. Make up a big batch of your vegetables or grains, and freeze in individual portions.

You need freezer space and a source for your raw foods as well. In larger cities, pet-supply shops may stock frozen raw bones, turkey necks, tripe, and packages of raw meat mixed with vegetables. If this option isn't available to you, find a good butcher.

Jean Hofve, DVM, offers suggestions for feeding raw at her Web site (`www.littlebigcat.com`). Yes, the site is primarily about cats, but you can find information about dogs as well. Dr. Hofve recommends pounding or grinding bones to alleviate the dangers of bone splinters and the difficulty in digesting the bone, especially for puppies.

An alternative to raw meat and bones is to cook chicken legs in a crock pot. Cover the legs with water, and cook on low for 24 hours. The extended cooking time reduces the bones to mush. Check to make sure that no pieces of bone remain, and cool before feeding.

Ask your veterinarian for his opinion. If he is against a raw diet, but you intend to feed raw, have your veterinarian run a blood scan on your Bulldog before you start the raw diet. Repeat the scan every six months. This monitoring allows your veterinarian to regulate the effects the diet has on the health of your dog. You don't want the issue of food to be the reason you lose a veterinarian who understands Bulldogs.

When to Feed Your Bully

You've decided to feed your Bulldog a premium kibble, a quality canned food, or a homemade diet. You've talked to your breeder, your veterinarian, and possibly a nutritionist. Now you need to decide *when* to feed your dog. Most breeders suggest feeding twice a day, no matter which meal method you choose. With an older dog, feeding twice daily gives him a chance to get more out of each meal because as a dog ages, his digestive system may not be as efficient. Remember that feeding twice a day means splitting the daily ration, not doubling it. You don't want an overweight dog.

An advantage to feeding at specific times is that if your dog isn't feeling well, skipping a meal is frequently the first sign that something is wrong with your Bully. With regular meals, you know right away if your dog isn't eating. If you have multiple dogs, being able to separate them and watch over mealtime ensures that all dogs get the proper nutrition and portion.

You may like the idea of *free feeding* — measuring out your dog's daily allowance of food and letting him choose the time to eat. For some households, this procedure works just fine. I can hardly imagine a Bulldog leaving morsels for later after he's found the food, but I suppose that it's possible.

Free feeding doesn't work with home-cooked meals, the BARF diet, or the canned-food diet. The food gets dried out and crusty and provides a cozy home for bacteria, which can lead to illnesses in your dog

If you have two or more dogs, free feeding doesn't work because you never know who is really getting all the food. One dog or the other may dominate and get more of, if not all, the food. Also, if you free-feed, medicines or supplements are harder to regulate for each dog because with multiple dogs, you need to make sure that the right dog gets the added ingredients.

Whatever you decide to feed your Bulldog, make sure that he always has access to fresh, clean water! Because Bulldogs may overheat, water is especially important. Change the water in your dog's bowl at least twice a day, and remember to wash the bowl. Water isn't clean and fresh if it keeps going into a slimy bowl.

Giving Your Bully Doggy Treats

No matter what kind of diet your Bully follows, a time will come when you want to give him a treat. All my dogs get a dog biscuit at bedtime, as well as one whenever they go out. After breakfast, each one gets a carrot stick. I carry treats in my pocket when I walk my female so I can practice sits and downs. At lunchtime, the dogs line up for their bite of cheese, and when we have pizza, they expect to share the crusts.

The luxury of liver treats

People who show their dogs frequently use cooked liver to get their dogs to look alert and happy in the show ring. Whether you show your dog or not, liver makes a great and healthy treat. Liver contains no sugar, flour, or preservatives, and you can freeze the extra, thawing just what you need.

You can make liver treats in two different ways.

1. Put your liver in a microwave-safe dish.

2. Cover the liver with a paper towel.

3. Microwave for 3 minutes on high.

4. Turn the liver piece(s) over, and cook for an additional 3 minutes on high.

   The result is a lot like shoe leather.

---

5. Cut the leather — I mean, liver — into small pieces, and use for training or for the occasional treat.

A second way to prepare liver treats is by using garlic. Dogs love garlic, and the smell tempts even the fussiest of eaters — not that there are many fussy Bulldogs.

1. Rinse the liver.

2. Put the meat in a pan of cold water.

3. Bring the water to a boil.

4. Boil for 20 minutes.

5. When the liver has finished boiling, place it on a cookie sheet.

6. Sprinkle the meat with garlic powder.

7. Bake in the over for 20 to 30 minutes at 300 degrees.

8. Remove the cookie sheet from the oven.

9. Let the liver cool completely.

10. Cut the meat into bite-size pieces.

11. Store the leftovers in the freezer.

12. Make sure to thaw the liver treats before giving them to your dog.

For easy cleanup, cover your cookie sheet with aluminum foil, and put the liver on the foil. When the liver has cooled, you can remove the foil and just toss it in the trash.

Remember: Don't overfeed liver treats. Too much liver can cause loose stools.

Special treats for dogs abound. The store shelves line with all kinds of goodies, from hard biscuits to soft, bone-shaped treats to all kinds and shapes of rawhide chews. Rawhide chews, however, must be approached with some caution, as discussed in "Looking at Chew Toys," later in the chapter. Breeder advice is *no rawhide for your Bully.*

Sharing People Snacks with Your Bully

It's fun to give our dogs little bits of people food now and then, and most dogs can make you believe that they're starving when food is around. Sharing is fine within reason. Just remember a few pointers when sharing snacks with your Bully:

✓ **Limit treats to no more than 10 percent of your dog's total diet.** If your dog is gaining weight, cut back on the treats, and add a bit of exercise. Dogs soon discover when their behaviors produce treats, so try cutting the size of the treat in half. Adding exercise is harder with a Bulldog than, say, a Labrador Retriever. You don't want to stress your dog or get him overheated, but maybe you can work in another trip around the block.

✓ **Pay attention to the kind of treats you're giving your dog.** A bit of lean turkey at Thanksgiving is fine, but don't overdo the generosity with the rich gravy and spicy stuffing. A spoonful of pumpkin is a healthy treat, but pumpkin pie isn't.

✓ **Share your popcorn.** When you make popcorn for an evening snack, set aside a helping that is unbuttered and unsalted for your dog.

✓ **Add vegetables to the diet.** Carrots make a tasty chew toy, or throw a few green beans on top of your Bully's food. You've given him a treat with no fat and fewer calories.

✓ **Give your dog some *pupsicles*.** Most dogs love the occasional ice cube. Get your Bulldog used to munching ice because the cool cubes can help keep him from overheating on a hot day.

When your Bully is behaving, pop out a pupsicle, and watch his eyes light up. After your Bulldog adjusts to munching on cold cubes, alternate pupsicles and regular ice cubes. For details on how to create these treats, see the sidebar "Making pupsicles."

Making pupsicles

One of my friends encourages the ice cube habit by making what she calls "pupsicles":

1. Mix a can of low-sodium chicken or beef bouillon with a can of water (use the same can the broth came from).

2. Pour broth mixture in ice cube trays, and freeze.

3. Cover with aluminum foil to prevent heavy freezer burn.

You can also use dry bouillon cubes. Just reconstitute according to directions, mix with water, and freeze.

What Not to Feed Your Bully

In addition to all the fun foods you can share with your Bully, another list exists of foods that your Bully should never ingest. I know that your Bully buddy can be convincing, but never, ever give your Bulldog any of the following items:

✔ **Alcohol:** Don't give your Bully alcoholic beverages. A drunken dog isn't funny, and even small amounts of liquor can result in alcohol poisoning, which can lead to death.

✔ **Chocolate:** Chocolate contains theobromine, which can be fatal. The darker the chocolate, the greater the danger.

The American Animal Hospital Association notes that 2 to 3 ounces of baking chocolate can kill a medium-size dog. And 1 to 1½ pounds of milk chocolate can have the same effect. Don't panic if you drop a chocolate chip on the floor or your dog steals an Oreo, but keep that box of holiday chocolates out of reach of your dog, and be extremely careful with baking chocolate.

✔ **Coffee and tea:** Both contain caffeine and theobromine.

✔ **Macadamia nuts:** Don't serve these treats to your dog. Eating too many Macadamia nuts can cause paralysis. Symptoms include a mild fever and an upset stomach. Depending on the size of the dog and how many nuts he eats, within 12 to 24 hours, his back legs become paralyzed. The front legs are either unaffected or minimally affected, but the back legs no longer work. Within 72 hours, the dog is fine, as though nothing ever happened.

The good news —the paralysis goes away without lasting effects. The bad news — some dogs may be euthanized because they're misdiagnosed as having a severely injured disc, particularly among breeds where injured discs frequently occur. So keep the Macadamia nuts away from your Bully, or better yet, switch to cashews, which don't harm your pooch. I had a dog who managed to reach and devour an entire bowl of cashews. She suffered no ill effects.

✔ **Nicotine:** Tobacco products are deadly, so make sure that your Bulldog doesn't eat any cigars, cigarettes, snuff, or chewing tobacco.

✔ **Onions:** No one wants a Bulldog with onion breath, but that's not the only reason to keep your dog away from onions. Onions can cause hemolytic anemia. Symptoms of this type of anemia include pale mucus membranes, loss of energy, and lack of appetite. Your dog may also feel the cold more and try to find a warm corner. The dog may have a fever or a faster heart rate. Treatment may include a blood transfusion and/or vitamin B-12.

✔ **Xylitol:** Xylitol, an artificial sweetener, can cause a sudden drop in blood sugar, resulting in depression, loss of coordination, and seizures.

Looking at Chew Toys

Dogs enjoy a chewing workout now and then, but be careful what you offer your Bulldog. If you give your dog a real bone, make sure that it's fresh and raw. Never give your dog any kind of cooked bone, because bones can splinter and cause serious intestinal damage. Make sure that the bone is large enough for your dog as well. A dog can easily swallow a small bone that may get stuck in his throat or cause an upset stomach. If you want to give your dog a real bone, stay with him while he enjoys it so you can intervene if a problem arises. Another disadvantage of real bones is that they're messy. You aren't going to want to let your dog have a real bone on the living room carpet.

If you have more than one dog, bones may cause a fight. Dogs get possessive of bones, so if you have multiple dogs, make sure that you feed bones separately to prevent problems.

Nylon bones are an alternative to raw bones because they don't break or splinter. Small shreds of nylon that your dog may swallow pass harmlessly through the digestive tract. Nylon bones also get bristly at the ends, acting a bit like a toothbrush as your dog chews, removing plague buildup. Nylon bones don't stain carpet or floors, and dogs are less possessive of a nylon bone. Again, make sure that the size fits the dog.

Hard rubber toys, especially the kind with a place to hide cheese or peanut butter (Kongs), may also give your dog chewing exercise, but be careful that your dog doesn't bite off large chunks of the toy and swallow them. Different dogs treat toys differently. Supervise your dog until you know what kind of a chewer he is.

Rawhide comes in a variety of shapes and sizes, but for Bulldogs, rawhide is dangerous. Bulldogs tend to chew and soften rawhide and then pull more into their mouths, never actually biting off a piece. When they swallow, this long piece of rawhide can become impacted in the intestines (or bowel), causing problems. Take the end of a rawhide and pull it away from your Bulldog, and you're apt to pull a piece 12 inches or longer out of his mouth. Stay away from rawhide.

Special Diets for Your Bulldog

The important concept to remember is that not all foods are right for all dogs. If your Bully has large, smelly stools, look for another food. If a food is causing a minor problem, trial and error can help you find a better food. Your friend's recommendation for her Bulldog may give your dog diarrhea. If your dog's reaction to food is frenzied scratching and chewing at himself, loss of weight, and skin and coat problems (coat is dull and dry), he may have food allergies, and you need to visit the veterinarian. Your vet may put your dog on a one-protein food, like duck or venison, and then gradually move to foods with another ingredient or two until the cause of the allergy is determined.

Remember that your dog needs to be happy, healthy, and hungry for more of what you're feeding. If your Bulldog's coat is shiny and glossy; if his stools are firm and small, with no obnoxious odor; and if he is healthy, the food you chose is doing its job. Don't be afraid to ask questions, and do some research to find the ideal meal for your Bulldog.

You may have seen the senior pet foods on the shelves in your local grocery store, supercenter, or pet store. Senior foods are formulated to help control weight in an older dog whose metabolism has slowed with age. Stores may also carry "light" foods for less active dogs, no matter what their age. If you decide to switch to a food for seniors, pay attention to your dog's skin and coat. Some dogs develop dry, flaky skin because of the reduced amount of fat in the food. Mixing a senior food with a regular food may help, or you may need to add a tablespoon or so of oil to your dog's food to help keep his skin moisturized.

Many reasons exist for why your dog may not be able to eat regular dog food or even a meal you prepare yourself. Fortunately, many dog food companies produce specific canned and dry diets especially formulated for specific illnesses and diseases:

- ✔ **Cancer:** Dogs with cancer typically need a food with a moderate amount of fat, moderate to high protein, and low carbohydrate, with increased amounts of omega fatty acids.

- ✔ **Diabetes:** If your dog has diabetes, he may need to switch to a diet high in complex carbohydrates. Ask your veterinarian for a recommendation.

- ✔ **Heart disease:** Dogs with heart problems may benefit from diets low in sodium.

✔ **Kidney disease:** As dogs age, kidney problems may trigger special dietary needs. Except in acute kidney disease, a low-protein diet is no longer considered ideal. What does seem to help kidney disease is less phosphorous in the diet, and low-protein foods are also usually lower in phosphorous than regular diets. Contrary to popular belief, high-protein diets don't cause kidney damage.

For a dog with kidney disease, your veterinarian may recommend canned food over dry because canned food contains more water, and the more water your dog gets, the better. If you still prefer to feed dry, add as much water to the food as you can and have your dog still eat it. Adding water to the canned food is a good idea, too.

✔ **Liver disease:** Put a dog with liver disease on a low-protein diet.

✔ **Pancreatitis:** A dog diagnosed with pancreatitis needs a food low in fat.

✔ **Staining:** Staining is a common complaint from Bulldog owners. Tear stains and saliva stains (pink or red staining of the neck, face, or feet) may derive from your Bully's diet. Feeding a different brand of food may help. Chicken- and turkey-based diets seem to cause fewer issues than lamb or beef, but the individual dog's metabolism plays a role.

If you've been feeding your dog a homemade diet, and he now needs a special diet, you can still make meals instead of buying the commercial product. Visit www.2ndchance.info/homemade diets.htm for recipes for special diets for dogs with heart, kidney, urinary tract problems, diabetes, obesity, and allergies.

Chapter 8

Grooming Your Bulldog

*B*ulldogs aren't difficult to groom; you don't need a lot of fancy brushes, combs, or clippers. But Bulldogs still need occasional grooming — all dogs benefit from brushing and baths. Grooming time also allows you to check your dog for cuts, scrapes, or unusual bumps. Regular clipping of nails and checking of eyes and ears can catch any little problems before they become big problems.

Proper grooming keeps your dog an appreciated member of the family (and a better smelling one to boot). Grooming equals good health, and the time you spend grooming your dog helps to form a bond between you and your Bully.

Brushing Your Bulldog

Brushing removes dead hair and skin, spreads oil throughout the coat, and stimulates blood flow.

Bulldogs don't have elaborate coats or thick fur, so you don't need a lot of different types of brushes to brush your Bulldog completely and thoroughly. To brush your Bulldog properly, however, you need the following items:

> ✔ **Squirt bottle for water:** Spritzing your dog's coat before brushing keeps the hairs from breaking. Add a dash of Listerine to help clean the coat.

✔ **Bristle brush:** Boar's bristle brushes are expensive, but they last forever.

✔ **Curry comb:** This comb's stubby rubber nubs loosen and remove head hair.

Brush from the nose to the tail. It's best to have your Bulldog standing when you're brushing him, especially if you're getting him ready for a show and want his coat to look as nice as possible (see Chapter 11, and also the sidebar in this chapter, "Putting your Bully on the table"). When your Bulldog is standing, certain portions of him are more easily reached. However, if your Bully isn't going to a show and prefers to recline during the brushing process, that's perfectly okay.

To brush your Bully:

1. **Spritz him lightly with water from your squirt bottle.**

2. **Use the curry comb to work through his fur to remove loose and clumped hair.**

3. **Use the bristle brush to brush away all the loose hair.**

Don't forget to brush his legs and tail!

Your bed makes a wonderful grooming surface. I recently discovered this fact because the weather was way too hot outside to set up the grooming table. We have a fairly high bed in our bedroom, and we keep a sheet over the bedspread because one of our dogs sleeps with us. The dog needed grooming, so I hoisted my boy up on the bed and brushed away.

The bed provides a big surface for both you and your dog. You can sit on the edge of the bed and easily groom his feet. The bed also offers a soft platform to encourage your Bully to roll over on his side for brushing. That is virtually impossible on a grooming table without ending up in an argument. After grooming your dog, pull off the sheet, shake the hair in the trash, and throw the sheet in the washer.

Make sure that you use a rubber mat or some other type of non-skid surface for a base when grooming your Bully. You don't want your dog to panic because he can't grip a smooth surface, and you don't want him sliding off.

Putting your Bully on the table

At the top of my shopping list is a grooming table. The older I get, the more I don't want to kneel to do anything. A grooming table also helps you control your dog. He can't easily scoot away from you during the grooming process if he's on a table.

Planning on showing your Bully? Then you need a grooming table. If you don't plan to show, you may not need a specific grooming table, but do think about what you can use in your own home: a rubber mat on top of the clothes dryer, a work bench in the basement or garage, a sheet on top of your kitchen table.

Getting the Skinny on Skin Care

The Bulldog breed tends to be more susceptible to skin problems than other breeds. Problems range from dry, flaky skin to serious allergies to mange. A dog with fleas may end up with hot spots. But Bulldogs' face wrinkles require the most attention and care in the grooming process.

Wrinkles are beautiful

Wrinkles give a Bulldog his characteristic look and add to his charm, but these face folds need to be kept clean and dry. Some dogs' wrinkles need cleaning only a couple of times a week, but other dogs need their wrinkles cleaned every day. Because air can't get into the bottoms of the wrinkles, skin in the fold can become red, raw, and infected. If you notice a smell or any goop in the wrinkles, you need to clean them more often.

Use a damp cloth, cotton balls, or baby wipes. Baby wipes with aloe are a good choice because the aloe soothes the skin and helps moisturize, or you can mix water and dog shampoo. If you use shampoo, mix a tiny drop of it in a cup of warm water, and use a cotton ball to dab the wrinkles with the solution. Afterward, make sure that you rinse the wrinkles well to prevent further irritation. No matter what you choose to clean your dog's face, make sure that you thoroughly dry the wrinkles when finished. Use some petroleum jelly in the deep wrinkles to soothe the skin and add a moisture barrier.

Popular drying agents like powders or cornstarch aren't recommended for Bulldogs because they can clump on and irritate the skin.

When wrinkles appear raw or irritated, use a general antiseptic ointment or a diaper-rash cream to treat the area. And while you're taking care of the wrinkles, put a dab of petroleum jelly, vitamin E, or Bag Balm on your Bully's nose to help maintain the softness.

Acne — not just for teenagers

Your Bulldog doesn't have to be a teenager to get acne. Wrinkles make a lively place for bacteria to grow, and this growth may result in pimples on your dog's face and chin. Plastic dishes can also cause this problem, so I recommend using ceramic or stainless steel. Most of the time, minor breakouts respond to gentle washing and a daily treatment of antibiotic cream. You can also use a product called Oxyio, available in most drugstores. Acne that doesn't seem to go away merits a visit to your veterinarian. He may prescribe an oral antibiotic for your dog to help clear up the problem.

Alleviating skin allergies

If your Bully has skin problems — redness, flakiness, itchiness — for no apparent reason that you can think of, he may have allergies. Canine allergies — just like human allergies — stem from foods, molds, and pollens and cause itchy skin. Discomfort can be seasonal and chalked up to "something in the air." Continuous irritations can result from a number of reasons, but your dog's food is the most likely culprit.

If you suspect that your Bully's skin problems are due to allergies, make a trip to the veterinarian. He may run tests to pinpoint the cause of your dog's discomfort, or he may suggest a food made of all one product. These special diets have just one ingredient, like duck. Then, by gradually adding other foods, you can determine the exact cause of the allergy. Allergy food testing is a lengthy process, and fortunately, most dogs don't need to go this route.

Halting hot spots

A flea-saliva allergy in your dog may drive him to continuous biting and scratching, which can create hot spots. *Hot spots* are red, weeping sores caused by dogs biting their own skin. I use a triple antibiotic salve on hot spots, and the ointment seems to work. When hot spots don't get better within a few days or continue to get larger, check with your veterinarian.

You also need to manage the flea infestation in your dog. For more on controlling fleas, see "Making fleas flee" in Chapter 14.

Managing mange

Mange, a persistent, contagious disease of the skin causing inflammation, itching, and loss of hair, poses another skin problem in
Bulldogs. If you suspect that your dog has mange, take him to the
vet right away to determine what's causing the mange and what
treatments are needed.

Two types of mange, both caused by tiny mites, may affect your dog:

- **Sarcoptic mange:** Symptoms accompanying Sarcoptic mange
  include intense itching and, with advanced cases, skin lesions
  and hair loss. Treatments are done internally with a prescrip-
  tion of ivermectin and externally with sulfur dips to help ease
  the irritation. Using a monthly flea and tick preventative effectively protects your pet against mange-causing mites. Make
  sure to disinfect the dog's bedding thoroughly or simply
  throw it away.

- **Demodetic mange:** The second type of mange passes from
  the mother to her puppies and affects puppies between the
  ages of 3 and 10 months. With Demodetic mange, you may
  notice hair loss around your dog's eyes, lips, or forelegs.
  Extreme cases include hair loss at the tips of the ears. A special shampoo may be recommended, and ivermectin comes
  in handy again. Demodetic mange, if not widespread on the
  dog's body, may go away on its own. If the mange spreads sig-
  nificantly beyond small, localized areas, treatment can last up
  to one year. Veterinarians diagnose Demodetic mange through
  skin scrapings, but this type of mange doesn't cause the itching that Sarcoptic mange does.

Bringing up the rear

Your dog's tail doesn't need much attention, but on some Bulldogs,
the tail sits in a pocket that can harbor bacteria. If your dog has a
tail pocket, meaning that there's a thick fold of skin surrounding the
base of his tail, make a special effort to keep that pocket clean and
dry with daily wiping. For a tight tail pocket, you may need to use
cotton balls instead of a washcloth or a baby wipe. After washing
the tail pocket, make sure to dry it thoroughly. Rub a bit of antibiotic cream in the pocket for added protection. A bit of petroleum
jelly acts as a moisture barrier, just as it does for wrinkles. If the tail
seems irritated or infected, your veterinarian can give you an anti-
fungal ointment, as tail infections are frequently yeast infections.

Puppy Pedicures

If you walk your dog on paved roads or cement sidewalks, you may be one of the lucky few who never need to clip or grind his dog's nails. Otherwise, like the rest of us, include nail care in your grooming routine.

If, for some reason, you can't deal with trimming or grinding your dog's nails, hold your head high, and take your Bully to a groomer for his pedicure. No matter how those nails get short, make sure trimming happens. Long nails spread your dog's foot *(splaying)* and make walking difficult.

Cutting the nails

Nail trimming doesn't rank high on your Bulldog's list of most popular events for dogs. However, your Bully doesn't feel pain when you clip his nails unless you accidentally cut the *quick* (a tiny vein that runs through the center of your dog's nails), so don't let your dog tell you otherwise.

From the puppy stage, start trimming and get your Bully used to having his feet handled, even when you're not preparing to do the nails. Hold a paw in your hand. Give your pup a treat, tell him he's wonderful, and then let him go so that he associates paw handling with happy moments.

You need to buy a pair of special nail clippers intended for dogs. You get what you pay for, so invest in a good set. Ask your breeder or your veterinarian for recommendations.

When you do start to clip the nails, use sharp clippers, and cut quickly. Do one foot at a time in the following pattern: Trim nails, give treat, release to play, repeat pattern. The pattern helps your dog release the anxiety associated with trimming. The break time allows you to recoup between trimmings, especially if you're worried about hitting the quick.

Cut nails where they curve around to a point to avoid the quick. (If the thought of hitting the quick terrifies you, take off tiny amounts of the nail at first.) See Figure 8-1 for proper placement of the cut for nail trimming. If your dog has white nails, you can see the quick, which somewhat resembles a smaller, dark nail inside the actual nail, and avoid cutting it. If your dog has black nails, you'll need to make an educated guess, but the general rule is never cut the nail past the pad of the foot. With regular trimming, the quick shrinks, and over time, the risk of hitting the quick lessens.

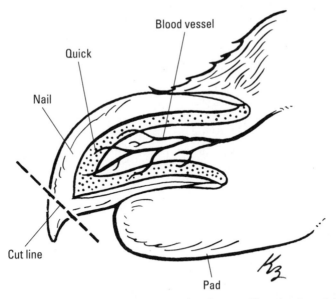

Figure 8-1: Where to trim your Bulldog's nails to avoid cutting the quick.

If you do happen to hit the quick, use a bit of styptic powder (available at your local pet-supply store or at a drugstore) to stop the bleeding. If you plan to trim your Bulldog's nails yourself, purchase styptic powder to have on hand in case of bleeding. If bleeding occurs, coat the end of the nail generously with styptic powder, and keep the paw elevated until the bleeding stops.

Grinding the nails

If, for whatever reason, you just can't cut the nails yourself, don't feel bad. I can't either. I can rip fleas apart with my nails, clean oozing wounds, and scoop out eye and ear gunk, but I just can't clip nails. However, I *can* grind nails.

A *grinder* is a motor-driven tool with an abrasive round drum. Think of a small version of a power sander, and you have the idea. The grinder acts as a file and grinds away the unwanted nail. Many dogs who hate having their nails cut don't mind the grinder at all, and when using a grinder, the risk of cutting the quick is eliminated. (Ask your breeder to recommend a grinder.)

Get your dog used to the grinder gradually. Turn on the grinder when you're grooming your dog, so he gets used to the motor's noise. Hold a paw against the handle of the grinder, and let him feel the vibration. When your dog seems comfortable with the noise and shaking of the tool, try a nail. Just as recommended with nail cutting, grind one set of nails at a time, and take a break. Give treats (offer a variety of treats). In no time at all, your Bulldog quietly lets you grind his nails without a fuss.

The "Eyes" Have It

Generally, the grooming process doesn't include regular eye care. But occasional dust and dirt particles from the outdoors cause eye irritations. To rinse out your Bully's eye(s), squirt a mild eye solution in the eyeball. Pet-supply stores carry many brands of eye solutions, or ask your vet to recommend one. Eye problems greater than the minor particle in the eye should always be referred to a vet. A scratched or swollen eye with seeping requires a veterinarian's examination.

Tear stains, on the other hand, can be treated at home. Your Bulldog's tears run down his face and can leave stains. Not all Bulldogs get eye stains, but if yours does, the discoloration isn't harmful to your dog. If you'd prefer your Bulldog's face stain free, check with a groomer or your veterinarian for stain-removing products, or try these helpful products and concoctions:

- **Boric acid or ointment:** Gently rub the stain with a piece of cotton soaked in boric acid, or use a dab of boric acid ointment, which you can find in most drugstores.

- **Hydrogen peroxide and cornstarch:** Make a thin paste of hydrogen peroxide and cornstarch. Apply carefully to the stain, let dry, and then brush off. Apply daily.

- **Tear stain remover, diaper rash cream, and medicated body powder:** Clean the tear-stained area with the tear stain remover dry. Apply a thin layer of diaper rash ointment, and dust with medicated powder. Tears tend to roll off instead of staining the face.

Ears to Good Health

Make checking and cleaning your dog's folded-open ears another part of your grooming routine. Potential infections grow anyplace where air can't freely circulate, so it's best to keep your Bully's ears clean to prevent problems. You can buy ear-cleaning products or use a cotton ball soaked in hydrogen peroxide. Gently clean the earflap and just inside the ear.

Never, ever push and poke into the inner ear of your Bulldog; you can seriously injure him.

Ear mites, while not common, can be a problem with regard to ear health, as they can cause redness, swelling, and bleeding from constant scratching. Pay attention when your dog shakes her head or scratches at her ears. These indicators relay messages of potential problems. If you suspect a problem with your dog's ears, schedule a visit with your veterinarian.

The Whole Tooth and Nothing but the Tooth

Tooth decay plagues humans more than dogs, but that doesn't mean that dogs aren't susceptible. Bulldogs can develop plaque, which, if not removed, hardens to tartar. Possible complications from tartar include abscesses of the gums. Or the bacteria from abscesses can circulate in your dog's system and lead to pneumonia or heart, liver, or kidney problems.

Brusha, brusha, brusha

If you start cleaning your dog's teeth when he's a puppy, he'll soon get used to the routine. Toothbrushing may not be your favorite activity to share with your dog, but statistics show that 75 percent of all dogs have some kind of periodontal problem by the age of four. So include your Bulldog's mouth and teeth in every health check.

Your veterinarian can give you recommendations on what products to use on your dog's teeth and can show you the proper way to keep your Bully's teeth clean. To brush your dog's teeth, you can use:

- Gauze wrapped around your finger
- Pretreated wipes
- Smaller plastic brushes that fit over your finger
- Special dog toothbrushes

Most veterinarians and pet-supply stores also sell special pastes that come in a variety of flavors for brushing your dog's teeth. Make sure that you use a paste made especially for dogs; never use human toothpaste for your dog's dental care.

Professional cleaning

Eventually, your veterinarian may recommend a professional cleaning for your dog's teeth. This procedure entails anesthetizing your dog so that the vet or technician can remove tartar buildup and clean and polish your dog's teeth. If cracked or broken teeth are found, they can be pulled during the procedure.

Not all dogs are alike, of course. Some dogs may need their teeth cleaned every six months; others may go their entire lives without a professional cleaning. Your veterinarian checks your dog's teeth during the annual checkup, but if you ever notice the following problems, contact your vet:

- ✔ Different breath or more intense breath than normal
- ✔ Excessive drooling
- ✔ Lack of desire to chew on toys or bones
- ✔ Pawing at the mouth
- ✔ Trouble eating hard food

When treating older dogs, veterinarians usually recommend blood tests before the cleaning to ensure the dog's safety under anesthesia. The blood tests may help your veterinarian detect other health problems as well.

Bathing Your Bully: Water, Water Everywhere

Your Bulldog may not need a bath often, especially if you keep him clean with regular brushings and wrinkle cleanings, but one day your dog and your bathtub will need to meet. Unless you have a large stationary laundry tub in your basement, use your own tub as the designated bathing area. Get organized, gathering every item you need before you find and heave your dog into the tub.

Preparing the bathing area

Before you start your Bulldog's bath, collect the following supplies:

- ✔ **Baby wipes:** Used for cleaning wrinkles.
- ✔ **Cotton balls or swabs along with commercial ear-cleaning solution:** If you haven't already cleaned your Bully's ears on the grooming table, choose bathtime as the time to do it.

✔ **Dog shampoo:** Don't use human shampoo, no matter how much you like the smell — the pH balance in shampoo differs for dogs.

✔ **Flexible spray nozzle, pan, or pitcher:** Attach the spray nozzle to the faucet, or use a pan or pitcher to pour water over your Bully. (Spray nozzles are easier to use and get all the soap out of your dog's coat.)

✔ **Grooming apron or an old sweatshirt:** This is for you to wear. Be prepared to get wet. Your dog *will* shake one or more times, and you *will* get wet.

✔ **Hair dryer:** Use either a special dog dryer or your own. Remember to set the dryer on low or air only.

✔ **Rubber mat:** Prevents the dog from slipping in the tub.

✔ **Stack of towels:** Get more than you think you need. Use a couple to kneel on, or get a pillow or a rubber pad to protect your knees.

After you've gathered all your supplies and before you put your dog in the tub, run the water to the desired temperature — warm enough to be comfortable but not too hot. If you try to place your pooch in the tub and the water runs too hot at first, you may scald your dog's paws, and cold water may shock your dog into a panic. Test the water temperature on the inside of your wrist, just as you do a baby bottle of formula. When in doubt, go cooler rather than warmer.

Preparing your pup

Now go get the dog. Bathtime usually ranks at the bottom of any dog's list of favorites. Inevitably, your Bulldog sees right through your loving voice and desire to pick him up for a simple cuddle and knows to run and hide.

So you may have to put him on a lead, pick him up, or lure him with treats to get him into the bathroom with you. But after you have him cornered and you're both in the bathroom, close the door. If you own other pets, you don't want them wandering in and distracting you or the dog, and after you suds up your Bully, you don't want him escaping to spread suds and water throughout the house.

Ideally, avoid shampoo near your dog's face, and clean the face separately. Before you hoist your dog into the tub, you may want to protect his eyes and ears:

✔ Some groomers recommend a drop of mineral oil in the eyes to protect Bulldogs against soap, but others feel that the oil just spreads the soap.

✔ Put cotton in your dog's ears to prevent water and soap from leaking in the ear canal. Cotton works if you can keep your dog from shaking her head vigorously and dislodging the cotton. So try the cotton if you want to, but if your dog persists in shaking, just be careful around the ears. Use a damp cloth to wipe the ears clean, and don't use any shampoo at all around the ears.

Because of your Bulldog's short, upturned nose, water can easily trickle into the nose and from the nose into the lungs. A Bulldog can easily drown in a small amount of water. If you're using a spray nozzle, be careful not to get water in your dog's nose.

Washing your Bulldog properly

Now you're ready to begin bathtime:

1. **Lift your dog into the tub.**

   No matter how low your tub, don't allow the dog to climb in on his own. Bulldogs slip easily and may hurt themselves.

2. **After he's in the tub, wash the face wrinkles first.**

   Use water only, and clean his face and earflaps. If you purchased special ear cleaner, use that now.

3. **Wet your dog all over.**

4. **Squirt shampoo on your hand, and begin to lather your dog.**

   Scrub gently, paying close attention to dirty spots and sensitive areas of the body.

5. **Rinse your dog thoroughly.**

   Rinse. Repeat. Rinse again; rinse a third time. And rinse again. Leaving any trace of soap on your dog causes skin irritation and itching.

6. **Rinse him some more.**

   Drench areas around the tail, especially if your dog has a pocket for his tail. Thoroughly douse your dog with water behind the elbows, between the toes, and on his stomach.

   Use some vinegar in the final rinse to get rid of any soap scum and leave your Bulldog's coat shiny and squeaky clean.

7. **Let your dog shake off.**

   I prefer letting him shake while he's in the tub. You'd be amazed at how much water a dog can shake off. Hold up a towel (or close the shower curtain), and let your Bully shake that water in the tub instead of all over your bathroom.

8. **Lift your dog from the tub.**

   Don't let him scramble out on his own.

9. **Dry your dog thoroughly.**

   Use a couple of towels to get him as dry as possible. Then finish drying in one of two ways:

   - When bathing in the summer, your Bulldog can air dry.

   - Follow a winter bath with a thorough drying that may include the use of a hair dryer. You don't want your Bully to chill.

     If you opt for a hair dryer, and you don't own a special dog dryer, use the lowest setting possible. The "air only" setting (if it's an option on your dryer) offers the best experience for your dog. Bulldogs have very sensitive skin, and you can easily burn your dog with too high a dryer setting.

Never cage-dry your Bulldog. Cage drying involves putting your Bully in a crate with a dryer blowing hot air into the crate. Bulldogs overheat in cage-drying situations.

After you clean and dry your dog, you may want to keep him indoors to enjoy his clean, shiny coat. After he's outdoors, the odds increase that he'll head straight for the nearest mud puddle.

Removing the sticky stuff

You may occasionally find that your dog gets into something that you can't easily get off. Here are some helpful household products to remove the goo:

- ✔ **Baby oil.** Rub a small amount of baby oil on your fingers and then rub into the stain.

- ✔ **Hairspray.** Soak hairspray on the spot and then peel or pick off the sticky goop.

- ✔ **Ice cubes.** Use an ice cube to freeze the sticky spot. The substance becomes brittle and flakes off your dog's coat. Be careful not to hold ice too long on any one area.

✔ **Nail-polish remover.** Soak a cotton ball with nail-polish remover and then apply to the sticky spot.

✔ **Peanut butter.** Try applying peanut butter on gooey substances.

All these ideas work, although my favorites include the ice cubes and peanut butter. No matter what method you choose, make sure that you protect your dog's eyes and wash and rinse the spot(s) completely. These products may cause skin irritations if left on too long.

Bathing in a pinch

Your Bulldog desperately needs a bath, but you're out of dog shampoo. What do you do? Make your own. Try the recipes and hints below to get you out of those sticky situations when shampoos and removers aren't readily available.

Homemade shampoo

16 ounces Dove liquid dishwashing detergent

16 ounces water

16 ounces apple-cider vinegar

4 ounces glycerin

Combine ingredients in an old shampoo bottle (or large cup), and swirl together. You can leave out the glycerin (which you probably don't keep on hand), but in that case, reduce the amount of soap. You can make shampoo for now and save some for later. If you don't want a large quantity, keep the recipe proportions the same but reduce the amounts.

Recipe adapted from www.abigslice.com.

Oatmeal shampoo

If your Bulldog suffers from dermatitis, try making a shampoo that includes oatmeal.

1 cup oatmeal

1 cup baking soda

1 quart warm water

Mix oatmeal and baking soda, and pour into water. Oatmeal shampoo makes a soothing rinse for your ailing Bully.

If your dog gets stuck with gum, tree sap, or road tar, remove all or most of the substance before trying one of the items from the previous list.

Grooming allows you to notice anything out of the ordinary going on with your dog, from lumps and bumps to rashes or areas of hair loss. Use this time to check for external parasites as well. See Chapter 14 for more information on parasites.

Part III

Training, Working, and Traveling: The Busy Bulldog

The 5th Wave   By Rich Tennant

Andy has doubts about the canine-osmosis training he's signed up for.

In this part . . .

This part is about work and play. Read about how to housetrain your Bully and then teach him some basics, so that he's always a joy to live with. Take training further, and consider the Canine Good Citizen test, conformation showing, obedience, rally, agility, tracking, and therapy dog work. When it's time for a break from all that training, take a vacation. Does your Bully stay at home or pack a bag too? Keep reading, and find out.

Chapter 9

Housetraining Your Bulldog

. . . .

In This Chapter

▶ Tackling the basics of puppy training

▶ Contemplating crate training

▶ Spreading the news: Paper training

▶ Digging up the dirt on litter training

. . . .

*U*nless you plan on living outdoors for the entire life of your Bulldog, you need to housetrain your pup — that is, teach him where to "go." This chapter deals with the different ways to train your puppy to be reliable in the house and get your Bully to do his business outside rather than inside. Be patient and consistent, and housetraining may be easier than you thought.

Wait and get a puppy when someone can be around to train him. If you anticipate that your puppy may spend most of the day alone during the first few weeks that you bring him home, with no one to let him out or help him understand housetraining, pick a time to bring home your Bully when schedules allow for potty breaks for your pooch.

Housetraining 101

A regular, consistent schedule helps train your puppy quickly. Have a handy-dandy schedule to follow (see "Working out a training schedule," later in this chapter), but remember that you're not dealing with a machine. That means that, although you may be following the schedule, your puppy follows his feelings (or urges).

Be prepared to make a few schedule changes to compensate for your puppy's individual quirks, but as soon as you settle on your schedule (the sooner, the better), stick to it like glue. Puppies (and adult dogs) like routine, and if your training methods are consistent, your puppy achieves the routine he wants, and housetraining runs more smoothly.

Remember the following consistency tips when housetraining your Bulldog puppy:

- ✔ **In the beginning, always use the same door to go out to the yard.** Make sure that everyone in the family uses the same door. By using this method, when your puppy is old enough to let you know that he wants to go out, he'll always go to the same door.

- ✔ **Use the same area of the yard.** This trick helps your puppy discover the smell of urine and know that he's come to the right place. Dogs rely on their sense of smell, so use this sense to your advantage. Just make sure that the area you choose in the yard is really where you want him to go.

  Some friends of mine got a puppy in the winter and got in the habit of taking him out on the deck and letting him go in the snow. As the weather warmed up, the snow receded, and the dog, having been trained to the snow, followed the snow line across the yard, each day having to go farther and farther before he would go. The deck seemed like a good idea at the time, but because dirt wasn't available to catch and hold the scent, the dog was convinced he had to go only on the snow.

- ✔ **Keep your puppy warm and cozy at night.** If your puppy gets cold, he may wake up, and if he wakes up, he may have to go out.

- ✔ **No matter where your puppy goes, as long as it's outside, praise lavishly.** Your neighbors may think that you're crazy, but make a huge fuss over your puppy when he goes. Give him a treat. Play with him after he goes — but not before. Puppies can be easily distracted, and if you take him outside and start to play, he may forget to go until he's back inside.

- ✔ **Always go out with your puppy.** After he's trained, you can open the door and let your Bulldog out in your securely fenced yard, but right now, you need to go with him so you can guide him to the right spot and praise him for doing what he does. Initially, always take your puppy out on a lead. Puppies run fast and can scoot under a bush or a porch before you know it. If you're ready to leave for work, you're not going to appreciate having to get on your hands and knees to retrieve your puppy. Besides, if he's on a lead, you can keep him in the proper area and focused on the job at hand.

- ✔ **Remember that during potty training feeding time plays an important part in the schedule.** As your dog gets older, you may decide that you like the idea of *free feeding* — putting down the daily amount of food and leaving it for your dog to enjoy whenever he feels like it. This feeding option is your choice, but while your Bully is a puppy and until he's house-trained, feed scheduled meals. This procedure helps you know when he's likely to need a trip outside. Also, regulate treats. Too many treats or too much variety may lead to a touch of diarrhea. Bulldog puppies truly can't control diarrhea, and that means extra cleanup for you.

Working out a training schedule

No matter what method you decide to use when you housetrain your puppy, a schedule makes the process easier on everyone. A schedule means that every family member knows what to do and when, and your puppy also quickly learns the schedule. You may even want to write the schedule down and post it on the refrigerator so everyone has a reminder of what's next.

Puppies are small. That means that the rest of their body parts are small too — including their bladders. Puppies can't physically hold as much for as long as an adult dog. Puppies also need to learn control. A schedule helps them discover that control.

Puppies already have a built-in schedule. They need to go to the bathroom when they first wake up; they need to go 10 to 20 minutes after eating; and they need to go after a play session. Considering that your dog's a puppy, she may also have to go anytime in between, but these times present a starting schedule for your refrigerator door.

Your schedule should fit your family, of course, but may look something like this:

✔ **6:00 a.m.**

Take puppy outside. If you're crate training, don't open the crate door and coax your puppy to follow you through the house. Pick the puppy up, and take her to the designated spot in the yard. She may not make it that far on her own before she goes.

✔ **6:15 a.m.**

Feed the puppy.

✔ **6:30 a.m.**

Take the puppy outside.

✔ **6:40–7:00 a.m.**

Play with your puppy.

✔ **7:00 a.m.**

Take the puppy outside. When you come back in, put your puppy in her crate or designated area. Get ready for work or school.

✔ **8:00 a.m.**

Take the puppy outside one more time before everyone leaves the house. Return your dog to her training space.

✔ **Noon**

Take the puppy outside.

✔ **12:10 p.m.**

Feed the puppy. Eat your own lunch.

✔ **12:30 p.m.**

Take the puppy out again. Play with the puppy if you have time.

✔ **12:45 p.m.**

If you played with your puppy, take her out again. Place her in the crate or sectioned area before you leave.

✔ **3:00 p.m.**

Kids are home from school. Take puppy outside. Play with puppy. Take puppy out again.

✔ **5:30 p.m.**

Take puppy outside. Feed puppy.

✔ **5:45 p.m.**

Take puppy out after feeding. Leave puppy in crate or training space while fixing dinner and eating. Take puppy outside again.

✔ **7:00 p.m.**

Take puppy out. Play with puppy.

✔ **7:15 p.m.**

Take puppy outside.

✔ **11:00 p.m.**

Take puppy out one last time before bedtime.

If your puppy sleeps soundly overnight, sleep in until 7:00 a.m. If you go to bed before 11:00 p.m., though, be prepared to get up in the middle of the night.

The sample schedule may look like a lot of trips out, and it is, but remember that the fewer accidents your puppy has in the house, the faster she knows that she needs to go outside when nature calls.

Also, make up the schedule that fits your family's lifestyle. If no one comes home at noon, see if your schedule can be changed to accommodate the noon break, or recruit a neighbor. The same goes for the 3:00 p.m. outing. If you don't have children, see whether someone in the neighborhood can help. If everyone leaves the house by 8:00 a.m. and no one returns until 6:00 p.m., you won't be able to use a crate to train your puppy, and you may try to use one of the other methods.

Keep up this routine until your puppy stops making messes in the house and starts letting you know regularly when he needs to go out. This regular notice happens before the puppy reaches 6 months of age, but keep in mind that many puppies go through a "relapse" period before they're 1 year old, where they start having accidents in the house again and need to be retrained. Don't get discouraged: It's all part of the growing-up and maturing process that all puppies go through. As long as you're persistent and patient with your training, your puppy can become successfully housetrained.

Watching for the warning signs

Recognize the signs that your puppy is getting ready to go. Generally, adult dogs are more apt to add these variations to the process. Puppies frequently don't realize that they have to go until they *really have to go*. Still, any of these activities may give you a clue that the time's come to pick up your puppy and get outside *now*.

Look for these signals:

- ✔ **The preliminary dance:** Generally, your dog performs a preliminary "dance" — usually quite short — before he needs to go.

- ✔ **The sniff and circle:** Most dogs tend to sniff a bit and circle before they actually go.

- ✔ **The back-and-forth pace:** Your Bully paces back and forth; usually, the length of the area paced gets shorter and shorter until he finally goes. When outside, he may get close to a shrub or tree.

- ✔ **The whine:** Another indicator — the whine. Listen for it! Sometimes the whine can be subtle. When your dog is a puppy, the whine can be a warning that he needs to go to the bathroom. As dogs get older and we condition our ears to the whine, we allow the noise to go on longer. Don't ignore your puppy's cry for a bathroom break.

- ✔ **The stance:** Some dogs even like to stand by the door when they have to go out. They don't bark, whine, or make a sound. If you haven't seen your pup in a while, look for the stance at the back door.

Considering and Conquering Crate Training

Unless you're lucky enough to be home with your dog all day, you probably need to set up a "bathroom break" system for your dog for when you're away. If some member of the family can reliably let your puppy out at regular intervals, use a crate for housetraining.

Crate training includes definite advantages. For starters, your puppy prefers not to go where he sleeps. Second, if your puppy does have an accident in his crate, he's confined the mess to a small, contained, easy-to-clean area, not in the middle of the living room rug.

Dogs quickly establish routines; and if you follow a schedule of times when your puppy runs around and times when he's in the crate, he soon knows to "hold it" until he goes out. See the section "Working out a training schedule," earlier in this chapter, for a schedule that gives you information on when to crate your dog.

The disadvantage of crate training is that someone must regularly be available to follow the schedule you've set.

 A crate is a tool, not a way to ignore your puppy. A young dog can't wait for more than four hours before he has to go to the bathroom. To make him wait longer means that he may pee in his crate, and after that becomes a habit, housetraining your puppy can be even harder.

Preparing for Paper Training

If crate training just isn't feasible because of time constraints, you may opt for paper training. Choose a room or an exercise pen to confine your pup to one area. A laundry room or bathroom works well because of the typical linoleum flooring, or you can mark off part of your kitchen.

 Be aware that your puppy may decide that linoleum is a wonderful teething toy. I've never understood how dogs can get any kind of grip on a smooth linoleum floor, but believe me, they can.

Cover the entire floor of the chosen area with several layers of newspaper. You may want to put down a piece of plastic first to further protect your floor in case any waste products soak through the paper. If the area is large enough, include your puppy's crate in the space, with the door open, as a place for him to rest. Supply water and several toys.

When you clean the area, remove the top couple of layers of paper, leaving the lower layers. Enough scent remains to tell the puppy where to go. You may want to take a section of soiled paper out to the yard and stake it down so your puppy understands where to go outside. After several days, cover a smaller area of the floor. If your puppy consistently uses the paper instead of the uncovered part of the floor, reduce the newspaper coverage again. Continue this process until you've removed all the paper. Don't try to rush the process. You don't want your puppy going on the exposed floor. Take the process slowly and easily until you know that he understands about going on the paper.

During this time, continue to take your puppy to his outdoor toilet area when you're home. By the time you've reached the stage where no newspaper remains on the floor, your puppy should be both old enough to hold it and make the connection that he needs to be outdoors when he has to go. He isn't ready for the run of the house yet, but he's well on his way.

Going Indoors Rather Than Outdoors

You may want to train your puppy to go inside. If you live in an apartment on the tenth floor and you're six blocks from the nearest park or dog run, inside potty training is another option. Keeping your Bully inside doesn't mean that that you don't have to train. Just because your dog is an indoor dog doesn't mean that you want him using your entire apartment as one big doggy bathroom.

Papering the floor

Paper train your puppy by using the same techniques mentioned in "Preparing for Paper Training," earlier in the chapter, except that you never totally eliminate the papers. Decide on where you want your dog to always use the bathroom, and follow the above method, ending by leaving enough paper to always accommodate your dog. To help define and contain the papers, add a small wooden or plastic frame.

Padding the tile

Puppy pads, which remind me of disposable diapers, are an alternative to papers. Pads are flat with a plastic backing and scented to encourage dogs to use them as a potty area. Place them on the floor, just as you would a newspaper. Unlike with newspaper, you need only one layer.

If you think that you'd like to use pads for your Bully, large washable pads are available for training. Pads come in different sizes: 2 x 2, 3 x 3, and 4 x 4 (all measured in feet). I recommend one of the larger sizes for a Bully. Pads are washed after each use and then air-dried. You need four or five pads at the minimum so that you have some to use when others are drying. The 3 x 3 pad runs about $35, and the 4 x 4 is about $55. Although this option is certainly more expensive than newspaper, the reusable factor is a great touch. Each pad can be washed approximately 300 times.

Boxing the mess: Litter boxes

Dog litter presents another choice for your indoor dog. Dog litter is different from cat litter, so if you decide to go for litter, make sure that you buy dog litter. Dogs, especially males, tend to use their hind legs to scratch and scuff the dirt — or, in this case, the litter — after they've used the bathroom. Cat litter flies all over the place, whereas the special dog litter doesn't fly around as much.

Train your puppy to use a litter box in the same way you train to use paper:

1. **Place the litter box in your puppy's enclosure.**

2. **Put papers all over the floor.**

3. **Cover the papers with a thin layer of litter.**

4. **Gradually reduce the area covered by paper and litter, closing in on the litter box.**

Using a crate also works for litter-box training. Follow the schedule at the beginning of the chapter, except that instead of taking your puppy outdoors, take him to the litter box. Remember that the litter box isn't a play area. Leave your puppy in the box for a few minutes, but if he starts playing or digging, put him back in his crate for a while and then try again.

If you plan to use a litter box, keep the container clean. As needed, scoop the litter and waste, and add fresh litter. At least once a week, empty the litter box, scrub it clean, and refill with fresh litter. Unlike when you clean up an accident, an ammonia-based cleaner is fine. After all, if the ammonia attracts your dog to the litter box, that's where you want him to go. See "Cleaning Up after Bully," later in this chapter.

Teaching Your Bully to Go on Command

After you housetrain your dog, you may occasionally need your pup to go to the bathroom quickly and on command, even if he's not at the door asking to go out. For instance, you may be going out for the evening and want to make sure that he's empty and comfortable while you're gone. Or when pouring rain keeps your dog from wanting to go outside, you need to be able to tell your dog to go.

Although some dogs never catch on, most dogs eventually make the connection between a word or phrase and the act of urinating. Start by choosing whatever expression you like: "Go potty," "Do your business," or any saying you're comfortable with.

I've read that you shouldn't use the phrase "Hurry up" because if you're in the house and you're telling a family member to hurry up, your dog may think that you're asking him to lift his leg. I happen to use "Hurry up" or "Hurry and go," and so far, I've never had a problem indoors, but still consider the warning.

When you take your puppy out, use the phrase you've chosen. When he goes, praise him. Use the phrase every time, and eventually, the idea sticks.

The battle of the sexes

The potty command works better with females, who are apt to be fussier about where and when they go, than with males. Walk most boys anywhere near a tree or bush, and they seem more than willing to take the hint. Boys don't usually care where they go.

Female dogs, on the other hand, can be picky. If human, they'd carry little tissue toilet-seat covers with them. I once walked a female puppy for 45 minutes in the pouring rain. We were in a strange place, so her scent was nowhere to be found. Remember, nothing can be done when this situation happens. You can't yell or jerk the lead or do anything negative. You can plead with your puppy, but I know from experience that does no good at all. You have to keep walking and get soaked and work on teaching your puppy to go on command. Believe me, when she finally went, an abundance of enthusiastic praise poured out of me!

Cleaning Up after Bully

Sadly, after a puppy does his business, his owner then has business of her own: cleaning up.

Cleaning up indoors

No matter what method you use to housetrain your puppy, accidents occur, which means cleaning time for you. A consistent schedule for feeding, playtime, naps, and walks helps reduce the number of accidents.

1. **Start by removing as much of the mess as you can.**

   On carpeting, pick up solid waste.

2. **Blot the area with paper towels.**

   If your puppy wets, fold several paper towels and place them over the spot.

3. **Step on the towels, and rock your foot back and forth to blot up as much liquid as possible.**

   Repeat, repeat, and repeat until the paper towel comes up dry. Owning stock in a paper-towel company may make you feel better about the number of paper towels you use.

4. **When most of the liquid is blotted up, apply your cleaner of choice, and follow the directions.**

To save some money, use old rags or cloth towels to sop up accidents and messes. You may want to run the washer immediately to prevent the stinky rags from lying around.

Never use ammonia-based cleaning products to clean floors. No matter how thoroughly you clean and rinse, an odor residue remains, and ammonia is a base component of urine. The trace of ammonia odor in the cleaner may be undetectable to you, but you can bet that your puppy smells it, and he will return to the scene of the crime. The market sells dozens of products designed specifically to deal with dog-accident stains and odors. Oxygen-based cleaners also work well. In a pinch, use white vinegar and club soda to help with stains. If the accident occurs on linoleum or tile, wipe up the problem and then use a cleaner.

Are you your dog's maid?

Many books tell you to never let your dog see you clean up. Supposedly, cleaning up after your pet teaches your Bully that you're his maid. I'm not clear on the reasoning here. First of all, I *am* my dog's maid. I've yet to see him wash his bedding, sweep up hair, or wash his own bowls. And I've never noticed that watching me clean up makes him go in the living room instead of outside.

I put my dogs elsewhere if one of them has an accident, but the reason isn't because I don't want them to watch. While you clean up after a puppy, you can't watch the puppy, and believe me, your dog doesn't need much time to get into trouble or to leave another puddle or pile while you're cleaning up the first one. Put your pup in his crate so you can concentrate on cleanup.

If an adult dog has an accident for some reason, I'm not happy. I hate coming home from dinner at a wonderful restaurant and having to clean up a mess. So I get the dogs out of the way. I'm not in a good mood, and I don't want to take my frustration out on the dogs. And dogs being dogs, they like to know what you're doing down on your hands and knees. They like to get their heads and paws right in your space to check everything out (because being on the floor naturally means that you want to play). I don't need their help at that point, nor do I want to play. So they get shut in another room or put outside until I've cleaned up, and I can take a deep breath and be happy to see them again.

Cleaning up outdoors

Figure outdoor cleanup into your duties as well. No matter how much you love your dog, you're not going to want your yard to be one big litter box, and no one loves stepping in what the dog's left behind. If you want to enjoy your yard, or if your children play in the yard, invest in a set of *pooper scoopers* — long-handled implements, with one half being a bit like a dustpan and the other side having either a rake-type head or a flat blade like a small shovel. Scoops make quick cleanup possible without having to bend over. Then deposit the waste in a lined trash can or into a doggy septic system.

A doggy septic system is easy to install. Just dig a hole anywhere in your yard (preferably out of the way) and place the system in the hole. These systems depend on enzymes that turn the waste into liquid that leaches away into the ground. The cost of one of these systems runs between $40 and $70.

The drawback to septic systems for dogs is that they don't work in cold weather because the ground is frozen.

Using the bag system for pickup

If your yard is small, and you choose to walk your puppy, you still need to pick up the puppy's waste. Carrying a set of pooper scoopers with you on a walk isn't practical, so carry plastic bags for cleanup. Recycle the plastic sleeves that cover your newspaper, plastic bread bags, and plastic bags from the grocery store. You can also purchase small bags, called scrap bags, at the store that easily stick in your pocket.

When your dog goes, take out a bag and put your hand in it; pick up the waste; and then pull the bag forward, over your hand and the waste (turning the bag inside out). Tie the bag closed, and throw it in the trash.

If you're reusing bags from the grocery store or newspaper, make sure that they're free of holes before you use them or take them with you on a walk. Do I need to say why? Yuck!

You may want to take an opaque bag from the grocery to put the individual waste bags in. I don't know about you, but our walks can get long, the dog can go several times, and I prefer not to be seen swinging multiple sacks of excrement in my hand. The grocery bag at least masks the mess until you get home.

Although this system may gross you out at first, trust me, it becomes second nature, and you don't have a choice. If you have a dog, part of your responsibility includes cleaning up after him. No one else wants the job, and if you're walking in a public area, no one should have to worry about stepping in your dog's business. Also, think about your neighbors. Leaving little "surprises" in their yards isn't the way to build rapport.

Try to walk your dog to a neutral area before he goes, or if that isn't possible, steer him to the grassy area between the sidewalk and the street instead of letting him wander onto a neighbor's lawn. Even if you pick up, your neighbor may not want your dog going on her property. If none of these options are convenient, stay in your own yard until your Bully has gone; then go for the exercise part of your walk. (But still, don't forget the bags.)

If the bag method truly bothers you, even with the protection of the opaque bag, use disposable cardboard kits with small handles. The contraption works like a small scoop, and the handles close and seal the box for throwing away. The disposable kit costs more and isn't as handy as stuffing a few bags in your pocket, but the choice is yours.

Chapter 10

Mastering Good Manners and Basic Commands

In This Chapter

▶ Adjusting to a collar and lead

▶ Teaching basic commands

▶ Attending puppy classes and day care

▶ Contacting the professionals

*Y*ou don't need to have a champion obedience dog, but your dog should know basic good manners. Many untrained dogs are unhappy, and usually, so are their owners. Dogs are pack animals and rule followers. A dog with no understanding of the rules is confused and unsure of himself. He may try to make his own rules or lead the pack, which in this case is your family.

A Bully with good manners knows when, if ever, she's allowed to get on the furniture, to beg at the table, and so on. Your dog should also know to let people go through doors first. The more rules your dog knows, the more secure she'll be, knowing that you're in charge.

This chapter covers basic training tips; how to solve problems; the importance of socialization and getting your dog out to meet other people and dogs; and, if you face a difficult behavior problem, when and where to seek professional help.

A Few Things to Keep in Mind While Training

For general socialization, take your puppy places. Carry her into the bank with you. The tellers may pet her and even give her treats. Go to a mall, and take a walk around outside (most malls ban dogs from inside). People think that puppies are cute, and someone may want to pet her. Give her treats. If you don't have children, find children in your neighborhood who may like to play with your puppy for a while.

Here are a few general tips that you can apply to all the training ideas in this chapter:

✔ Always stop on a positive note. If your dog isn't "getting" the new lesson, go back to a command she knows how to do. If your dog always sits promptly, end the lesson with a sit. Give a treat and a lot of praise, and go back to training when you've both rested.

✔ Don't be afraid to try commands because you don't think they work. With practice and plenty of treats, you can train your Bully to obey your commands.

✔ During training time, stuff your pockets full of treats, and always have treats on hand for rewards. You don't want to ask your Bully to do something and then go find the treats. He may forget why he's getting the treat.

✔ Think of a release word to let your dog know that he can stop whatever you had him doing. Make your release word happy and short. Many people say "Okay" or "All right." Whatever you use, be consistent. Don't say "Okay" one day and "That's fine" the next.

Following the Leader: Lead and Collar Training

The first step in training your Bulldog is getting your little darling used to wearing a collar. At first, purchase an adjustable, flat, buckle nylon collar because this type of collar is inexpensive, and your puppy soon outgrows it. For more on buying collars for your dog, see Chapter 5.

Collaring the culprit

Your Bulldog needs to be comfortable wearing a collar because a collar and lead keep you connected to your Bully when you go for a walk, to the vet, or to the bank. A Bulldog (at least at full size) is too big for a cute little tote bag. If you want to go somewhere with your Bully, you will both be more comfortable if your Bulldog moves under his own power. Also, the collar is an excellent tool for grabbing your Bully when you need to.

To start out, buckle the collar loosely around your Bully's neck (that is, the collar must be tight enough to not fall off your dog, yet not be so tight that it presses into his neck), and let him get used to it. At first, make sure that you supervise your pup. He may want to wriggle out of the collar by rubbing or scratching it off. You don't want him to get stuck on a piece of furniture without anyone around to release him. After your Bully adjusts to the piece of fabric around his neck, feel free to leave the collar on all the time.

Attach your dog's rabies tag and identification tag on his collar. If you lose him, the ID tag may assist in bringing him home.

Being gentle but firm with the lead

After your puppy accepts the collar, attach a lightweight lead to the collar, and let your pup drag the leash behind him. Keep an eye on him during this process to prevent the lead from catching on nearby objects, getting tangled, or being chewed by your dog.

When your puppy finally gets used to the lead, pick it up by the end. Start moving away from your pup, calling her as she comes. Keep the lead loose, and don't drag your dog. Encourage her to walk with you by using treats and a lot of praise. Keep training sessions short and positive. Your first walk may be just down the driveway, but those first steps are a beginning.

Be patient. Don't fight with your dog. Just remember to have a pocketful of treats and to set aside a lot of time. When you start getting impatient, stop any lesson instead of continuing a battle of wills with your pup.

Knowing the Basic Commands

Having a dog with manners is a bonus. The basic commands, like Sit, Come, Down, and Stay, can make living with your dog more pleasant. You can teach the basic dog commands, but not every method works with every dog or for every owner/trainer. If you don't fully understand a particular method, or you're not comfortable, you can't teach your dog effectively.

I have a "haunch" you can teach your Bully to sit

The Sit command is one of the easiest and most useful commands to teach your young Bulldog. Encourage your Bully to sit by using food. Find his favorite treats, and get your Bully's attention.

1. **Take a treat, and show it to your dog.**

2. **Tell him to sit.**

3. **Move your hand back over his head.**

   He follows your hand and the treat back, tipping his nose up and sinking down on his haunches.

   If you hold the treat too far above your dog's head, your Bully stands up and tries to reach the goody or stands on his hind legs. This error in technique may teach your dog the wrong command or to put his paws up on you for the treat. You want him to sit, so keep your hand low.

4. **Praise him, and give him the treat.**

5. **Repeat this process several times.**

6. **Then end the session.**

Work on Sit four or five times during the day, keeping sessions short and treats plentiful, and always end on a positive note. Before long, your Bully is eagerly sitting whenever you give the command. The Sit command can easily be worked into your everyday routine. Tell your Bulldog to sit, and you can

- ✔ Easily snap on his lead instead of trying to catch him as he bounces with delight at the prospect of a walk.

- ✔ Check his ears for dirt.

- ✔ Lift a paw and clean off mud. This command comes in handy when bringing in your Bulldog from the rain.

- ✔ Put his food bowl down. Having your dog work for his supper never hurts. Food is an excellent motivator.

Come to me, my Bully!

Come is another of the basic commands. You don't always want to go get your Bulldog when you need him. You'd like to say his name and the command, Come, and have him respond reliably. Begin teaching Come almost immediately. Here are your first steps:

1. **Call your puppy in a happy, excited tone of voice.**

2. **Back away from him.**

3. **Odds are good he bounds after you.**

4. **Pet and praise him, and give him a treat.**

You can practice this feat under different circumstances:

✔ At mealtimes, call your Bully. His reward is his bowl of food.

✔ After he's used to a collar and lead, work with him on the lead. Again, call him in a happy tone, and run backward away from him. When he comes, reward him.

✔ As you enjoy walks together, and your Bully is beginning to understand the command Come, call him when he is distracted, sniffing a bug, or just wandering in the grass. Say his name; call him; and give the lead a gentle tug. Don't haul, jerk, or drag him. Encourage him with your voice and with treats.

When you're at the point where your Bully comes to you in the house and on a lead, start practicing in the yard. To begin:

1. **Leave the lead or a long rope attached to the collar.**

2. **Call your pup.**

3. **If he comes, praise him, and let him go back to whatever he was doing.**

    You don't want him to think that when he comes to you, playtime is over. Coming to you is just a break and a chance for a cookie.

4. **If he doesn't come at first, pick up the trailing lead; give a gentle tug, and repeat the command.**

    After he comes, praise him, and let him go back to what he was doing.

Don't ever call your dog for unpleasant news. (If you want to punish him, go to where he is.) Don't call him to give him medicine. Don't call him for a bath. Don't call him because you've just found one of your good shoes that he's partially eaten. If he is digging a hole in the middle of your prized petunias, call him, and when he comes, pat and praise him. Don't punish him because he's destroyed your flowers. Punishing at this point turns into punishing him for coming. Praise him for obeying, and replant the flowers later.

Call your Bully for dinner or a walk. Call him for a grooming session if he enjoys being brushed. Call him for no reason at all, and give him a treat when he obeys. If you're patient and consistent, and never call your Bulldog for unpleasantries, your dog comes to you whenever you call, no matter what he's doing.

Teaching the Down command

Before working on this chapter, I checked seven training sources and came up with five different methods for teaching the Down command, and they all work. Many people combine methods to find one that works for both them and their dog.

Some methods require some form of physical manipulation, like pulling or pushing, and with a Bulldog, the struggle may turn into a contest of wills and strength.

Because food keeps a lesson happy and doesn't result in a physical battle, I use it to teach the Down command. Here's how I like to teach Down to my Bullies:

1. **Start with your dog in a Sit.**

2. **Show your dog the treat.**

3. **Move your hand slowly down in front of your dog and slightly away, giving the Down command.**

4. **With luck, your dog slides into a Down.**

5. **Make sure to praise and reward him.**

I've seen this method work, but with dogs with short legs, I've also seen them pop right back up. They follow the treat all right, but only their head is down. If your Bully pops up like a jack-in-the-box, don't despair, and don't give him the treat. Keep the treat in your closed hand on the ground. Your puppy may paw or nibble at your hand, but don't give in. Eventually, when all else fails, your puppy briefly lies down. As he starts to lie down, give the command Down, and quickly give him the treat.

Teaching the Stay command

Another helpful command is the Stay command. The command Stay is often the most difficult for a dog to grasp. Young puppies have a difficult time because their attention spans are short. Puppies dislike sitting for any period of time, let alone for long stretches, and they prefer to be up and playing with you. Understanding your puppy's fidgety nature helps you gain more patience for this part of training. To start the Stay command, follow these simple steps:

1. **Attach the lead to your dog's collar.**

2. **Have your Bully sit on your left side.**

3. **Hold the lead in your right hand.**

4. **Lean over, and extend your left hand and arm in front of your dog's nose, with your palm facing the dog.**

5. **Give the command Stay.**

6. **Step in front of your dog.**

7. **Return to your dog's side.**

8. **Praise, and give treats.**

Gradually increase both the distance between you and your dog and the amount of time you stay in front of him. If your dog breaks his Sit, return to him, and gently replace him in the Sit with no additional commands.

 Don't rush this process, and always return to his side before you praise him. Some dogs are wonderful at the Stay until you move; then they think that they can move as well.

When your dog improves at the Stay on the lead, he can try training without the lead. If you're planning to compete in formal obedience, start returning to your dog on his left instead of his right and walking around him to get back into position by his right shoulder. Your dog should maintain his Sit until you release him.

Combining the Down and Stay commands

After your dog sits and stays, he can work on Down and Stay. Follow the same procedure as above, but with your dog on a Down. Here's what to do:

1. **Attach the lead to your dog's collar.**

2. **Have your Bully Down on your left side.**

3. **Hold the lead in your right hand.**

4. **Lean over, and extend your left hand and arm in front of your dog's nose, with your palm facing the dog.**

5. **Give the command Stay.**

6. **Step in front of your dog.**

7. **Return to your dog's side.**

8. **Praise, and give treats.**

Your dog should catch on quickly because the steps are the same, except that your dog is lying down. The Down and Stay commands combined can be a magical combination. Here are some of the benefits:

✔ A dog who obeys these commands is less likely to be kenneled when company arrives or when he may otherwise be in the way.

✔ If you're frantically trying to get Thanksgiving dinner ready (or any other dinner, for that matter) and on the table, Down your dog in the corner and tell him to Stay. You can work without worrying about tripping over the dog.

✔ If you're bringing in the groceries from the car (and sometimes in the rain), and your Bully is happy to see you, but she is making you trip, say hello to your pup and then give the Down and Stay commands. Finish bringing in the groceries. Make sure to reward her for obeying the command.

✔ If your dog runs across the road, you may not want to use the Come command. Having her come to you means that she has to cross the road again, putting her in danger of getting hit. But you don't want her to get even farther away. Give the Down command, and your well-trained Bully drops to the ground. Tell her to Stay; then you can cross the road at a safer time, and snap the lead on your dog's collar.

In an age of fenced yards and leashed walks, the danger of a dog's running out into traffic is less, but accidents happen. Your dog can slip out an open door, and even your stocky Bulldog may reach the street before anyone can catch her.

Wait for me!

Wait is another command I like: a smaller, softer form of Stay and less formal. Wait is a temporary command and doesn't need a formal release. Because the command isn't formal, a particular way to teach Wait doesn't exist. Wait means calm down a minute, and be patient.

Here are a couple of ways to start teaching your Bully the Wait command:

✔ **If your Bully loses a treat under the table or couch.**

My dogs frequently knock dog biscuits under furniture and can't reach them. I can, but not with the dogs' heads between me and the furniture. If you're trying to retrieve the dog biscuit from under the couch, your dog discovers that if he doesn't wait, he doesn't get the treat. Give him a firm but gentle push to get him out of the way and say, "Wait." Retrieve the cookie, and tell him "Okay."

✔ **If you're trying to leave the house.**

Use the Wait so your dog doesn't go through the door with you. If your dog's on a lead, say "Wait" as you go through a door, restraining him so he has to wait for you to go through the door first.

Some trainers argue that putting your dog on a Sit or a Down–Stay accomplishes the same goal as Wait. They're right! But sometimes I just prefer a less formal command.

Leave It!

Leave It can be a bit harder to teach to a Bulldog, whose instinct is to hang on forever, but it can be done. Teaching your dog to Leave It or Drop It is useful when she has something you wish she didn't have.

The best way to enforce Leave It is to offer to trade your dog what's in her mouth for something she wants more. Use tasty treats you know that your dog loves. Wait until she has an item in her mouth, like a toy or a ball. Say "Leave It" or "Drop It," and show her the treat. When she spits out the toy to get the treat, praise her and give her the goody. Repeat this exercise throughout the day, and she quickly catches on that the command means that she's getting a tasty treat.

I can't live without this command. The Leave It command can save your sock or shoe from being chewed; and if your dog knows the Leave It command, when the day comes that your Bully picks up something dead and disgusting, you won't have to pry her jaws open; she willingly gives the carcass up without a fight. Give the command, and she spits it out by herself. Remember to give her a treat.

One of my females once tried to bring a dead chipmunk into the house. Fortunately, I saw what it was and gave her the Leave It command before she made it indoors. She dropped the chipmunk and then followed me inside for her treat. On a less gruesome note, I quickly trained my male dog to leave another dog's stuffed toy in exchange for a dog biscuit. He was happy, and the toy lasted longer because he didn't have a chance to disembowel it.

Mixing up your training

When your dog understands the Stay command, start mixing up your training. Go back to his side, and at other times, call him from the Stay. Use the Down–Stay when you're working in the kitchen or when the family is eating. Down is a comfortable position and a way to teach your dog manners.

Put your dog on a Sit–Stay before walking in- and outdoors and before he gets fed. Have your Bully sit before someone pets him. Having your Bulldog work for treats or other rewards is good practice. This process helps him know that you're the leader of the pack.

Training your dog can be fun. Incorporate Sit and Down into a game of hide-and-seek. Put your dog on a Stay, and go into another room before you call him. Playing games adds fun to the training and mixes things up. Your Bulldog learns how to stay whether or not he can see you or whether you're in a specific room or in a line with other dogs at an obedience class.

Conquering Common Behavior Problems

No dog is perfect, but with training and patience, you can get any dog close! Don't despair if your dog bothers people by jumping up, begging, or barking, but do address the problem. You can teach your dog to behave. If you don't have the knowledge or what you try doesn't work, don't give up. Find a professional to help. Just like you contact a doctor when you're sick or have a broken bone, contact a professional dog trainer or behaviorist if you have a problem with your dog. For more on finding help, see the "Finding Help" section, later in the chapter.

I beg you: No begging!

Begging is like water torture. The first few drops seem like nothing at all, but eventually, the water has you screaming. Puppies are so darn cute that when they look at you with those big, pleading brown eyes during dinner, you want to give them a tiny bite of your sandwich. Resist, my friend; resist! Harden your heart — and resist. What is cute once in a puppy paves the way for continual daily begging for the life of your dog, and after you start, you can't explain to your dog that begging is okay when the family is at the table but not when a dinner party arrives.

is proud Bully displays the famous Bulldog profile.

photo by Theresa Crowley

Bulldogs are clean dogs, but they should be bathed regularly.

Bulldogs have a reputation of being sedentary, but they do like to play and should get some exercise.

ost Bulldogs tend to be rather laid-back.

Bulldogs are inquisitive and always interested in what people are doing.

Healthy and happy puppies come from responsible breeders and healthy, happy adult dogs.

hese Bulldog puppies already have many of the facial characteristics typical
f adult Bulldogs.

hey may appear grumpy, but most Bulldogs are actually very sweet-tempered.

These Bulldogs are the result of many years of conscientious and responsible breeding.

photo by Anthony Ficarotta

A well-trained Bulldog is ver[y] well-behaved on a leash and a joy to take on walks.

photo by Theresa Crowley

NEW CD
OBEDIENCE
PENN TREATY
KENNEL CLUB

Bulldogs can be trained to master a variety of activities and disciplines, including obedience, tracking, and agility trials.

Canines are hard-wired to return to a spot where they receive food. Researchers discovered that when a wolf caught a rabbit at a specific spot, he revisited that spot dozens of times in the hope of catching another rabbit. Similarly, you can create a monster in your own home. Give your Bully a bit of food from the table once, and he will return to the scene again and again.

Make a household rule to never, ever feed your dog from the table, and follow through. If you feel that your dog has to have a sliver of the Thanksgiving turkey, put the food in his bowl away from the dinner table.

If you never feed your Bully from the table and he still sits next to you, staring soulfully into your face, ignore him. If you can't comfortably ignore him, put him at a distance and use that Down–Stay you practiced, or put him in his crate.

Begging isn't limited to the table. If you have snacks while you're watching television, your Bully wants his share. Sharing a handful of popcorn is okay, but after you start, your Bully will always be there, so think about the repercussions of sharing before you do it.

Begging can also develop accidentally. One morning I threw a handful of Cheerios on the floor, and I enjoyed watching the dogs act like mini vacuum cleaners. The show was fun, so I threw more Cheerios on the floor the next morning. By the third morning, I wasn't even having cereal, but that didn't stop the dogs from expecting theirs. A handful of Cheerios became part of the morning routine.

Moving can break bad habits, but you can't move every time your dog starts an annoying habit. We broke the Cheerios habit when we moved. We were in a strange place, and the dogs had never been given Cheerios there, so they didn't expect them. So if your dogs have some bad habits that you've created, and you're moving in the near future, be thankful, and think twice this time before you scatter that handful of cereal or let your dog lick the ice cream bowl.

Jumping isn't always joyful

Bulldogs aren't known for being bouncy and jumpy, but in case your dog is a jumper, think about stopping the habit. Watching your dog jump for joy when you arrive home may make you feel happy. But you may not be quite so happy when you're all dressed up to go out, and your dog jumps up with muddy paws, ruins your nylons, or gets tiny white hairs all over your blue slacks. The jumping up doesn't seem as cute as it once did.

Even if you never mind your Bulldog jumping up on you, your visitors may not find the habit quite so endearing. Bulldogs are solid, heavy dogs, and your dog can knock over a child or an older person and cause injury.

First, make sure that everyone in the family understands that jumping isn't allowed. You're never going to break the habit if half the family lets your Bully jump; then your corrections and efforts confuse him. Your dog doesn't understand why jumping up is all right sometimes and not always.

Start teaching your Bully not to jump by ignoring him. When you come home, and he jumps up to greet you, turn sideways to him, and totally ignore him. Don't pet him or talk to him or push him off you. Eventually, he figures out that jumping up isn't getting him the attention he wants. When he stops jumping, use the Sit command, and pet him.

If you're expecting company, tell your guests ahead of time to ignore your dog and pet him only when he's in a Sit position. Pretty soon your dog realizes that jumping is a totally worthless activity.

After you've trained your Bully not to jump, you can train him to jump up on command. If you're practicing agility or doing tricks in the back yard, jumping up can be a fun part of these activities. But always remember to begin with no jumping as the rule.

Digging up the yard

The good news is that Bulldogs aren't terriers, who are notorious for digging. For even more good news, the word on the street is that Bulldogs aren't diggers. The bad news is that young dogs may still dig. Bulldogs may also dig holes to lie in to keep cool. Unless your Bully is a determined digger, you may want to patiently fill in the occasional hole and wait for him to mature. Monitor the digging so your dog isn't digging up and eating bulbs, many of which are toxic to dogs.

If you're simultaneously trying to preserve your lawn and have a dog, and your particular puppy does enjoy some excavation time, consider giving your dog his own digging spot. Think of the spot as a sandbox for dogs. Mark off an area with low boards; add some sand or dirt; and introduce the spot to your dog. You can make the introduction by burying dog biscuits just under the sand's surface or putting a few drops of bacon grease on "the digging spot." Before long, your dog figures out that the box makes a great digging place.

If you don't want to create a special area, you need to watch your dog whenever he's out. If he starts to dig, tell him no and offer a ball or toy in exchange. Bulldogs don't generally get too upset with a verbal reprimand, but know what your own dog can tolerate. My parents had a dog who was digging up a storm, and they firmly said, "No digging." Their tone of voice really upset him, and for the rest of his life, they had to spell the word "digging," or he looked like he had just been scolded.

Keeping the peace: No barking!

Bulldogs aren't known as barkers. They were never guard dogs or watchdogs, so barking wasn't bred into them. But if your Bully is a barker, his barking can lead to problems with neighbors and complaints that your dog is the noisy one on the block.

Figuring out the distractions

If your Bulldog does bark when you'd rather he didn't (or the neighbors rather he didn't), take a look at the reasons for the barking:

- ✔ **Animals:** If your backyard has rabbits, squirrels, or other furry friends, maybe the distraction of other animals is what is making your dog bark. Give your dog something to do, and he's less apt to bark at activity on either side of your fence.

- ✔ **Boredom:** If your dog is left out in your yard for extended periods of time, he may be barking because he's bored. Give him something to concentrate on, and when he's finished, he may take a long nap. Ideally, don't leave your Bulldog outside so long that he has to resort to barking to entertain himself.

- ✔ **People:** If he's barking at people, consider a solid fence. Dogs aren't as apt to bark at what they can't see. If children pass by your home, make sure that they aren't teasing your dog through the fence.

- ✔ **Separation anxiety:** If your dog barks when he's left alone in the house, he may have separation anxiety. Leave him with a *Kong,* a heavy rubber toy stuffed with peanut butter or cheese. (For more information on Kongs, see Chapter 5.)

  Videotapes of solitary dogs have shown that they're the most anxious during the first 10 to 15 minutes of being left alone. If your dog has an occupier during those minutes, chances are he'll be fine the rest of the time.

- ✔ **Traffic:** Your Bully may like to bark at passing traffic. Certain cars make noises that can make your Bully bark wildly. You can manage this noise by looking for ways to incorporate sound insulation into your house. For example, thick fabric drapes help reduce noise more than blinds or thin drapes do.

✔ **Weather:** Don't leave your dog outside during weather extremes. Your Bully may be telling you that he is too hot or too cold.

Barking in the house

If you leave your Bully inside the house all day, and his bark can wake the dead, try the following routine to lessen the barking:

1. **Go through your normal schedule of getting ready to leave the house.**

2. **Go out the door.**

3. **Count to ten.**

4. **Go back in you house.**

5. **Leave again.**

6. **Gradually extend the amount of time you're gone.**

7. **Return if your dog starts barking; otherwise, extend the time.**

This process is time consuming. The procedure may take you days or even weeks to train your dog not to bark when he's alone. But believe me — your neighbors will thank you.

When the doorbell rings, and your dog barks, tell your Bully to bark just as he starts barking. Then praise him and give him a treat, or if you're clicker training, click and treat. Before long, he expects the treat and may even stop barking before you praise and give him the treat. Start adding the word "Quiet," "Stop," or whatever word you've chosen as the command to stop barking.

If none of these tips works, and your neighbors still say that your dog barks incessantly, contact a professional trainer for advice.

Finding Help

Don't hesitate to get help if you feel that you need it, whether the problem is minor or major. The sooner you get help, the more likely the problem can be treated and corrected or kept from escalating into a bigger problem. Discover the ways in which you can get help to ensure that your Bulldog is a well-mannered companion.

Clicker training

Clicker training was first used with sea mammals. Handlers used metal clickers to communicate. You can't put a collar and lead on a dolphin! The system involves positive reinforcement and shaping of an animal's behavior. Every time the animal performs an action approximating what the handler is looking for, the handler clicks and treats. The animal soon associates the click with getting a goody and offers behaviors in an attempt to hear that click. The book *Dog Training For Dummies* contains information on this and other types of training.

Basic obedience classes are offered in most communities. Local shelters frequently offer classes. Personally, I find classes a way to discover new information. A class translates what I've read into a visual display, and because the instructor expects progress each week, I train regularly.

The earlier you start socializing and training your dog, the better. Many puppy socialization or kindergarten classes admit puppies before they've received all their shots. To find a class, check veterinary offices, local kennels, or your area humane society. If you can't find a class, start the basics at home, and remember that all training methods require patience and consistency.

Puppy classes

If your Bulldog is generally good, but you need help teaching him or need a way to socialize him, enrolling in a puppy class may be the solution. Puppy kindergarten classes aren't the same as formal obedience lessons. Puppy classes combine play with socialization.

In class, your puppy realizes how to interact with other dogs and people. One simple exercise at puppy kindergarten consists of people sitting on the floor in a circle with the puppy in the middle. The people take turns calling the puppy and giving him a lot of pats and praise. The puppy understands to trust people and to let them willingly touch him.

Day care

If you discover that your Bulldog's behavior problems relate to your puppy's lack of play time, consider doggy day care two or three times a week. Day-care centers provide supervised play for your dog and give your puppy something to do when you're not at home. Day care is another way to socialize your Bully with other people and animals to alleviate barking and behavioral problems.

Obedience classes

For older dogs, obedience classes help teach the basic commands. Classes in your area may be at the YWCA or YMCA, at your local shelter, or at a boarding kennel. Trainers may have their own facilities, or a local kennel club may offer classes. Many boarding kennels know of classes, even if they don't offer them, or you may find a class posted on a bulletin board at your veterinarian's office or at a pet-supply store.

Professional trainers

If you're dealing with a specific problem, you may want a professional trainer to come to your home to work with you. A dog who barks constantly needs some attention at home instead of in an obedience class. Professional trainers may be listed in the phone book, or again, you may find them on a bulletin board. If you have doggy friends, ask them for recommendations. They may know someone who specializes in working with individuals.

Doggie Psychology 101: Hiring an animal behaviorist

If your dog has a problem that goes deeper than excessive energy or lack of basic training, call out the big guns. If your dog is aggressive or overly fearful, you may not be able to overcome the problem without professional help. First, make sure that your pup doesn't have any physical problems. A dog in pain may snap or bite or try to avoid human contact, and these actions can be confused with having a behavior problem.

If your trip to see a veterinarian rules out a physical problem, you need to figure out what is wrong with your Bully. Let me just say that this behavior is highly unlikely from a Bulldog, but exceptions do exist. At this stage, help is right around the corner. That help is in the form of an animal behaviorist.

An animal behaviorist may be compared to a psychologist or psychiatrist for people. A trainer may also be a behaviorist, but just because someone has been training dogs for 20 years doesn't make him a behaviorist. A trainer may be able to help you, but if you need a behaviorist, talk to your veterinarian and see if she can recommend someone. Other dog people in your area may also have suggestions.

Finding a behaviorist can be tricky because national standards for certification don't exist. When you contact a professional, ask for credentials, and get references. If possible, talk to former clients of the person you're considering. You can also get help finding a behaviorist (in the unlikely event that your Bulldog's behavior warrants this level of professional help) in your area at any of the following professional associations:

- ✔ **American Veterinary Society of Animal Behavior (AVSAB):** For information on the AVSAB, go to www.avma.org/av.sab. The AVSAB is a group of veterinarians who share an interest in understanding, teaching, and treating behavior problems in animals. The AVSAB is committed to preserving and improving the human–animal bond wherever it exists. Members range from those who are casually interested in animal behavior to board-certified specialists.

  The AVSAB has two levels of membership. The first level is open only to veterinarians. The affiliate membership is open to others who have been approved by the executive. Affiliate members must have a PhD in animal behavior or a closely related field and be currently active in research and/or practice of applied animal behavior.

- ✔ **International Association of Animal Behavior Consultants (IAABC):** The IAABC is yet another organization you can contact. Its Web site is www.iaabc.org. The IAABC's goal is conveyed in its mission statement: "To assist companion animals and educate their humans to interrupt the cycle of inappropriate punishment, rejection, and euthanasia of animals with resolvable behavior problems."

  Lynn Hoover, president of IAABC, notes that members have diverse backgrounds, but all have "the knowledge, skill, and ethics base" needed to work with both dogs and their families and to collaborate with the family veterinarian.

- ✔ **Animal Behavior Society:** Visit www.animalbehavior.org, the site for the Animal Behavior Society. This group is a professional organization for the study of animal behavior. The society recognizes that "animal behaviorists can be educated in a variety of disciplines, including psychology, biology, zoology, or animal science. A professional applied animal behaviorist has demonstrated expertise in the principles of animal behavior, in the research methods of animal behavior, in the application of animal behavior, principles to applied behavior problems, and in the dissemination of knowledge about animal behavior through teaching and research."

Classifying behaviorists

Before making a decision on a behaviorist, take a look at the profession requirements and the educational background of the position. A dog trainer who decides to call herself a behaviorist may have trained hundreds of dogs, but that doesn't make her a behaviorist, any more than the newspaper's advice columnist is a psychiatrist. Behaviorists can be certified at two levels: Associate Applied Animal Behaviorist and Certified Applied Animal Behaviorist.

Associate Applied Animal Behaviorist

An Associate Applied Animal Behaviorist's education must include a master's degree from an accredited college or university in a biological or behavioral science, with an emphasis in animal behavior. Undergraduate and/or graduate coursework must include 21 semester credits in behavioral-science courses, including six semester credits in ethnology, animal behavior, and/or comparative psychology, and six semester credits in animal learning, conditioning, and or animal psychology.

The applicant must have a minimum of two years of professional experience in applied animal behavior and must demonstrate the ability to perform independently and professionally in applied animal behavior. The candidate must also include personal evidence of independent studies, data analysis, formulation, and testing of hypotheses and professional writing.

An applicant must also show experience working interactively with a researcher, research assistant, or an intern. This collaboration must include working on a particular species with a Certified Applied Animal Behaviorist prior to working independently with the species in a clinical animal-behavior setting.

Certified Applied Animal Behaviorist

The Certified Applied Animal Behaviorist category has more rigorous educational and experience requirements than the Associate Applied Animal Behaviorist category.

A certified Applied Animal Behaviorist must have a doctoral degree from an accredited college or university in a biological or behavioral science, with an emphasis in animal behavior. The degree must include five years of professional experience or a doctorate from an accredited college or university in veterinary medicine, plus two years in a university-approved residency in animal behavior. Three additional years of professional experience in applied animal behavior are also required. Any of these degrees must include the same coursework requirements as the Associate Applied Animal Behaviorist degree.

The applicant must also demonstrate a thorough knowledge of the literature, scientific principles, and principles of animal behavior. Candidates must document original contributions or original interpretations of animal-behavior information and show evidence of significant experience as a researcher, research assistant, or intern working interactively with a particular species with a Certified Applied Animal Behaviorist prior to working independently with the species in a clinical animal-behavior setting.

Chapter 11

Showing and Showing Off Your Well-Trained Bulldog

*Y*ou and your Bulldog can enjoy many activities together. This chapter highlights some events that you can accomplish with your well-trained pet. Note the word "well-trained." These fun activities also mean a lot of work. You need to train your Bulldog to pass the exercises in the Canine Good Citizen test and in obedience competition. A conformation dog show may look easy, but you need to coach your Bulldog for that, too.

Becoming a Canine Good Citizen

The title of *Canine Good Citizen (CGC)* is one of the easiest titles that your well-trained Bulldog can earn, and after your Bully passes the test given by a certified tester, you can proudly put *CGC* after her name. This notation tells everyone that your dog is, indeed, a good citizen. All dogs benefit from training, and earning a CGC means that your dog has the manners she needs when you have visitors or when you go somewhere with her. A CGC title may mean that your dog can stay in a motel room with you because the desk clerk knows that your dog behaves.

Preparing for the CGC test

Most of the things you need to teach your Bulldog for this test you can do yourself, but some kennel clubs offer classes just for the Canine Good Citizen test. You may want to see what's available in your area. I find that a class helps me because the instructor expects a certain amount of progress each week, so I can't put off the training.

Preparing your Bulldog for the CGC test also gives you an idea of whether you want to continue with more formal obedience. Bulldogs aren't the easiest dogs to train in obedience, but you and your Bulldog can do it. Plus the two of you get to spend quality time together.

Although you can certainly train your Bulldog yourself at home, joining a class has the advantage of following someone who can help you with problems and familiarize your Bulldog with other people and dogs.

If you decide to join a class, take your time finding one that's right for you and your Bully. Consider whether you want to use clicker training. Clicker training uses positive reinforcement through a clicker and food. When your dog does what you want, you mark the behavior by clicking and giving a treat. Some trainers use a combination of food rewards and corrections. See Chapter 10 for more information on training.

To find out about reputable classes of any sort, ask friends who have dogs, or contact your local kennel club. Sometimes boarding kennels, local YMCAs, and local humane societies offer classes. See whether you can visit a class before you sign up. People train dogs by using many different methods, and you want to make sure that you're comfortable with whatever method your instructor uses.

If an instructor yells at or hits any dog, run — don't walk — from the class. Yelling and hitting only confuse the dog and may make a dog aggressive or fearful. A first-rate instructor knows how to train without raising her voice or her hand.

Classes usually run eight to ten weeks. After you and your pooch master the basics, you usually can take an advanced class for competing in obedience trials. If your class instructor doesn't offer such a class, she can likely recommend someone who does.

Taking the CGC test

When you're ready to have your dog tested, you notice that the American Kennel Club (AKC) wants your dog *and* you to be good citizens. Before taking the Canine Good Citizen test, you have to sign the Responsible Dog Owners' Pledge. This pledge states that you agree to take care of your dog's health, safety, exercise, training, and quality of life. You also agree to be responsible for cleaning up after your dog in public places and never letting your dog infringe on the rights of others.

After you sign the pledge, you and your dog are ready for the test. The CGC test has ten steps; here they are:

- ✓ **Your dog must allow a friendly stranger to approach.** In this test, the evaluator walks up to you and your dog to greet you, ignoring your dog. Your dog must show no sign of resentment or shyness and must not break position or try to go to the evaluator.

- ✓ **Your dog must sit quietly and allow the person to pet him.** With your Bully sitting at your side, the evaluator pets him on the head and body. You can talk to your dog during this exercise. Your dog may either sit or stand, but he must not show shyness or resentment.

- ✓ **Your dog must allow someone to groom him.** You supply the brush or comb, and the evaluator runs it lightly over your dog's body. The evaluator also examines your dog's ears and gently picks up each front foot.

- ✓ **You must take a walk with your dog on a loose lead.** This test isn't a formal heeling exercise, so your dog doesn't need to be on your left side and doesn't need to sit when you stop.

- ✓ **You must walk your dog through a crowd.** You and your Bully have to walk around and closely pass at least three people. Your dog may show interest in the strangers but continue to walk with you without being overly exuberant or shy. Your dog shouldn't jump on people in the crowd or strain on the leash.

- ✓ **You must ask your dog to sit and stay down; then you must leave your dog and return to him.** In this exercise, the evaluator replaces your leash with a 20-foot-long line. You can leave your dog in a Sit or a Down position for the Stay command, and you can issue more than one command to Stay.

- ✓ **You must call your Bully, and he must come when called.** You walk 10 feet from your dog, turn to face him, and then call him.

- ✓ **Your Bulldog must behave politely around other dogs.** You and another handler, each with your dogs, approach each other, stop, shake hands, exchange pleasantries, and continue on for about 10 feet. The dogs should show no more than casual interest in each other, and neither dog should go to the other dog or his or her handler.

✔ **Your dog also tests on how he reacts to distractions.** In this test, two distractions take place. Because many people who have their dog tested for the CGC are also interested in therapy-dog work, the distractions are frequently wheelchairs or a person using crutches or a walker. To test how well your dog recovers from being startled, the evaluator may throw the crutches to the ground or knock over the walker.

✔ **You must tie up your dog or hand him to someone to hold, and go out of sight for three minutes.** Your dog can move about but must not whine, bark, or pull to go after you.

If, at any time during the testing, your dog growls, snaps, bites, attacks, or attempts to attack a person or another dog, he fails the test.

When you and your Bulldog become official Canine Good Citizens, you may want to do more obedience training. The following sections give you some ideas of more ways to show off and have fun with your Bulldog.

Exploring Conformation Shows for Your Bulldog

Conformation shows originally began as a way to evaluate breeding stock, so judges look at each dog and how closely he conforms to the official breed standard. (The breed standard describes the ideal dog; see Chapter 2 for breed standards.) Even if you bought your Bulldog as a pet, you may think about the fun you can have showing your dog in the conformation ring.

You've probably seen parts of dog shows on television, and if that looks like fun to you, talk to your breeder and other Bulldog lovers about your Bully's potential as a show dog. If people who know the breed say that your dog isn't show quality, don't feel bad; your dog is still your best buddy, and you can do other activities as a team. If your dog is show quality, you can enter your dog in shows and earn points toward a championship.

Show-quality dogs compete for championship points. To earn a championship from the AKC, your dog has to win 15 points.

Depending on the number of Bulldogs competing, you earn between 1 and 5 points at any given show. Winning 3, 4, or 5 points is called winning a *major.* You need to win at least 2 majors under 2 different judges as part of your 15 points. If your dog accumulates more than 15 points but still hasn't won 2 majors, he isn't a champion.

If you decide to enter your dog in a conformation show, ask your breeder for help, or find someone in your area to be your mentor. The breeder or a mentor helps you enter shows and gives you advice in several areas:

- ✔ Deciding what to take with you to shows
- ✔ Determining what judges may like your dog
- ✔ Filling out entry forms
- ✔ Handling your dog in the ring
- ✔ Revealing grooming tips, too
- ✔ Wearing the appropriate attire

Understanding conformation classes

Conformation shows have six classes, and each class is divided by sex. Male dogs only compete against other male dogs, and female dogs compete against only other female dogs. Here are the six classes:

- ✔ The puppy class, which further divides into puppies 6 to 9 months and 9 to 12 months
- ✔ Dogs 12 to 18 months
- ✔ Novice (open to all dogs who haven't yet won three blue ribbons)
- ✔ American Bred for dogs bred in America
- ✔ Bred by Exhibitor for dogs bred by the person showing
- ✔ Open (for all dogs, regardless of who's showing them, where they were born, or how many wins they've had)

The winners from each class compete for *Winners Dog* (the award for the males) or *Winners Bitch* (the award for the females). The Winners Dog and Winners Bitch earn championship points.

The final step — the judging for *Best of Breed.* The Winners Dog and Winners Bitch return to the ring with any champions entered, and from these dogs, the judge selects the Best of Breed.

Figure 11-1 gives a more graphic representation of how an AKC dog show, in particular, progresses from classes to Best in Show.

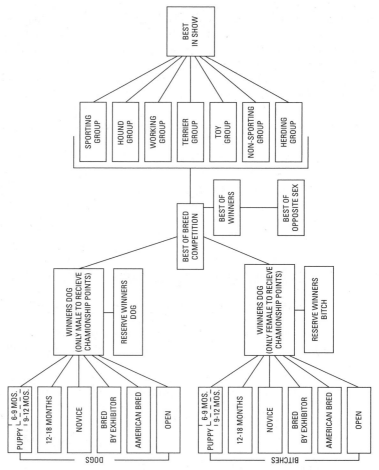

Figure 11-1: The progression of an AKC dog show from breed classes to Best in Show.

Dogs who are already champions don't compete in the regular classes. They enter the Best of Breed class and compete against the Winners Dog and Winners Bitch. The Champions don't earn any more points, but when dogs are "specialed" (entered after they're champions), the goal becomes earning group placings and Best in Show wins. The more wins, the higher the dog's standing in national rankings. A high standing adds prestige to the kennel and gets more people to want to use the dog at stud, and the breeder can ask for a higher stud fee. For winning bitches, their puppies have more value.

Westminster

Two Bulldogs have won Best in Show at the prestigious Westminster Kennel Club Dog Show. The first Bulldog, Ch. Strathtay Prince Albert, won in 1913 and was the first nonterrier to win. Ch. Strathtay Prince Albert beat almost 200 other Bulldogs to win Best of Breed before going on to win his group and, ultimately, Best in Show. The second Bulldog to achieve this honor was Ch. Kippax Fearnaught in 1955. John Rendel of the *Times* called him "a picture of power," and the judge said he was "the best Bulldog I've ever seen."

If your dog wins Best of Breed, he continues to group judging. Group judging consists of seven groups: working, sporting, terrier, toy, nonsporting, hound, and herding. The Bulldog is in the non-sporting group. Your dog joins all the other breed winners from the nonsporting group (see Chapter 2). All group winners are then judged a final time, and one dog wins Best in Show.

Scoring your Bulldog

The point system is part of the official breed standard (see Chapter 2) and shows you how a Bulldog scores in the ring. This point system guides a judge in his evaluation of your dog. Judges place a heavy emphasis on the head, which counts for 39 points, and on the body and legs, which add up to another 39 points. Other parts of the dog deserve attention, but this point schedule shows how important the head and body are in an ideal Bulldog. For a complete rundown on how dogs are scored, see the sidebar "Scale of points."

Junior Showmanship

If your child wants to show your Bulldog, *Junior Showmanship* is designed to give younger handlers a chance to compete.

Junior Showmanship divides into two classes: novice and open. Junior competitors who haven't won three first-place awards with competition components compete in the novice class. Juniors who have won three first-place awards with competition present compete in the open class. Classes divide further into junior and senior classes. Junior classes are for boys and girls who are at least 10 years old and under 14 years old on the day of the show. Senior classes are for boys and girls who are at least 14 years old and under 18 years old on the day of the show.

Scale of points

The AKC uses the following system to score dogs in dog shows:

General properties–22	Chops–2
Proportion and symmetry–5	Jaws–5
Attitude–3	Teeth–2
Expression–2	**Body, legs, etc.–39**
Gait–3	Neck–3
Size–3	Dewlap–2
Coat–2	Shoulders–5
Color of coat–4	Chest–3
Head–39	Ribs–3
Skull–5	Brisket–2
Cheeks–2	Belly–2
Stop–4	Back–5
Eyes and eyelids–3	Forelegs and elbows–4
Ears–5	Hind legs–3
Wrinkles–5	Feet–3
Nose–6	Tail–4
Total 100	

Disqualification — Brown or liver-colored nose.

The dog who the junior shows must belong to the junior or to a member of the immediate family and must be eligible for show in regular conformation or obedience classes. Bitches in season can't be shown.

Showing a dog requires more than the dog!

Showing your dog isn't cheap. Entry fees are around $25, but you also have to pay for your transportation, meals, and hotel room. You don't want to waste your money, so make sure that you and your dog are ready to show.

Preparing your dog for competition

To ensure that you and your Bully are ready for competition, check into handling classes, where you discover the correct speed for your dog as he moves around the ring and how to wear your armband (on the left arm). At class, you study the various patterns a judge may use as he evaluates your dog. A judge may ask you to move your dog in a triangle, an L, or a simple Down and Back. Classroom practice helps alleviate mistakes in the show ring. Most local kennel clubs offer inexpensive handling classes that usually range in price from $3 to $10 a session.

Although handling techniques vary a bit among breeds, some methods are basic. For example, you need to know how to get your Bulldog to *stack* — stand solidly — and hold still while the judge looks him or her over. Also, your dog must allow a stranger — the judge — to run her hands over him and to open his mouth to check his bite (although some judges ask the handler to show the bite). Your dog must trot around the ring with you so that the judge can observe his gait. Never stand between your dog and the judge.

In conformation, judges examine low-built dogs on a table to make evaluating them easier. Because Bulldogs can be too big to put on a table, judges may request a ramp, which raises your dog to a comfortable height for the judge. To prepare for this possibility, get your Bulldog accustomed to walking up a slight incline and standing quietly on a narrow platform. Most handling classes don't have a ramp, so build your own at home.

The more you practice, the more comfortable you and your dog become in the ring. Before you take the plunge into a real show, try to attend some *matches*. Matches run like shows, but they're smaller and more informal, and don't offer any points. Entry fees run from $5 to $10. A match gives your dog, and you, an idea of what a show is like and gives you practice — without spending a lot of money.

Grooming your dog beautiful

Conformation shows are sometimes called *beauty pageants*. In the conformation event, judging is based on your dog's build and how he moves; however, having him look his best never hurts.

Bulldogs need minimal grooming, but make sure to clean your dog. Trim his nails, and brush his coat. No judge wants to run her hands over a dirty dog. Take pride not only in your dog's structure but also in his appearance. For details on how to groom your dog properly, see Chapter 8.

Dressing for success

When you dress for a competition, comfort is key. You have a long day ahead of you, and not wearing the right clothes or shoes makes the day even longer. These few hints keep you comfy all the livelong day:

✔ At spring or fall shows, wear layers. A sweater that keeps you comfortable in the morning may roast you by afternoon.

✔ Carry a raincoat in your car, no matter what the weatherman says!

✔ Make sure that you wear comfortable shoes that have nonslip soles. And remember: High heels are *always* a mistake!

Now on to the clothing specifics of the events. In conformation, the attire tends to be more formal. Men typically wear sports coats and ties, and women wear dresses, although a pantsuit is acceptable. In extremely hot weather, men can shed their coats, especially if the judge takes off his coat. For women, a pantsuit is acceptable. No matter what you wear, try to wear a color that contrasts with your dog's coat. For instance, if your dog's coat is red or dark brindle, avoid wearing red, burgundy, or any other color that hides your dog's color.

In obedience, attire is a bit more casual, but men still frequently wear jackets and ties. Women prefer wearing slacks and rarely wear skirts or dresses in obedience events. Unlike conformation competitions, handlers try to match the colors of their dogs in these events. After all, if the judge can't see clearly where the dog ends and your slacks begin, maybe she won't notice your dog's crooked Sit!

The agility competition is the most casual event as far as dress goes. In the case of warm weather, competitors wear shorts. Because your dog works away from you in agility, matching or contrasting your dog's coat doesn't matter.

What to bring to the show

Dog, check. Self, check. But what else do you need to bring with you to the show? Well, many people take a grooming table and a box of supplies to a show, but if you groomed your Bully that morning or the night before, you may not need much more than your dog and his show lead.

Show leads are typically thin and light so the handler can easily bunch it up into his hand. The presentation is better than having a heavier lead dangling from the hand or flapping in the breeze. A thinner collar allows more of your dog's neck to be seen. The lighter equipment makes for a cleaner, more elegant look and also implies training and control because you're using such light equipment.

Don't forget the bait — the food tidbits you use to keep your dog alert in the ring. Also, don't forget a lot of water for your little guy or gal. I take at least a gallon of water a day. If the weather is hot, and you attend an outdoor show, take more water, both for wetting your dog down and for him to drink. Don't assume that water is available at the show site.

Take beverages and maybe a picnic lunch for yourself. Food vendors sell concessions at most shows but not always, and the food generally consists of hot dogs and hamburgers. If you stay at the show through your dog's dinner hour, pack his food as well.

In hot weather, you may want to bring ice packs for your dog or a special coat you can wet down that helps keep him cool. Tuck the ice packs under a towel, and let your dog lie on them or curl around them. Any dog can suffer from the heat, but the short-faced Bulldog is even more susceptible.

Never, ever leave your Bulldog in a closed car, even on an overcast day. Even on a cloudy day, a car's interior temperature can soon climb to a killing temperature. Take your dog with you to get your armband. If you need a bathroom break, find someone to hold your dog.

Tackling Obedience Trials

If you and your Bulldog complete a basic obedience class and enjoy working in obedience, think about trying for the Companion Dog (CD) title. The CD title is one of several obedience titles based on progressive levels of training.

Many of the exercises for the CD test are similar to the ones in the CGC test, though they're more structured. Each exercise contains definite patterns; you give only one command and can't talk to your dog otherwise. Some of the exercises are performed with your dog off lead. Although you can train your dog at home, an obedience class helps if you decide to enter competitions. Additionally, a class can help your dog get used to the long Sits and Downs in a line with strange dogs.

Receiving your Companion Dog title

All obedience titles are earned at obedience trials, which are usually held in conjunction with conformation shows. You fill out your entry form and include the entry fee, which is around $25.

To earn a CD title, you and your Bulldog need to get qualifying ribbons under three different judges. A qualifying score in obedience earns 170 out of a possible 200 points, with the dog scoring at least half the possible points in each exercise. The exercises include

- ✔ **Heel on lead and figure eight (40 points):** During the heeling exercise, the judge gives you instructions, such as forward, right or left turn, fast, slow, normal, and halt. You and your dog must execute each command, with the dog always on your left in the heel position. For the figure-eight test, two stewards form "posts" 6 feet apart, and you and your dog move around them in a figure-eight pattern.

- ✔ **Stand for examination (30 points):** The stand for examination is just that — you must remove your dog's lead, leave him standing, and move away while the judge lightly touches your dog.

- ✔ **Heel off lead (40 points):** In this exercise, you and your dog execute instructions given by the judge off the lead. These commands include forward, right or left turn, fast, slow, normal, and halt. Your dog must always remain on your left side in the heel position.

- ✔ **The recall (30 points):** On the recall, you put your dog in a Sit, tell him to Stay, walk about 35 feet away, and turn to face your dog. When the judge gives you a signal, you call your dog, who should move eagerly toward you and sit in front of you. When the judge signals again, you command your dog to Heel, and he should do so.

- ✔ **The long Sit (30 points):** The long Sit is a group of exercises in which all the dogs and handlers competing line up in a row. All handlers put their dogs in a Sit, tell the dogs to Stay, and then move across the ring and turn to face the dogs. In the long Sit, your dog must remain seated until you return to him in one minute.

- ✔ **The long Down (30 points):** The long Down is another group exercise in which all the dogs go in a Down position. The handlers instruct their dogs to Stay, move across the ring, and turn to face the dogs. In the long Down, the dog must remain lying down for three minutes.

Group exercises are a good reason to join a class. A class helps your dog get used to other dogs, and your instructor may use distractions to help teach the dogs not to move until given the command. If your dog can handle classroom distractions, he may be fine in the ring.

Earning your Companion Dog Excellent title

If you and your Bully work well as a team in obedience and have won the necessary three qualifying ribbons to be awarded a CD, you may want to work toward the Companion Dog Excellent (CDX) title. To do so, you need to qualify with three different judges.

If you decide to pursue a CDX, have your veterinarian examine your dog first. Bulldogs, unlike other breeds, have lax joints, and unstable joints may lead to jumping injuries.

In CDX competition, your dog performs versions of the exercises he's already mastered for the CD title:

✔ **Heel and figure eight off lead (40 points).**

✔ **Recall exercise (30 points):** At the CDX level, as your dog moves toward you, he must drop into a Down at your signal. Then you call your dog again, and he finishes the recall.

✔ **Long Sits (30 points):** The long Sit lasts for three minutes, but this time, you leave the ring — out of sight of your dog. You have no way of giving your Bully the evil eye if he looks like he's going to change position!

✔ **Long Downs (30 points):** The long Down lasts for five minutes, and once again, you leave the ring — out of your dog's sight.

So far, the CDX exercises extend from the ones you and your dog have already mastered for the CD title. But now you add a few new tasks to the list of required exercises:

✔ **Retrieving on the flat (20 points):** In this exercise, your dog waits at your side while you throw a dumbbell and then, at your command, retrieves the dumbbell.

✔ **Retrieving over a jump (30 points):** The AKC regulations state that the minimum jump height for Bulldogs is "the nearest multiple of 2 inches to ¾ the height of the dog at the withers." The regulations also state that the minimum jump height is 8 inches. So your Bully probably has a 12-inch jump.

✔ **The broad jump (20 points):** This jump is twice as long as the height of the high jump. If your Bulldog jumps a 12-inch high jump, he needs to jump 24 inches in the broad jump.

Your Bulldog may not see the point in going over a jump at all. Many Bulldogs seem to enjoy just going through a jump rather than over it, even though the jump is possible, as seen by your dog's jump on the couch everyday at home.

Slowly teach your dog to jump consistently. Start your training with low jumping, getting your Bulldog used to jumping on command. Keep the jump low until your dog is comfortable, and raise the height gradually. Pushing your dog can lead to injury and may make him refuse to jump at all. With the broad jump, start small and work up to the required width.

Striving for the Utility Dog title

Many handlers and their Bulldogs have gotten the CD title, and several have gotten the CDX, but not too many have earned the Utility Dog (UD) title. One reason may be that the tests for this title involve more jumping, and another reason may be that the title has a scent test and a retrieve test. In both tests, the dog must pick up an article and return with it to his handler. A Bulldog can be trained to retrieve and, even with his short nose, detect your scent. But many Bulldogs don't want to give up what they have in their mouths. Bulldogs were bred to hold on and never let go, no matter what. A long time has passed since they've had to get a death grip on a bull's nose, but that instinct to hang on is still there. Teaching a Bulldog to let go can be a challenge. Still, if you like challenges, enjoy obedience, and won't consider any breed other than a Bulldog, here's what you and your pooch need to do to earn a Utility Dog (UD) title:

✔ **Signal exercise (40 points):** During the signal exercise, all commands to your dog are hand signals. As you're heeling, the judge issues several commands, including "stand your dog" and "leave your dog." When the judge signals to down your dog, have your dog sit from the down position and then "come" and "finish," all by using hand signals.

✔ **Scent discrimination, metal article (30 points), and scent discrimination, leather article (30 points):** In this exercise, your dog has to select the one article out of nine that has your scent on it. You supply these articles — five metals and five covered in leather. The articles have a dumbbell shape, and each has a number.

The judge indicates which article number to use for your scent, and the remaining articles are placed on the ground. While you and your dog have your backs to the articles, you place your scent on either the metal or the leather article — whichever the judge indicates. The judge takes that article by using tongs or his clipboard and places it with the other articles on the ground. At his signal, you and your dog turn toward the articles, and you send your dog to retrieve the scented article. You repeat the process with the remaining article.

✔ **Directed retrieve (30 points):** In the directed retrieve, while you and your dog have your backs to the steward, she drops three white gloves in a line. Next, you turn to face the row of gloves, and the judge indicates which glove your dog has to retrieve.

You can purchase sets of three Bulldog-size gloves from vendors at dog shows or order them through catalogs. When I first got into dogs, I thought that handlers had to buy two pairs of gloves and throw one away, which seemed a real shame. I also wondered how anyone knew what size glove to buy. What a relief when I found out that they came in various sizes and in sets of three!

✔ **Moving stand and examination (30 points):** For this exercise, your Bulldog heels beside you until the judge gives you the command to stand your dog. Without stopping, you command your dog to Stand while you continue to walk ahead another 10 to 12 feet, where you stop and turn to face your dog. The judge examines your dog; then you call your dog to the heel position.

✔ **Directed jumping (40 points):** The exercise has two jumps: the high jump (a solid jump identical to the one in CDX competitions) and the bar jump (a single bar on two upright poles). You send your dog away from you, and at the command to sit, your dog should turn to face you and sit. When the judge indicates either the high jump or the bar jump, you direct your dog to do the designated jump. You repeat the process for the second jump.

Considering even greater Bulldog obedience challenges

The title of Utility Dog Excellent awards the dogs who receive a qualifying score in both Open B and Utility B classes at ten separate competitions. The Open B class exercises are those listed above for the Companion Dog Excellent title. The Utility B class exercises are the exercises for the Utility Dog title. As with all obedience titles, a Bulldog needs a qualifying score of 170 out of a possible 200.

If you and your dog are both happy with obedience, the next challenge is earning an obedience trial championship, or OTCH. This competition's award points are for the number of dogs you defeat in either Open B or Utility B classes, and you need 100 points to earn the OTCH. You win points only if you come in first or second in your class, and under three different judges, you must win a first place in Open B over six dogs or more, a first place in Utility B over three dogs or more, and another first place in either class under the same conditions.

So far, no Bulldog's earned an OTCH. Maybe yours will be the first!

Competing in Agility: Yes, Bullies Can Do It!

If the structure of obedience doesn't appeal to you or your Bulldog, consider agility. In agility events, your dog competes in running timed obstacle courses. Though they may not seem built for it, Bulldogs can and do compete in agility.

Three major organizations offer agility competitions:

- ✔ The American Kennel Club (AKC)
- ✔ The United States Dog Agility Association (USDAA)
- ✔ The North American Dog Agility Council (NADAC)

Each organization has its own set of rules and regulations, and they change periodically. Each organization also has three levels of competition. The AKC has Novice, Open, and Excellent; the USDAA has Starters/Novice, Advanced, and Master; and the NADAC has Novice, Open, and Elite. The AKC also has Jumpers with Weaves (JWW), a course with no contact obstacles (no dog walk, A-frame, or teeter-totter). The JWW contains jumps and weave poles and may have open and/or closed tunnels. Titles in JWW include Novice, Open, Excellent, and Master Excellent. You can also go on to win agility championships.

 If you worry about dog injuries or stress, you can enter the AKC preferred class, which includes 12-inch jumps rather than 16-inch jumps and an added 5 seconds to the time allowed to complete the course. NADAC also offers a 12-inch jump for Bulldogs. The USDAA doesn't offer these jumps, and in fact, if your Bulldog is over 16 inches at the withers, his jump height is 22 inches.

Because agility is a challenging and complex sport, the best advice is to put in the time at the novice level, making sure that your dog always touches the yellow contact area of the A-frame, teeter-totter and dog walk, so that missing that area doesn't become a problem at advanced levels. Waiting a bit and not pushing your dog too hard is a good idea, because you want to give a young dog plenty of time to finish growing and be in good physical condition. Agility is a demanding sport, especially for Bulldogs. Waiting until your dog is 18 months to 2 years old before actually competing is a good idea, because your dog needs time to get conditioned, to build up stamina, and to mature (Bulldogs take between 2 and 3 years to fully mature). Your dog must be at least 12 months old before he can compete in an AKC agility event. To compete in a NADAC or a USDAA competition, your dog must be at least 18 months old.

An agility course presents different obstacles for your dog to complete in a specific order and in a certain amount of time. The main obstacles in an agility course are

- *A-frame,* where the dog goes up one side of the *A* and down the other.

- *Dog walk,* which is a sloping board that leads up to another level board, which the dog walks across, and then another sloping board down that leads to the ground.

- *Seesaw.*

- Four types of jumps:

  - Broad jump

  - Panel jump, which looks like a wall

  - Bar jump

  - Tire or window jump

- *Pause table,* where, at the judge's direction, you must instruct your dog to sit or down for the count of five.

- *Open tunnel.*

- *Closed tunnel,* or *chute,* which consists of an open, rigid entry area and an expanse of cloth for the exit; the fabric has no support, so the dog must push through it to exit.

- *Weave poles,* which is a row of poles through which a dog "weaves," going between two poles, coming back through the next two, and so on. Weave poles aren't part of an AKC-novice course.

The A-frame, the dog walk, and the seesaw are all contact obstacles — that is, they all have a contact zone where the obstacle touches the ground and are usually painted yellow. The dog must touch this area as he gets on and off the obstacle to ensure that the dog doesn't injure himself by leaping on or off the obstacle.

Agility competitions can be fun for you both as long as you don't let your dog overheat. Many agility events have kiddie wading pools for cooling off the dogs, but make sure that you still carry plenty of water and ice. You also may consider investing in a special jacket that you soak in water and put on your dog to cool him off.

Do you want to know what to do with the ice? Carry ice to cool water; wrap ice in a towel, and put it in the crate with your dog; and offer ice to your dog to chew.

Sniffing Out the Fun in Tracking

Tracking isn't a competition usually associated with Bulldogs, but Bulldogs can earn tracking titles. Fewer than ten Bulldogs in the United States have attained tracking titles. However, a trainer in the Netherlands trains all her Bulldogs to track and says that they enjoy it. She says that a Bulldog works only if he likes what he's doing, so you have to make training fun, not work. Another roadblock is your Bulldog's shorter nose, so your dog may never reach the proficiency needed to do search and rescue. But if tracking sounds like fun to you, give it a try.

The AKC offers tracking tests and supplies a booklet of the rules and regulations. Tracking tests, like obedience tests, have entry fees, and tracking clubs organize the tests. Find someone in your area who tracks; subscribe to the *AKC Gazette* for a listing of events; or go to the AKC Web site, www.akc.org.

Tracking tests a dog's ability to follow a particular scent. *Variable Surface Tracking (VST)* includes pavement as well as other surfaces, such as gravel and grass. As with obedience titles, tracking has various levels of titles. Each level is based on the number of turns in the trail, the length of the trail, and how long the scent has aged before the dog starts to track it. (*Aging* is the amount of time between when the trail is laid and the dog is allowed to start tracking.) To complete any tracking title, two judges must certify that your dog has successfully completed the track for any given trail.

For all tracking titles, you need a harness and a tracking lead, which must be between 30 and 40 feet long.

Tracking titles include

   ✓ **Tracking Dog (TD):** For the TD title, a dog follows a track that's at least 440 yards long, has 3 to 5 turns, and has been aged at least 30 minutes and no longer than 2 hours. The track can't cross any paved area or body of water and has two starting flags — one at the beginning of the track and one 30 yards from the first one to indicate the direction in which the track was laid. The first flag lets you know where your dog picks up the scent. The second flag lets you know that you and your dog are moving in the right direction. At the end of the track is a glove or wallet, which the dog must indicate in some way. The dog may pick up the article, may sit or lie down, or otherwise show that he has found the article.

✔ **Tracking Dog Excellent (TDX):** Your dog must have a TD title before he can compete for a TDX. For the TDX title, your dog must traverse a track at least 800 yards long, containing 5 to 7 turns, and aged at least 3 hours and no more than 5 hours. Two cross tracks cross the main track, and two obstacles — a stream, a fence, a bridge, a lightly traveled road, a gully — must also be in a TDX track. Along the way, your dog needs to find four articles.

✔ **Variable Surface Tracking (VST):** VST tracking tests your dog's ability to track over changing surfaces. A dog must already have a TD or a TDX title to compete for a VST title. In this test, the trail crosses three different surfaces, with one being vegetation and the other two a combination of concrete, asphalt, gravel, sand, hardpan, or mulch.

✔ **Champion Tracker (CT):** A dog gets the Champion Tracker title (CT) when he earns all three tracking titles.

Rallying Around!

Rally is a new sport based on obedience commands, but Rally is less structured than obedience trials. Handlers can talk to their dogs, pat their legs, and otherwise encourage their dogs without penalty. You can't touch your dog, but you can use hand signals. The dog walks on the left, but perfect "heel position" isn't required. Each dog-and-handler team's time is recorded in case the points end in a tie.

In obedience, a judge gives the commands, but in Rally, signs (between 10 and 20) direct you. After the judge gives the command "Forward," you're on your own to complete the exercises. Judges allow handlers a 15-minute walk-through of the course *without* their dogs so they know which commands the course includes.

Bulldogs compete at three levels of competition: Rally Novice, Rally Advanced, and Rally Excellent:

✔ In the Rally Novice class, the dog remains on lead at all times, and the team completes between 10 and 15 stations.

✔ In the Rally Advanced class, all exercises are judged off lead, and exercises contain between 12 and 17 stations, including at least 1 jump. The jumps are the same as those used in obedience, broad, high and bar jumps. Dogs less than 15 inches at the withers jump 8 inches; dogs measuring between 15 and 20 inches jump 12 inches; and dogs measuring over 20 inches jump 16 inches.

✔ In the Rally Excellent class, again, the dogs are off lead, except for the "honor" exercise. During the honor exercise, one dog either sits or Downs at the judge's direction and remains in that position while another dog-and-handler team completes the course.

The course consists of 15 to 20 stations and at least 2 jumps. A handler at the Rally Excellent level may not clap or pat his leg to encourage his dog, but multiple commands are still permitted.

A minimum score of 70 points, out of a possible 100, qualifies. A team may lose 3 to 10 points, or even receive a nonqualifying score, for handler error. The total deduction depends on the frequency and severity of the error.

A one-point deduction occurs for each of the following:

✔ Being out of position

✔ Delaying or resisting responding

✔ Having a tight lead

✔ Interfering (on the dog's part) with the handler's forward motion

✔ Sitting poorly

✔ Touching a jump, pylon, post, or person

In the case of the following incidents, a three-point deduction occurs:

✔ Barking excessively

✔ Giving a loud command or intimidating signal

✔ Knocking over a post or pylon

✔ Lacking control

✔ Repeating a station

A 10-point deduction is taken for

✔ Hitting a jump

✔ Performing a station incorrectly

A judge may also deduct one to ten points for lack of teamwork.

Nonqualifying (NQ) scores include

- Being substantially out of position/not completing the honor exercise

- Eliminating in the ring during judging

- Failing to attempt a station

- Failing to meet minimum requirements

- Having an unmanageable dog

- Knocking off the bar from the uprights and/or using a jump as an aid in going over

- Maintaining a consistently tight lead

Working with Your Bulldog as a Therapy Dog

If you refer to your Bully as a couch potato, and you aren't competitive enough to enjoy any formal events, consider having your dog become a therapy dog. *Therapy dogs* visit healthcare facilities. A dog may do as little as sit and be petted, or a dog may be actively involved in patient care. Throwing a toy for a dog to retrieve can be part of physical therapy. A therapy dog may also visit schools. Children love to read to dogs, and dogs love to be read to, and they never care if a child makes a mistake. Therapy dogs also visit survivors after a disaster. The dog doesn't find victims but offers comfort to the victims and to the rescue workers as well. Disasters add stress to life, and the presence of a calm, loving dog can help people cope. Bulldogs make great therapy dogs because they're calm and because they love people.

Therapy dogs and their handlers traditionally visit nursing homes and hospitals, but your dog may be the perfect canine for a visit to the local school. Most Bulldogs are calm and steady with children. If you don't have children of your own, make sure that children don't frighten your dog. Many schools have programs where children can read to a dog. The reading program gives the child practice and supplies a listener who doesn't criticize them.

Although you can make nursing home, hospital, and school visits with a "regular" dog, some organizations, like Therapy Dogs International and the Delta Society, register therapy dogs. For more information, check out their Web sites: Delta Society, www.deltasociety.org, and Therapy Dogs International, www.tdi-dog.org.

To become a registered therapy dog, your Bully has to pass a test similar to the Canine Good Citizen test. The test includes exercises with a person using a wheelchair, crutches, a walker, or all three.

If one of these organizations certifies your dog, he gets a special ID tag for his collar, and you may get a laminated wallet card to show as proof of his certification. The agency also may provide insurance coverage for visits in case your dog accidentally harms someone and may offer guidelines for taking your dog to hospitals or other healthcare facilities.

One drawback to having Bulldogs as therapy dogs is that people in wheelchairs or beds can have a difficult time reaching them. Plus Bulldogs' weight makes putting them in someone's lap nearly impossible. So that your Bully can provide a little TLC, consider teaching him to put his front paws up on the side of a wheelchair or bed, but always check with the facility manager first for permission to do so.

Whether your dog is registered with an agency or not, take proof of vaccinations with you when you make your visit. You may not need the proof, but sometimes administrators want to make sure that your dog has his necessary shots, especially rabies. Make sure that you've cleaned your dog and trimmed his nails. Trimming your dog's nails is important: Remember, older people have delicate skin, and your pooch's nails can easily bruise or tear their skin. Make sure that your dog is clean; no one wants to pet or smell a dirty dog!

Chapter 12

On the Go: Taking, Leaving, or Looking for Bully

*Y*ou want your Bulldog with you, but you need to know the best way to travel with him. Don't worry — I give you the overview on transporting your Bully, packing for him, and finding great destinations he'll love accompanying you to. I also tell you what to do when you have to leave your Bully behind. And this chapter contains tips on what to do if the unthinkable happens and your Bulldog gets lost.

Investigating Your Travel Options

Many methods of transportation exist to move us from point A to point B. How you decide to reach your vacation destination is up to you. The most popular methods of travel are probably by car or plane. But whatever you decide, consider your Bulldog's comfort when making plans.

Traveling by car

If your Bulldog isn't used to riding in a car, now's the time to accustom him to it. Some dogs equate riding in a car with going to the veterinarian's office. They resist getting into the car, and they're not happy after they get in. They may whine, bark, or even throw up. It's hard to blame them. I wouldn't be happy about a car ride, either, if the trip always ended at the doctor's office.

If your car has leather seats, place an antiskid mat underneath a blanket to prevent your Bully from sliding around when you slam on the breaks or accelerate. Sudden movement and slipping can injure your Bully.

When your Bully's in the car, either put him in the crate or attach the harness. Whatever means of restraint you use, offering more treats aids in the process. To get your Bulldog used to riding in the car, try these steps:

1. **Start slowly, and be patient.**

2. **Open the doors on each side of the car.**

3. **Coax your Bully in the car with food and then out the other side.**

4. **Don't try to restrain him or keep him in the car.**

5. **When he's willingly going through the car, shut the door on one side.**

6. **Invite him in with food and then let him out again.**

7. **If he's happy to stay in the car for a bit — great — but don't shut the door yet.**

After your Bulldog is happy hanging out in the car for a while, take a car ride or two, but make the trips short. Follow these easy steps to ease your Bully into taking those car trips:

1. **Take your dog for a short drive around the block.**

2. **Give your Bully a treat, and let him out of the car.**

3. **Gradually increase your drive time.**

4. **Drive your dog to a park and then go for a walk.**

5. **Drive up to a bank drive-through window where dog biscuits are given.**

If you take your Bully places that are fun and where your pup gets treats, eventually, your Bulldog will understand that not all trips lead to the veterinarian's office.

Remember, you absolutely, positively can't leave your dog in a closed car while you go sightseeing. Even with the windows down, a car in the summer can get dangerously warm for a Bulldog. If you're planning on crating your dog, the crate will get even hotter while you're away having fun. Parking in the shade is no guarantee of coolness either, because shade moves, and your car may soon be in the sun.

Sightseeing with your Bully

Part of the fun of a car trip can be stopping to visit roadside attractions, but sightseeing can be harder if you brought the dog along. If you take your Bully along, plan your trip to include dog-friendly sights as well.

If you absolutely can't leave your dog at home, some theme parks and attractions have kennel facilities. You can enjoy the park, and your dog can stay safe and cool.

Using a crate

If your dog is crate trained, have him ride in a crate in the car (if you have a big-enough car). Your Bully is safer and more comfortable in his crate. Many times, crates have water or food dishes attached, so your Bully can have a refreshing snack on your trip. Also, your dog's crate likely has his scent on it; this scent can lessen the frightening factor of the car and make your dog more willing to take a trip. Depending on the type of interior you have in your vehicle, your Bully's mess may be easier to clean if he's confined to a crate. If he gets sick, urinates, or defecates, these messes will be limited to a small crate instead of in your back seat.

Using a harness

If you haven't crate trained your Bully, or if you drive a compact car, consider investing in a seat harness — you don't want your Bully flying through the air or escaping from the car into traffic if you have a car accident.

Airbags are as dangerous to a dog as they are to a small child. Don't let your dog ride in the front seat, even with a harness. Securely fasten your Bully in the back seat.

Traveling in the air

If you're flying to your vacation destination and still want your Bully to go with you, plan ahead. Think about where you're going and what the weather is like. Most airlines fly dogs only if the destination's temperature is under 85 or over 45 degrees Fahrenheit.

All airlines are different, and the rules change frequently, so make sure that you get all the information you need well before your planned flight. Besides the limits based on temperature, some airlines have a limit as to how many dogs they accept on a particular flight. In addition, many airlines have different rules for Bulldogs than for other breeds. Make sure that you specify that your dog is a Bully.

Bulldogs can become dangerously stressed during air travel. Have your veterinarian rule out elongated soft palate, stenotic nares, and small-trachea problems before you schedule a flight. Dogs with restricted airways should not fly. (For more on these issues, see Chapter 14.)

Riding in cargo

People with smaller pets have the option of taking the dog in the cabin with them, but unless you're traveling with a Bulldog puppy, your Bully's crate isn't going to fit under the seat, and he won't be allowed to fly in the cabin. Plan your route carefully. Plane transfers are harder on your dog, and a chance exists that she can get lost en route.

An overnight flight (red-eye flight) lessens the risk of overheating and may also be less chaotic.

If you decide to fly with your dog, you need to abide by a few rules to ensure your Bully's safety:

- ✔ **House your Bully in an airline-approved crate.** Plastic models are better than metal because metal tends to absorb more heat; remember that heat is especially dangerous for a Bulldog.

- ✔ **Tape a label on the crate that lists your destination, name, address, telephone number, and dog's name.** You may also want to include your veterinarian's phone number. If you have a cell phone, be sure to include that number on the label.

- ✔ **Place absorbent bedding in your Bully's crate.** Shredded paper under fleece is a good choice because fleece is comfortable for your Bully, and liquid that your dog expels runs through the fleece and is absorbed by the paper shreds.

- ✔ **Don't feed your dog for at least 12 hours before the flight.** A little urine is easier to clean up than feces.

- ✔ **To keep your Bully cool, freeze water in your dog's water dish, and place the dish in the crate.** Your dog can either lick the ice or drink the water as the ice melts. Frozen water prevents spilling and keeps your Bully cool on the flight.

- ✔ **Don't tranquilize your dog before a flight.** If your dog gets hot, he may be too woozy to compensate for the heat by panting.

✔ **Run a bungee cord over the door of the crate to keep the door from opening if the crate is dropped or bumped.** Luggage shifts, and items fall over. You don't want your Bully wandering around the cargo section of the plane while the plane is in flight.

Dropping off and picking up your passenger

Make sure that you understand exactly how and when your dog is loaded on the plane, and where and when you can pick her up when the flight lands. Be polite, but be persistent. If you don't actually see your dog board the plane, ask the gate counter agent to call the ramp to make sure that your dog is on board.

Pick up your Bulldog promptly at your destination. If you don't get your dog in a reasonable amount of time, ask about the delay. Ask again. Ask before your plane has taken off. Having your dog with you is the point of the trip, not having him fly to another city without you.

Packing for Your Pooch

Packing your Bully's bag for your vacation is just as important as packing your own bags. The first item in your dog's travel bag should be his shot record. If you're crossing state lines, leaving the country, or staying in a state or federal park, you may be required to show proof of your dog's vaccinations, particularly the date of his most recent rabies shot. Here is a list of items you should have with you when traveling with your Bulldog:

✔ **Medication:** If your Bulldog is on any kind of medication, take enough for the trip. If you plan to be away during the time for your Bully's monthly heartworm medicine, don't forget to take that medication too.

Even if your own home is flea and tick free, the place that you are going may not be. Ask your veterinarian for a preventive flea medication.

✔ **Food and water:** Think about the long the trip, and take food and water for your pal (and for yourself too, if you want).

- **Make sure to pack your dog's regular food.** Don't take the chance that your dog's brand of kibble isn't available everywhere. Carry enough food for the entire trip.

- **Carry a food dish and a water dish.** This will make Bully feel more at home.

- **Bring water from home.** This prevents doggy tummy upsets from unfamiliar water. If your trip is so long that carrying enough water is impractical, mix water from home with water on your travels so your dog gets used to changes gradually.

- **If you're traveling in the summer, bring a cooler with ice to help keep your Bully cool and happy.** Freeze plastic jugs of water to have both ice and water as the ice melts.

✔ **Toys:** Pack your dog's favorite toy. Travel is stressful. Making sure that your Bully has his teddy bear each night helps him adjust.

✔ **Towels:** Take extra towels. Dogs always find the patch of mud or the puddle in the parking lot. Take more towels than you think you need.

✔ **First-aid kit:** Take a small first-aid kit. Pack a few basics like disinfectant, gauze pads, and antibiotic cream. Make sure that you pack an extra blanket in the car. For information on first-aid kits, see Chapter 15.

Bulldog-Friendly Places to Stay

If you already have a destination in mind, you still need to know how to find a good place to stay. Whether you're looking to camp or stay in a hotel, the following sections give you some good tips for making the experience a good one for all involved.

Finding a pet-friendly motel

If you're going to take your dog with you on vacation, you have to plan ahead. Although many motels happily welcome dogs, many more don't. Make your reservations well in advance, and make sure that your dog will be an accepted guest at the hotel where you want to stay. After a long day of driving, you don't want to be turned away from your motel.

The AAA publishes a guide called *Traveling with your Pet,* which lists thousands of pet-friendly places to stay. But if your favorite resting place isn't in the book, give it a call and find out what the policy is regarding pets. If you're camping, check with campgrounds about their policies too.

Sometimes, smaller places that aren't part of a chain allow a dog if he's crated or has had obedience training. Find out the policies of the hotels in the area you are staying. Never be afraid to ask. What can it hurt?

Many motels and hotels charge a fee for a dog. Find out about the fees ahead of time so the extra money isn't a shock.

Protecting your pooch in the room

Crating your dog while he's in a motel room alone is a good idea. Even the best-trained dog may be anxious in a strange place, and sometimes anxiety can mean a chewed chair leg or a puddle on the carpet. Also, when your dog is safe in his crate, he can't accidentally escape if the room door is opened. A crated dog means that housekeeping can enter safely, too. Your dog may be the biggest lover in the world, but a stranger doesn't know that.

If you're leaving your dog in the room while you go sightseeing or out to eat, turn on the television or radio. The noise helps calm your dog and masks outside distractions that may make your dog bark.

Cleaning your room yourself

When you stay at a hotel, you may expect your room to be clean and tidy when you return from a day of fun in the sun. To make your stay happy for everyone involved — you, your dog, housekeeping, and the management — you may want to consider cleaning your room yourself.

Try these tips to keep the peace:

- ✔ Put out the "Do not disturb" sign.

- ✔ Make your bed yourself.

- ✔ Travel with a sheet so you can cover the bedspread. Dog hair on a bedspread is hard to remove, and believe it or not, hotel bedspreads aren't washed between guests.

  If you don't want to carry a sheet, ask housekeeping for one. They'd rather launder an extra sheet than have to clean the bedspread. The sheet also keeps the spread clean if your Bully's paws are a bit dirty.

- ✔ Bring your own towels. If your Bully gets dirty or muddy, use the towels you packed. Don't use the hotel's towels.

  If you're staying more than a night or two and need clean towels for yourself, talk to the front-desk staff. You can probably arrange to leave the hotel's dirty towels in the corridor and have clean ones dropped off.

✔ Stay at a place where the room door opens to an indoor corridor instead of directly outside. If your dog gets out the door, he's still in the building.

✔ Keep a piece of plastic under your dog's food and water dishes to prevent carpet stains.

If you're staying anywhere more than a night or two, leave a tip for housekeeping on the first day. Tipping makes the staff more receptive to working around your dog.

Camping with your Bulldog

A wonderful way to combine a vacation and your love of dogs is to go to a dog camp with your Bully. The number of dog camps is growing, so a camp may be within driving range of where you live. Dog camps generally offer dorm-style accommodations, and activities are doggy-based. Camps differ but may offer classes on obedience, agility, herding, animal massage, first aid, and nature walks. Some may have a pond or lake for swimming. You can participate in events like a costume parade or bobbing for hot dogs. Craft classes may give you a chance to make a dog collar or lead for your Bully.

Whatever is offered, the atmosphere at camp is dog friendly and leisurely, and human food is generally excellent and one of the attractions — no charred hot dogs around the campfire (although a campfire may happen one night). The dog camp I attended had hearty breakfasts of pancakes, bacon, sausage, and eggs, and lunches and dinners were superb. Dogs, much to their regret, keep to their regular kibble.

More Great Vacation Spots for You and Bully

Besides dog-friendly camps and hotels (see the previous section), a fun getaway for Bulldogs is anyplace with water. Bulldogs love water, but unfortunately, most of the breed swim like a rock. In addition, Bulldogs' upturned noses make drowning a real danger. With those warnings out of the way, a vacation on the shores of a small lake or near the ocean may be just the getaway you're looking for. Your Bully loves walks along the shore, cooling his tootsies in the waves or wading a bit. Keep your dog on a lead so you can keep him out of deep water.

Don't let your Bulldog drink salt water. Salt water causes your dog to be violently ill. Let your Bully play in the ocean, but don't let him drink the water.

Dog-friendly bed-and-breakfasts make a relaxing getaway and generally offer more freedom for your dog, as well as more lawn area.

If you travel a lot or want to go only where your dog is welcome, check out *Doggone* — "The newsletter about fun places to go and cool things to do with your dog." This publication prints six times a year and lists a variety of places you can visit with your Bully. Subscribe to *Doggone* by visiting the Web site at `www.doggone fun.com`, or call 888-DOGTRAVEL.

Leaving Your Bully Behind

Sometimes, taking your Bulldog on your vacation just isn't practical. A trip through the Southwest in July is definitely not Bulldog friendly. A trip to Europe is probably better without the added worry of your dog. And sometimes, even on a short trip, you want to stay out late, sleep in, and spend hours touring the area without thinking about feeding or walking your dog or worrying about his comfort.

Whether you're boarding your dog or hiring a pet sitter, leave the number for your veterinarian, as well as a contact for long-term care should something happen to you. And tell your veterinarian about the arrangements. See whether the office will bill you if either the kennel owner or the sitter takes your dog in for treatment. Planning ensures that your dog gets the care he needs, and questions about fees and payments won't arise.

Boarding your Bully

A boarding kennel can make your vacation not only dog free but also worry free. Just like your dog's crate isn't a jail cell, a boarding kennel isn't a jail. Think of a kennel as summer camp. Sure, you may see wires and locked doors, but those cages mean that your dog isn't wandering loose and getting into trouble.

You need to check out kennels to make sure they're up to your standards and will take great care of your beloved Bully. Here are some tips:

  ✔ **Visit the kennel without your dog.** Look at the fencing. The fence should be in good repair, with no holes or pieces of protruding wire. I prefer a kennel where the lower half of each pen is solid for more separation, but I wouldn't rule out a kennel with chain link to the floor if I liked everything else about the place.

✔ **Make sure that all the dogs have fresh water available and clean food bowls.** The place should be clean. A kennel may smell a bit doggy but not like urine or feces. The pens should be picked up and the outside play area clean.

After you have toured the facilities, ask some questions about what you saw and what you expect from the kennel:

✔ **What's the playtime policy?** Some kennels put dog-friendly dogs together for a bit of playtime. Ask what criteria staff members use to determine how the dogs get along. If you don't want your dog to be part of a playgroup, say so.

✔ **What kind of food do you serve?** Most kennels feed quality food that agrees with most of the dogs they board. If your dog is on a special diet, or you don't want his food changed, ask about supplying your own food. An extra charge may be assessed. Kennel owners are happy to meet the needs of their clients, but remember that you may have to pay for the duties that take more time or if you need storage space.

✔ **Will you be able to give my Bully her medication?** If your dog is on medication, let the kennel operator know. If your dog has any condition that needs watching, tell the manager. Write out any special instructions, and give the kennel staff more information rather than less.

Leave your veterinarian's number in the case of an emergency.

✔ **What is the kennel policy if a veterinarian is unavailable?** What's the kennel's backup plan? When I leave a dog at a kennel, I always state that I want any problem treated aggressively. I'd rather pay for a trip to the veterinarian that was unnecessary than have something happen to my dog because I told the kennel operators to "wait and see."

✔ **Can I bring in bedding and toys for my dog?** Most kennels let you supply these items for your dog. I suggest washable towels. Some dogs get nervous in a kennel, and they demonstrate their anxiety by chewing on their bedding. I've seen expensive wicker beds turned into matchsticks. Save the plush foam bed for home, and send towels to the kennel.

✔ **What are your hours of operation?** Be clear on the charges and on the hours for dropping off and picking up your Bulldog. Some kennels offer pickup and delivery service, so ask about that if you're interested.

✔ **Does your staff prefer one breed over another?** Make sure that the staff likes Bulldogs. Some people may dislike or fear certain breeds. Make sure that the staff understands what a Bulldog needs and is willing to accommodate those needs.

To make the boarding-kennel stay a bit easier on everyone, try out these simple tips:

✔ **Ease your dog in by boarding her overnight or just for a weekend.** A "trial run" gives your dog a chance to experience the kennel and the people who are in charge, yet she's home again fairly soon. The younger the dog, the more easily she adapts to the kennel environment, so whether you're planning a vacation anytime soon, think about boarding your dog. Waiting until your Bulldog is older makes the boarding experience more traumatic for her (and maybe for you too!).

✔ **Supply a record of your dog's vaccinations.** Some kennels also require a bordatella, or "kennel cough," injection before you can leave your dog for boarding. There are over 100 strains of kennel cough (infectious tracheobronchitis), but the ones most commonly seen are caused by an airborne virus that can spread rapidly in a kennel environment. Dogs with kennel cough develop a dry, rasping cough that lasts about 2 weeks. The disease isn't life threatening in a healthy dog, but there is a risk of secondary infection, like pneumonia, which is minimized by a course of antibiotics.

Hiring a pet sitter

An alternative to a boarding kennel is a pet sitter. With a pet sitter, your dog stays in her own home, and the sitter comes at specified times to feed, walk, and play with your Bully. Some sitters even spend the night at your home. The sitter's presence in and out makes your home look lived in, and many times a pet sitter also brings in the mail and waters your plants.

Choosing a pet-sitting business

Organizations, such as Pet Sitters International and the National Association of Professional Pet Sitters provide reputable sitters, but you can find sitters who don't belong to these organizations. The key is to find a *reputable* pet sitter. Don't think that everything will be fine because the neighbor's teenage daughter has volunteered to look after your dog. That method may be a cheap way out, but remember, you get what you pay for.

If you choose a pet-sitting business, the business should be bonded and carry insurance. Levels of service are based on how many times you need a sitter to visit your home and the needs of the dog/owner. A diabetic dog who needs insulin shots and six walks a day costs more to pet-sit than a young, healthy dog who goes out only three times a day.

Calling on Bully lovers

If you don't trust the neighborhood teenager, and the professional pet sitter is too expensive, an in-between pet sitter may be right up your alley (and budget). This sitter is usually a pet lover who has found sitting an enjoyable way to make some extra money.

Avoiding stranger anxiety

No matter who you select for pet sitting, the person should visit your home once or twice before you leave for vacation. Ideally, the sitter should also visit when you're still in town but not at home. Dogs react differently when you let someone into the house versus when someone comes in and you're not home. Make sure that your Bully recognizes the sitter as a friend.

Alleviating misunderstandings

The pet sitter should also know what the rules are. Put instructions in writing to prevent misunderstandings. If your dog is allowed on the couch, fine. If not, let the sitter know. If you limit treats for your Bully, tell the sitter. Give the sitter whatever information helps her give your dog the best care. If you never walk on a certain street because of a loose dog, let her know.

Knowing What to Do If You Lose Your Bulldog

Whether you're on a trip or at home, be prepared for the worst and have an action plan in case your Bulldog goes missing. In the event that your dog gets lost, he should always have proper identification. But no matter what methods you use for identification, if your dog should become lost, don't rely on tags, tattoos, or microchips alone to get your dog back. You need to make an effort to track him down.

Identifying Bully

If your Bully gets lost, his identification is all he has to link him back to you. I recommend that everyone have her pet both tagged and microchipped. Why two methods of ID? Well, if your Bully ends up a mile from your home, your neighbor can bring him right home or give you a call. On the other hand, tags can come off collars, and collars themselves may come off your dog. If your dog ends up in a shelter, and he's microchipped, he can be scanned and returned to you.

Taking tags into consideration

Tags are an easily visible means of identification. You have your Bully's rabies and license tags, so why not add one with your name and contact information?

Tags come in many different styles, even ones that glow in the dark. Most pet stores can order tags for you, and some even carry vending machines that allow you to custom-make dog tags on the spot. Most identification tags minimally list your phone number and may also include your address and/or your name. Many pet owners also put their dog's name on the tag.

Some people discourage identifying your pet by name; stealing your dog becomes easier because thieves can call your dog by name. You make the judgment call. If a thief is close enough to your dog to read her tag, he is also close enough to snap on a lead or pick up your dog, and he doesn't need to call her.

If you're traveling with your dog a long way from home for your vacation, make up an additional ID tag for your dog to wear, with your vacation address and phone number.

Here are some tips for making sure the information on your tag is as useful as it can be:

- Cylinder tags hold a piece of paper with your information and are handy if you move around a lot or travel with your dog, because you can change the information to reflect your local address.

- If your dog is staying home, make another tag with a local contact — the pet sitter or a friend who can pick up your dog if he is found.

- Include your cell-phone number on your dog's tag. Typically, with today's technologies, cell-phone numbers rarely change because they're used in all parts of the country. Listing a cell-phone number ensures the best possible contact number in the event that your dog becomes lost.

✔ Many people also put the word *reward* on the dog tag. The idea is that the finder may be more inclined to call the owner than to keep the dog or dump him at the pound. Be aware that just because someone calls saying he has your dog doesn't mean that he does. Money should never change hands until the dog is returned. If you suspect fraud or that your dog is being ransomed, contact local law enforcement.

Microchipping your dog

One of the most effective ways to identify your dog is with a microchip, which costs about $45. Microchips never fade or stretch, like tattoos, and can't fall off, like a tag.

The microchip is about the size of a grain of rice; the vet inserts the device just under the skin between your dog's shoulder blades. Special scanners can read the chip's information, which includes the registered agency and your dog's individual number. A veterinarian or shelter worker calls the agency for your contact information. Although different companies supply microchips, most veterinarians and animal shelters have scanners that can read the information on all chips. Ask your veterinarian about the microchip on your first visit. Tips on locating a good veterinarian are in Chapter 13.

Microchips have the advantage of being permanent. They can't get lost or become unreadable. The disadvantage is that a scanner is needed to detect and read the chip, and many people don't know about microchips. Although most veterinarians' offices and animal hospitals and shelters have scanners that can read the chips from the three major chip systems, the scanners are no use unless your lost dog is brought to one of these places to be scanned.

The paperwork that comes with a microchip includes contact sources in the case that your information changes. A fax number, e-mail address, and regular mailing address are included. If your contact information changes, use one of those methods to keep your info up to date. If your Bully is lost, you want your current location on file with the registering agency.

Tattooing your Bully

Many breeders tattoo their dogs, so your Bulldog may come to you with a tattoo. Before the rise of identity theft, many people used their Social Security number as the identifying tattoo. Now the number is usually your dog's registration number or a randomly chosen number (usually chosen by your breeder) that is stamped on all of your Bully's information.

A tattoo can prevent dog thieves from selling your dog to a research laboratory but may not help if your dog is lost in the neighborhood. The idea behind tattooing is that someone picks up your dog; recognizes the tattoo; and takes your puppy to a shelter, vet, or breeder who can research the number and return your dog to you.

Keep in mind that most people don't know to look for a tattoo as an identifier when it comes to dogs. Also, tattoos can fade and stretch as your puppy grows. Only one of my dogs came with a tattoo, and that dog's veterinarian records reflected the number tattoo; but as she's grown, the tattoo has stretched and faded. So this method may not be the most reliable way to identify your dog.

Looking for a lost Bulldog

Be aggressive. Do everything you can to let people know that your dog is lost and that you are the owner. Make up posters of your dog. If you have a scanner, a printer, and a computer, you can make your own posters, complete with a picture. Otherwise, have the local copy shop make the posters for you. Put posters on area bulletin boards, in veterinarians' offices, and at local stores. The following tips suggest items to include on your "Lost" poster:

✔ **Choose the best picture of your Bulldog for your poster.** Use a sharp black-and-white image of your dog. Keep a good photo of your Bully on hand in case of an emergency. Try to get an easily identifiable picture of your dog. If you have a dark brindle Bulldog, try to take a picture of him against a light background. If your Bulldog is mostly white, find a dark background.

   Keep up-to-date photos on hand.

✔ **List your phone number and the general area where the dog was lost.** For instance, in the vicinity of Green Park or between Maple and Elm Streets.

✔ **State the dog's sex and age.** Listing the age as an approximation with a description like "puppy" or "older dog with gray muzzle" may be more helpful than stating a specific age.

✔ **Mention that your dog may be wearing a collar.** Describe the collar, including the color. The collar may have come off or been taken off, but this info is still important to include.

✔ **List the colors of your dog.** This is especially important if your photo is black and white. If your Bulldog is brindle, you may want to say "brown and black," mention the striped pattern, or say "mostly brown" on the poster. Not everyone knows what brindle is.

✔ **Offer a reward.** But don't specify the amount on the poster.

Posters are an excellent way to get the most information out to the public. There are other ways to get the word out that your dog is missing:

✔ **Go door to door.** Ask your immediate neighbors to keep an eye out for your dog. Leave them a poster.

✔ **Recruit children.** They probably cover more territory on foot than the adults in your neighborhood do, and they may be more apt to notice a dog.

Don't actually encourage children to try to catch your dog. Ask them to come to you and lead you to the dog, or to tell their parents and have them call you. A lost dog is frequently a frightened dog, and you don't want him chased farther away. You also don't want to run the risk of your dog's biting someone out of fear.

✔ **Call area veterinary hospitals.** A chance exists that your dog was hit by a car and taken to a veterinarian. Call repeatedly.

✔ **Check with your local animal shelter.** Go in person, and look at the dogs. Don't rely on phone calls, and don't rely on having someone at a shelter call you.

 • **Leave your name and phone number, of course, but also check in person.** Notes can be lost, and shelter personnel may change. Hard as it may be to believe, the person you talk to may not know what a Bulldog is. He may have seen your dog and thought that she was a mixed breed.

 • **Go look at the dogs claimed as strays.** Go look at least every other day.

 • **Show the staff pictures of your dog.**

 • **Visit distant shelters.** If another shelter is 20 or 30 miles away, visit it too. Dogs, even Bulldogs, can travel amazing distances. In addition, if someone picked up your dog and dropped her off again or lost her, she can end up even farther away.

✔ **Run an ad in the lost-and-found column of your local newspaper.** Ask your area radio stations to announce your ad. Many newspapers and radio stations are happy to run these kinds of public-service announcements at no charge.

✔ **Notify your breeder.**

✔ **Check with Bulldog rescue.**

✔ **Notify your local Bulldog or kennel club.** Bulldog enthusiasts can be helpful resources, and if they see a stray Bulldog, they can contact the correct authorities to help you get your dog back. Dog people are generally eager to help other dog people.

Part IV
Keeping Your Bulldog Healthy

The 5th Wave   By Rich Tennant

"I don't mind him investigating canine health issues online, I just wish he'd save his bookmarks, remember to log off, and quit drooling on the keyboard."

In this part . . .

*T*his part is all about health: how to choose a veterinarian, what shots to give, and what diseases and parasites threaten your Bulldog. Health issues are specifically addressed, and I provide a chapter on canine first aid. In addition, what happens when your Bully reaches his senior years? Making his life comfortable in his old age is extremely important, so of course, you will find information on your senior Bully too.

Chapter 13

Knowing Your Veterinarian, Vaccinations, and Common Treatments

*F*inding a reputable veterinarian and starting a vaccination schedule are the first steps to ensuring that your Bulldog has a long and healthy life. There are many different vaccinations available to protect your dog; your and your veterinarian will decide together just which ones your dog will need. This chapter also deals with alternative care, allergies, and internal and external parasites that can affect your pet's health. There's information on holistic care and massage therapy, as well as how to protect your Bully from fleas and ticks.

Choosing a Veterinarian

Many choices exist today for your Bulldog's care. As you may have read in other chapters, choices abound for all categories: feeding, training, and even playing. Medicine is no different. Ideally, you want to choose a veterinarian before you pick up your puppy. Your breeder may also want to know who your vet is or if you have made the effort to look for one before you get your pup. You can just flip through the yellow pages and pick a name you like, but the results may be better if you take a little more time and care to select your veterinarian and weigh your options. You and your veterinarian work together to keep your Bulldog healthy for several years, and you want to have a good working relationship.

Counting the cost of veterinarian care

Many times people complain about the cost of a veterinary visit. So far, dog medicine is still cheaper than human medicine, but like people medicine, veterinarian medicine advances all the time. Veterinarians work hard to prevent illness as much as they do to cure it, and your vet may try to find the underlying cause of a problem and not just treat symptoms. This research into your Bulldog's condition may mean that the vet needs to take measures beyond a regular visit: blood tests, x-rays, and maybe even a trip to a specialist. You should ask your veterinarian for explanations and alternative solutions, and you can always seek a second opinion, but don't skimp when it comes to your Bully's health.

Some veterinarian offices offer payment plans for procedures that cost hundreds or thousands of dollars. Before you arrange for procedures for your Bully, ask your vet about payment options.

There are numerous pet health insurance companies that offer policies to cover some bills and emergencies. The AKC offers one now as well, and when puppies are registered with AKC, they are now automatically eligible for two months of free trial coverage. Plans vary as to what is covered, and most (if not all) will not cover what they consider to be congenital, hereditary, or breed-specific illness. However, they can really help defray the costs of injuries and acquired illness. Some will even cover cancer. All are applicable to broken bones, swallowed foreign bodies, poisoning, and more. As an unexpected emergency and subsequent bill may mean deciding between treatment or the agonizing decision to euthanize or give up a pet, veterinary health insurance is a very important consideration for most pet owners.

Your Bulldog will never ask for a pair of high-priced sneakers (although she may chew on a pair or two). You won't need to pay for an expensive wedding or for college tuition. Your car insurance won't go up because of your dog, and she'll never beg you for a car. Be thankful that veterinary medicine has advanced, and pay the bill.

Making an informed decision

Depending on the area where you live, your choices of vets may be limited. Assuming that you have choices, consider the following list when choosing a veterinarian:

- **Who do you know who owns a Bulldog?** If your breeder lives in your area, ask her what vet she uses and why. Ask other your local Bulldog club and dog people, and especially try to talk to other Bulldog owners.

- **Do you want to take your dog to a multidoctor or a single-doctor facility?** Taking your dog to a small practice may mean that the veterinarian knows your dog better, but if an emergency arises and your vet isn't available, the interim doctor won't know your Bully. In a multidoctor practice, you may not always see the same veterinarian, but if an emergency occurs, the on-call veterinarian has access to all your dog's health records.

✔ **Can you find a veterinarian who understands the potential problems of the Bulldog breed?** These veterinarians are more aware of what to look for when they're examining your puppy.

✔ **How far are you willing to drive?** A highly recommended veterinarian may practice 50 miles away, and you may not mind the drive for scheduled visits, but if your Bully has a serious problem, will that drive mean the difference between life and death?

Considering drive time doesn't mean that you should go to the veterinarian right next door if you don't like or trust him. Try a veterinarian somewhere in between the two extremes. Alternatively, you can choose to have a backup veterinarian (one you've seen once or twice and can use in emergencies).

✔ **What kind of emergency coverage is offered?** In a multiple-veterinarian practice, doctors likely have staggered hours. If only one veterinarian practices, how are vacations and off hours handled?

✔ **Is the staff friendly? Is the waiting room clean?** If possible, visit different veterinarians' offices. Ask how they handle emergencies, and find out what their hours are. When I need a veterinarian, I want to know that the staff believes me when I say that I have an emergency and not try to give me an appointment in three days.

✔ **Are you willing to go through trial and error?** It may not be possible to find the perfect veterinarian (if the *perfect* vet exists) without some trial and error. Friends may recommend a particular practice, but you just don't feel comfortable there. No matter how highly recommended a practice is, if you don't feel comfortable, don't stay.

✔ **What complaints have you heard?** If someone complains about a veterinarian, consider the complaint. Was it a one-time incident or something chronic, like a dirty exam room?

Questioning your veterinarian

You need to be comfortable with how your veterinarian treats your Bulldog, and waiting for an emergency is not the time to search for a doctor you like. Depending on your Bully's level of care, you may want to ask some of the following questions at your next visit:

✔ **What shots do you recommend?**

✔ **How frequently do you give shots?**

✔ **How do you place referrals?**

Most vet referrals tend to be for traditional specialists, such as orthopedics, dermatology, ophthalmology, and oncology. You should not only be appreciative when a veterinarian makes a referral, but also should actually insist on it or seek one on your own if your regular vet is floundering with an issue. (See the section "Finding a Specialist," later in the chapter.) Owners need to be advocates for their pets' health!

✔ **Do you practice alternative approaches to veterinarian medicine?**

- Do you use acupuncture or homeopathic remedies?

- If not, can you recommend practitioners should I consider alternative forms of medicine?

- If you're a strong believer in alternatives to traditional Western veterinary practices and the veterinarian you've selected is totally against them, find another practice.

Selecting Alternative Medicine

While some pet owners feel that traditional veterinarian medicine is the way to go, others may choose a more holistic approach to solving the ailments of their Bullies.

Holistic medicine approaches the prevention and treatment of disease through examining the whole of your Bully (not just the part that is wrong with her) and her physical and social environment. Our society is accustomed to synthetic drugs that stop symptoms quickly. But in many cases, problems recur because they are merely suppressed, not cured. Holistic methods seek to cure problems, not just treat the symptoms. This therapy results in a more permanent solution and a healthier pet. Holistic medicine embraces different categories under its approach:

✔ Acupuncture

✔ Applied kinesiology

✔ Behavior problems

✔ Chiropractic

✔ Contact Reflex Analysis

- ✔ Cranial Sacral Therapy
- ✔ Crystal therapy
- ✔ Energy healing
- ✔ Flower essences
- ✔ Glandular therapy
- ✔ Grief counseling
- ✔ Herbs
- ✔ Homeopathy
- ✔ Magnetic therapy
- ✔ Massage
- ✔ Metabolic balancing
- ✔ Myotherapy
- ✔ NAET Allergy Elimination Technique
- ✔ Nutrition consultants
- ✔ Orthopedic manipulation
- ✔ Reiki
- ✔ Tellington Touch
- ✔ Therapeutic Touch

For further information on holistic care, read *The Holistic Dog Book: Canine Care for the 21st Century* (Wiley).

Homeopathic care

Homeopathy follows the theory that like heals like. Homeopathic practitioners compare the theory of homeopathy with vaccines; "like" substances, weakened or killed germs, are used to prevent the disease the germs would cause if the germs were full strength. The like substances are diluted in several stages for safety and to prevent side effects, yet the substance is still powerful enough to act as a healing agent. Homeopathic remedies come in tablets, powders, granules, liquids, and ointments.

Homeopathic treatment consists of highly individualized plans of healing based on genetic history; personal health history; body type; and present status of all physical, emotional, and mental symptoms.

There are 235 homeopathic veterinarians listed at the American Holistic Veterinary Medicine Association Web site, www.ahvma.org. but this list is only for those belonging to the AHVMA. Many other veterinarians may also apply homeopathic treatment or combine it with traditional Western approaches to healing.

Consult your veterinarian or find a homeopathic veterinarian if you think this approach is right for your dog. "Do it yourself" treatment can do more harm than good.

Chinese herbal medicine

A doctor may have "TCM" listed after her name, indicating that she practices traditional Chinese medicine, including use of herbs in treatment. Herbal medicines may be gentler and safer than synthetic compounds when correctly used.

Don't dash off to the drugstore or health-food store and give your dog herbals just because herbs are "natural." Consult a veterinarian who understands the correct way to use herbs to heal.

Chinese medicine also uses certain herbal treatments. Herbs are pungent, sweet, sour, salty, and bitter. Pungent herbs help with circulation. Sweet herbs relieve pain and slow progression of diseases. Sour herbs are used to solidify. For example, if your dog has diarrhea, a sour herb would be prescribed. Salty herbs soften hardened tissue and are used for constipation. They may also help with muscle spasms and enlarged lymph glands. Bitter herbs are used with kidney-related diseases.

Acupuncture

More veterinary practices are going beyond traditional Western medicine to treat pets. Acupuncture is one of those practices that is gaining acceptance. Acupuncturists have treated animals for about 2,000 years and humans for more than 4,500 years. *Acupuncture* is the process of stimulating acupoints on the skin by using hair-fine needles and is said to improve healing.

Acupoints are areas on the skin that contain concentrated levels of nerve endings, lymphatics, and blood vessels. Acupoints are identified by their lower electrical resistance and are usually located in small depressions detectable by trained acupuncturists.

The healing power of plants

Bach flower essences are often mentioned along with herbal and homeopathic treatments. In the 1800s, English doctor Edward Bach began studying the healing properties of various plants. He eventually identified 38 flowers and trees with specific healing properties for emotional and behavioral problems, such as shyness, fear, and anxiety.

Rescue Remedy is a mixture of five of the single Bach flower essences and is effective in cases of shock, collapse, and trauma. Many holistic veterinarians recommend Rescue Remedy as a part of your dog's first-aid kit. Check your local health-food store for this product.

Studies have shown that acupuncture increases blood flow, lowers heart rate, and improves immune-system function. Acupuncture also prompts the release of neurotransmitters such as endorphins, the body's natural painkillers, and smaller amounts of cortisal, an anti-inflammatory steroid. This release of natural painkillers lessens the need for pain medication.

Additionally, acupuncture frequently treats chronic conditions like arthritis and allergies. Epilepsy may also be helped by acupuncture, as well as skin conditions and side effects from cancer.

Besides using acupuncture to treat specific conditions, "alarm points" on the body help indicate what is wrong with your Bully. No reaction may occur when an alarm point is stimulated, but if a problem with a specific organ exists, stimulating the alarm point may cause a reaction from your dog. He may try to bite.

Many acupuncturists use acupuncture to complement Western medicine. Doctors diagnose based on Western medicine and then use acupuncture to help ease pain and hasten healing. An acupuncturist may also encourage an owner to manipulate acupressure points at home between treatments. Acupressure is acupuncture without the needles.

To understand more about acupuncture or to find a veterinarian in your area who practices acupuncture, the International Veterinary Acupuncture Society lists certified veterinary acupuncturists by state at its Web site, www.ivas.org.

Finding a Specialist

A time may come when neither a general-practice veterinarian nor a holistic vet can help your Bully. You may need to take your dog to a specialist. Specialists practice in all medical fields, but common ailments that befall Bulldogs can be covered by a chiropractor and a masseuse.

Chiropractic care

Chiropractic treatment is the manipulating of the spine and connected bones. Chiropractic theory states that when the spine and bones are even slightly displaced, nerves become irritated. Chiropractors gently push the bones back into their correct places. If your Bulldog is extremely active (well, as active as he can be), the occasional chiropractic adjustment may be just what he needs. If you and your Bully practice agility, you may want to seek chiropractic care more often as a preventive measure against back pain and problems. Even a couch-potato Bulldog may benefit from an adjustment if he lands wrong jumping down from his comfy nest.

Many people take their dogs to chiropractors for humans if a veterinarian does not offer the service. If you choose this course of treatment, make sure that your regular veterinarian has examined your dog first to make sure that no other cause, like a tumor, may be pushing on your dog's spine and causing his pain.

For more chiropractic information, visit www.animal chiropractic.org, the Web site of the American Veterinary Chiropractic Association.

Massage therapy

Although massage therapy may not be considered a medical treatment (although it is in my book), it is a wonderful way to relax your dog. Linda Tellington-Jones developed a method of massage called the *Tellington Touch* or *Touch,* in which repeated massage movements generate specific brain-wave patterns that help your Bully who is suffering from anxiety, especially following injury or surgery. The calming effect of the massage helps promote healing.

Your dog doesn't have to be suffering from injury or recovering from surgery for you to give him a massage. A massage can soothe tired muscles and just plain feels good. Besides relaxing your dog, massage may strengthen the bond between you and your Bully.

When massaging your dog, pay attention to how he reacts. If your techniques seem to annoy or hurt your dog, stop! This tip may seem obvious, but you may love massage so much that you forget to make sure that your dog does too. If he whines, growls, or twitches, he may be trying to tell you that he doesn't like what you're doing. When you are pulling him out from under the bed for the daily massage, think about the moment you read this, and reconsider who benefits from that massage.

Massage is no substitute for veterinary care. Even after massage sessions, if your Bully consistently limps or is in pain, make an appointment with your veterinarian.

While you may not feel comfortable with every type of alternative to traditional veterinary care, you may come to appreciate a veterinarian who tries many different treatments to provide the best possible healthcare to his patients. Many alternatives are, in fact, complementary to traditional medicine. If your veterinarian does not use any complementary systems, ask for referrals if you feel that may help your Bulldog.

Knowing Your Vaccinations

A few years ago, "vaccination facts" would have been a no-brainer. Veterinarians vaccinated for just about everything that had a vaccine, and the shots were given every year. Combination vaccines were the norm, usually including five or six different vaccines in one shot. Ouch! Veterinarians gave the combination shot and rabies shot during the same office visit as well.

Circumstances are a bit different now. Veterinarians are moving away from combination shots that include vaccines against distemper, hepatitis, leptospirosis, parainfluenza, and Parvovirus. Many vets vaccinate only against distemper and Parvovirus and give the required rabies shot, giving other vaccinations based on what may be needed for a specific dog in a specific area. Veterinarians now may also split up the visits for shots.

A rabies shot is required by law in every state. While some states require the shot every year, others only have a once-every-3-years policy. Check with your veterinarian to find out the regulation in your state.

Talk to your veterinarian about her methods of vaccination and for what diseases she inoculates. Many veterinarians vaccinate young dogs or dogs who travel frequently, such as show dogs, every year, while older or stay-at-home dogs may receive vaccinations only once every 3 years.

Giving vaccinations at more than one appointment doesn't mean that your veterinarian is trying to get more money from you. Multiple visits may mean that your vet is concerned about your Bulldog and wants to prevent problems that may arise from multiple-vaccine shots. A mild reaction can be swelling at the site of the injection. If your dog has an allergic reaction, he may itch or have hives, his head and face may swell, or he may vomit or have diarrhea.

Administering puppy and booster shots

Depending on the age of your Bulldog puppy, he may have already received his first set of vaccinations. Schedule an appointment with your veterinarian so you can get your Bully's shots within the time frame of your breeder's health guarantee — typically, within 48 hours of bringing your puppy home.

Currently, many veterinarians give the first set of shots at 8 weeks, then 12 weeks, 16 weeks, and annually. Some veterinarians may recommend shots at 18 to 20 weeks and then annually. Check with your breeder to see what, if any, shots have been given to your puppy.

Some dogs have an allergic reaction to shots. The first time your puppy gets a vaccination, stay at the veterinarian's office for a while to see if your Bulldog is going to have a reaction to the shot. If he does, the staff is available to counteract the reaction.

Warding off diseases

What exactly are the diseases your dog may be vaccinated against? While many diseases and ailments may befall your Bulldog, you need to be proactive in your dog's care and vaccinate against certain viruses to help keep your Bully healthy for years to come.

Bordetella

Bordetella, or kennel cough, presents in over 100 varieties, and the bordetella vaccination protects against only a few varieties. If you plan on leaving your Bulldog at a kennel while you are on vacation or for any reason, most boarding kennels require the bordetella vaccination before your Bully can stay there. If you're traveling a lot or showing, you may also want to vaccinate against bordetella because kennel cough is highly contagious. If you decide that you want your dog to have this shot, keep in mind that even with the shot, your Bully may still develop kennel cough. Treat kennel cough with antibiotics, and while any disease is cause for concern, kennel cough is not usually serious. If your dog has a dry, hacking cough and has recently been around other dogs, he may have kennel cough. Check with your veterinarian.

Coronavirus

Coronavirus causes weeklong diarrhea and is contagious. Diarrhea may be orange-tinted and have a strong odor. This disease, while rarely fatal, causes dehydration. Talk to your veterinarian about the need for this shot. A healthy, mostly indoor Bulldog may never need this shot, but the vaccination is advisable for a show dog or a Bulldog who regularly encounters many other dogs.

Distemper

Distemper, which has a low recovery rate, is a dangerous and highly contagious virus. The threat for distemper is greatest for Bulldogs under 6 months of age and over 6 years of age. Symptoms include vomiting, coughing, and fever; the disease typically ends in death.

Hepatitis

A Bulldog with a mild to moderate case of hepatitis will have a fever and be lethargic. He may also be reluctant to move and have abdominal tenderness and pale mucous membranes. Bulldogs usually recover anywhere from 1 to 5 days after showing symptoms. In severe cases, your Bulldog may vomit, have diarrhea, and develop a cough. Sudden death may result. The virus spreads through the feces and urine of dogs.

Leptospirosis

Leptospirosis is a bacteria frequently transmitted through the urine of rats and mice. Symptoms include vomiting, fever, and a reluctance to move. Signs of renal failure may also exist. With renal failure, your dog may urinate more frequently, as the kidneys work harder and less efficiently, or your dog may stop urinating altogether. If you notice any of these symptoms, get to your veterinarian immediately. Severe cases of leptospirosis can be fatal. Protect your Bulldog against leptospirosis if you live in an area of exposure to urine of rats and mice; otherwise, you may be able to skip this shot. The leptospirosis vaccine in combination shots seems to increase the risk of a reaction in dogs, but a newer type of vaccine has been developed that causes less reaction and can be given as a separate shot. Consult your veterinarian.

Lyme disease

The deer tick spreads Lyme disease, a disease that causes lethargy, loss of appetite, and lameness. The disease can be treated with antibiotics. Some vaccination recommendations depend on where you live or what you're doing with your Bulldog. Lyme disease is more prevalent in the East. If you live in the East, you may want to have your dog vaccinated. Ask your veterinarian if this disease is a problem in your area.

Parvovirus

Parvovirus (Parvo) is another potentially fatal disease, particularly if the symptoms include vomiting and bloody diarrhea. Your Bully may show signs of a fever, lethargy, and depression. A dog with a mild case of Parvo may recover, but young puppies are highly susceptible and generally don't survive.

Early shots are important in the prevention of this fatal disease.

Rabies

The rabies virus attacks the central nervous system of Bulldogs and spreads through saliva. Common carriers in the wild include bats, foxes, raccoons, and skunks. Rabies is considered a fatal disease. After symptoms appear, a cure is not an option. Only vaccination, which is required by law for all dogs, prevents rabies.

Mulling Over Medicines

A time may come when your veterinarian will prescribe some form of medication for your Bulldog. Usually, the dosage will be in pill form. If it's an antibiotic, make sure that you give it all, even if your dog seems to have completely recovered. Using all the medicine ensures that the infection doesn't have a chance to flare up again.

Each day that you are giving the antibiotic, also give your Bully a spoonful of yogurt that contains active cultures. Antibiotics, besides going after the "bad guys," also destroy beneficial bacteria in your dog's intestines. The yogurt's active cultures will help replenish the good bacteria in your dog's system.

Pills are one of the easiest forms of medication to give a Bulldog. Many dogs gulp down a pill all by itself or if it's just lying casually on top of their food. If your dog is a bit more discriminating, wrapping a bit of food around the pill will make it acceptable. The food (anything that your dog eats quickly) can be almost anything that hides the pill:

- A pat of butter
- Canned food
- Cream cheese
- Hot dogs (Stuff the pill inside the hot dog)
- Yogurt

Peanut butter may not be the ideal choice for covering a pill. Peanut butter sticks to the elongated soft palate of your Bully, and the peanut butter may be hard to remove or cause choking issues for your Bulldog.

Liquid medications can be a bit harder unless they're flavored to appeal to your dog or are neutral enough to be accepted when mixed with your dog's food. If mixing with food doesn't work, pull your dog's lower lip out to the side to make a pocket, and squirt or pour in the liquid. Quickly close your dog's mouth, keep it shut, and gently stroke his throat until he swallows. You may need a helper for this project.

An eye problem requires drops or an ointment or both. The best way to approach the eye is from the rear:

1. **Straddle your Bully.**

2. **Stand pigeon-toed so that your feet are under your dog.**

   This stance prevents your Bully from backing out between your legs.

3. **Tip your dog's head back slightly.**

4. **Squeeze the drops into the inner corner of the eye.**

Dealing with dehydration

Severe vomiting or diarrhea can leave your dog dehydrated, and your veterinarian may suggest Gatorade or Pediolyte to replace the fluids your dog has lost. These fluids are fine suggestions except that in my experience, your dog won't like either one. Try them, by all means, but don't be surprised if your Bully turns up his nose even further.

My dogs consider ice cubes a treat, so I give those. If your dog won't crunch up enough ice cubes to do any good, offer chicken or beef bouillon. Besides the liquid of the bouillon, the salty taste may send them to their water bowl. Water drained from a can of tuna fish may flavor a bowl of water enough to get your dog drinking.

If you need to apply salve, follow the same procedure, except that you should start at the outer corner of the eye. Slightly pull the lower lid away, and put in the salve. Then hold the eye closed for a few seconds so that the salve will melt and spread over the surface of the eye.

Chapter 14

Recognizing and Tackling Bulldog Health Issues

*B*ulldogs are a unique breed and experience health issues that are common to the breed. This chapter highlights breed-specific conditions and how to recognize them, as well as addressing general health.

Generally, any problem that lasts longer than 24 hours needs a trip to the veterinarian. Also, any problem that gets progressively worse over several hours — such as loss of appetite, weakness, or fever — needs attention from your veterinarian.

The longer you have your Bulldog, the better you'll be able to tell whether a stomach upset just requires some cooked meat and rice to correct it or whether you need your veterinarian, but when in doubt, make the appointment. Bulldogs are sturdy dogs, but compared to a human, they don't weigh much. A dog can "go downhill" much faster than a human with a comparable health problem.

Spaying or Neutering Your Bulldog

After vaccinations (see Chapter 13), spaying or neutering is likely the first major health issue you'll have to address with your Bulldog. For various reasons, spaying or neutering is a good idea if you don't plan to either show or breed your Bulldog. Breeding is not for the faint of heart no matter what the breed, but with

Bulldogs, it is even harder. If you're thinking about breeding, skip to Chapter 18 immediately.

When a dog has an operation to become sterile, no matter what the gender, the animal is neutered. With a female, the removal of the ovaries is a *spay*. With a male, the removal of the testicles is *castration*. Commonly, though, while the term *spay* is still used with females, *neutering* applies to the operation performed on males. So I'm using the terms *spaying* and *neutering* as opposed to *spaying* and *castrating*.

Neither spaying nor neutering is particularly hard on a healthy young dog. Spaying takes longer because the surgery is performed abdominally. Neutering is easier and quicker because the testicles are external. If you're concerned about appearance, ask your veterinarian about a vasectomy, which is a more complicated operation.

Before any surgery, make sure that your veterinarian knows that a Bulldog may have problems breathing after the operation when the ventilating tube has been removed but the dog is not yet fully conscious.

When your Bully is neutered, he is first anesthetized; then an incision is made at the base of the scrotum, and the testicles are removed. When a female is spayed, a short incision is made in the abdomen. The veterinarian draws out the ovaries and uterus, ties off the blood vessels, cuts the uterus and ovaries free, and stitches up the incision.

With both operations, most veterinarians want to keep your Bully overnight to make sure that your dog recovers fully from the anesthetic. About ten days after the operation, you'll return to the veterinarian to have the stitches removed.

With a spay incision especially, keep an eye on it. If you notice any redness or puffiness, call your veterinarian. It can be a sign of infection. Also, keep an eye on your dog, and make sure she doesn't try to remove the stitches herself before it's time.

Watch your Bully's weight after spaying or neutering because the metabolism does change a bit. None of my females ever gained any weight after being spayed, but after neutering, my male did start to gain weight. Cutting back his food by about half a cup got him back to his normal weight.

What to know about male Bulldogs

Sometime between 6 months and 2 years, your male dog becomes sexually mature. (It may take a Bulldog 4 years to reach full physical maturity.) He'll start to exercise his authority a little more around the house (and the neighborhood):

- He may become more aggressive toward other males.

- He will definitely become more interested in females, especially females in season. Around such a female, he will pay more attention to her than to you. Because of this attraction, if an intact male gets loose, he's more apt to wander farther from home than a neutered male.

- He'll lift his leg to urinate more frequently on walks as a way to let other males know that the neighborhood is *his* territory.

- He may also start marking the house with his urine, which can be a hard habit to break.

Intact males are more apt to suffer from prostatic hypertrophy, which is a benign enlargement of the prostate. Neutering prevents prostate problems, may curb aggression toward other males, and may end marking in the house.

Some neutered males may continue to mark, but if marking is a problem, neutering is definitely worth a try. My male was constantly marking the furniture, and I went through rolls and rolls of paper towels and tried every cleaning product available. I was told that his behavior patterns were set and that it was unlikely that neutering would have any effect on his marking at all. When he was 6, I brought a female home, and not wanting to deal with keeping him away from her when she was in season, I had him neutered. He's never marked since.

What to know about female Bulldogs

If you have a female, look for her to come in season sometime between 6 months and 18 months. After her first season, she will cycle about every 6 months after that. Ask your breeder about the females in her pedigree, so you'll have a rough idea of what to expect.

A female is in season for 21 days but is receptive to a male for only 3 to 5 of those days. Females produce a bloody discharge while in heat, and how much discharge you see will vary, but you may want to keep your female in a room without carpeting while she's in season. If you also own a male, you may want to board your female. Keeping the two separate can be difficult, as males are persistent, and 3 weeks can seem like an eternity.

If you have a fenced yard and let your female out unattended, make sure ahead of time that your fence has no holes or gaps and is high enough to prevent any wandering males from jumping in. All the boys in the neighborhood will be interested, not just other Bulldogs. If you're walking your Bully, keep a grip on the lead, and be alert to the approach of any romantic males.

With females, besides the benefits of no unwanted litters, a spayed female has less chance of getting mammary tumors if spayed before her third season. After that, the incidence of tumors is not much different. Spaying also eliminates the risk of Pyometra, which is relatively common in Bulldogs and which can be life threatening, as well as other possible infections of the reproductive system.

Alleviating Canine Allergies

Allergies commonly occur, and you should keep an eye out for these sensitivities in your Bulldog. When you're checking your dog for fleas and ticks, look at his skin as well. Allergies cause itchy skin, so check for red patches, scratches, or anything that isn't clean healthy skin.

Dogs, just like people, can be allergic to food, mold, and pollen. If your dog seems to present problems during certain seasons, the allergy can be "something in the air." If the irritation continues, try checking other sources

Figuring out food allergies

Your dog's allergic reactions may derive from his food. If your Bully's reaction is not too severe, you may have time to try different foods. Look at the grain in your dog food, and switch to a food with a different grain. Corn, wheat, and soy grains most generally cause allergy problems.

If your dog's condition worsens or is severe, make a trip to the veterinarian, who may run a series of tests and also suggest a food made of all one product. These special diets have just one ingredient, such as duck, and by gradually adding other foods (a lengthy process, but a necessary one), you can eventually determine the cause of the allergy. See Chapter 7 for more information on food allergies and options.

Flea saliva

Your dog may also be allergic to flea saliva. If a flea has bitten your Bulldog, the bite may become irritated through biting and scratching from your dog. Prolonged agitation may cause a raw, red, oozy-looking spot called a *hot spot.*

Hot spots generally can be treated with a triple antibiotic ointment. If the spot does not get better or is left untreated, an infection can occur and then a trip to the vet will be inevitable.

Mold, pollen, fungus

Dogs, like people, can be allergic to airborne particles, such as pollen and mold and fungus spores. It can be hard to determine just what particular plant is causing the problem, other than to observe what time of the year your dog is bothered and what plants are in your area at the time. Talk to your veterinarian about whether or not your Bully may need an antihistamine.

Whether or not an allergy of any kind exists, if your Bully is continually licking or biting an area on his body, he may develop a hot spot, and you may want to get him checked out.

Preventing External Parasites

Depending on where you live and the time of year you get your Bully, you may already have encountered fleas or ticks.

Making fleas flee

Fleas are nasty little critters, and if your dog is allergic to flea saliva, they can make your pet miserable. Be aggressive when fighting fleas. In northern areas, where winter arrives with a lot of cold weather, expect a short break. If you live in a warmer climate, you face a year-round battle, but desert areas are virtually flea free.

The flea generally seen on dogs is a cat flea and is not native to this continent but is originally from Africa. It is becoming resistant to many flea-control products on the market.

If your dog is scratching, and you suspect fleas, check any white areas of fur and push the hair against the grain, or turn your dog over and check toward the hind legs, where the fur is thinner. When you push the hair away from the body, you may see a flea or two running for cover. If you don't see any fleas, check for small flecks of flea dirt. If you can't tell if what you're looking at is flea dirt or just a bit of regular dirt, collect some on a piece of paper or a paper towel, and wet it. If it turns red, it's flea dirt. Flea dirt is flea excrement, and it turns red from the blood it's been enjoying from your dog.

If you don't see anything on your dog but still suspect fleas, run a flea comb through your dog's coat. Flea combs have very fine, closely set teeth that trap fleas and flea dirt.

Fighting fleas with medicine

After you've determined that your dog has fleas, the war has begun. If your dog has a heavy infestation, start with a bath using a flea-fighting shampoo. Wash all bedding, as that is where the fleas lay their eggs.

If you decide to use a topical flea preventive, your veterinarian can help you choose the one for your dog. Many different products are sold on the market and through your veterinarian that can help you eliminate fleas:

- **Program:** Ingested monthly, this medication may be used safely with other flea-control products. Program acts as a birth-control method for fleas. The flea absorbs the medication from the blood of your dog, and Program prevents a cocoon from forming, so the flea larvae never develop into adults.

- **Frontline:** This topical preventive for fleas also fights ticks for 17 days.

- **Advantage:** I use Advantage, another monthly topical preventive, and have had good luck with it.

If heavy infestation occurs, bathe your dog with a flea-fighting shampoo before trying the topical medications. For your home, you should consider hiring an extermination company that specializes in fleas.

If you'd like to fight the fleas with fewer chemicals, try feeding your Bulldog garlic several times a week. You can buy garlic capsules, and most dogs love garlic, even if it doesn't repel the fleas. You can have too much of a good thing, however, so don't overdo the garlic.

Keeping the house and yard clean

Daily vacuuming works just as effectively as any spray in keeping the flea population down in the house. You can cut up a flea collar and put it in the vacuum bag to help kill the fleas. Also, change the vacuum bag frequently (when the bag is half full) to prevent a flea colony from growing in the bag. Wash your dog's bed, where most of the flea eggs accumulate, frequently. Combing your dog with a flea comb also helps trap the unwanted guests.

Help keep your yard flea free by planting marigolds. You can also use diatomaceous earth inside and out. Diatomaceous earth helps dehydrate the fleas.

Avon's Skin-So-Soft control bugs, even though the product was not invented as a bug repellent. Don't overdo it, but a light application helps control the blood-sucking pests. Be sure to monitor your dog in case he reacts to the Skin-So-Soft. Exchanging fleas for a rash is not the point in eliminating fleas.

Flea collars tend to keep your dog's neck free of fleas but don't do much over the rest of the body. You can, however, cut up a flea collar and put it in your vacuum bag to help kill fleas that you suck up. Change the vacuum bag frequently, or you'll end up with a flea colony in the bag.

Getting ticked off

Ticks may be a problem in your area. If you take long walks in tall grass or through brush, the likelihood of picking up ticks increases (for both you and your dog). Most ticks are relatively small, and you may find them on your dog by touch faster than by sight. Ticks feast on your dog's blood and create a large, dark bump buried in his fur. The bump is actually the tick itself.

Checking your dog regularly for ticks prevents further health problems for your dog. Don't leave ticks on your dog. Ticks can be hard to find even on a short-coated dog like the Bulldog, so be patient and thorough. If you don't think that you can get the tick off properly or just don't want to try, make an appointment to visit the veterinarian so he can perform the procedure.

Place a touch of rubbing alcohol on the tick to shut down the oxygen supply, and the tick may back out of your dog on its own.

You can remove ticks gently with tweezers, being extremely careful not to leave the head behind. Follow these procedures:

1. **Grasp the tick with the tweezers where the mouth parts enter the skin.**

   Don't use your fingers.

2. **Pull steadily and slowly until the tick comes away from the dog.**

   Dispose of the tick so that it can no longer affect your dog or your family.

3. **Wash the site after the tick has been removed.**

Never use a cigarette or burning agents to extract a tick. Undoubtedly, you would get the tick's attention, but you are also apt to burn your dog.

Four types of ticks can affect your dog: the Rocky Mountain wood tick, the American dog tick, the brown dog tick, and the deer tick. All of these ticks, with the exception of the deer tick, are the size of a watermelon seed. The deer tick is the size of a freckle. The Rocky Mountain wood tick is a more robust, husky tick with a rounded, thicker body.

The following diseases or conditions are spread by ticks:

✔ **Rocky Mountain spotted fever:** This disease is spread by the Rocky Mountain wood tick; this tick has been found in almost every state and in Canada. Symptoms can include fever, lethargy, vomiting, refusing food, and skin rashes.

✔ **Tularemia:** Highly infectious, tularemia is also considered a potential biological-warfare agent. Tularemia occurs naturally throughout the United States. Most cases have been reported from the central states of Missouri, Arkansas, and Oklahoma. There has been a decline in the number of cases over the past several decades. This disease is spread by the American dog tick.

✔ **Tick paralysis:** Certain ticks can cause a progressive paralysis, which is reversed upon removal of the tick. Recovery is usually complete. The paralysis isn't caused by a disease pathogen but by a toxin produced by the tick. Paralysis begins in the extremities of the body with a loss of coordination. It progresses to the face, with corresponding slurred speech and, finally, shallow, irregular breathing. Failure to remove the tick can result in death by respiratory failure. Most cases of tick paralysis are caused by the Rocky

Mountain wood tick in northwestern states. The American dog tick has also been known to cause tick paralysis.

✔ **Human ehrlichiosis:** This is a human disease that can also affect dogs. The disease causes fever, nausea, vomiting, rash, and weight loss. This is carried by the brown dog tick and the deer tick.

✔ **Human babesiosis:** This disease causes hemolytic anemia. The disease is most dangerous to puppies. Attachment to people is uncommon. Babesiosis is a malarialike illness caused mainly by Babesia microti, a protozoan parasite of red blood cells. Signs and symptoms include fever, fatigue, chills, sweats, headache, and muscle pain, beginning usually 1 to 6 weeks after the tick bite. This is carried by the brown dog tick and the deer tick.

✔ **Lyme disease:** This disease is spread by deer ticks. Ask your vet if this presents a concern in your area. You can obtain a vaccine for Lyme disease. Symptoms include a rash, usually spreading outward from the tick bite; muscle stiffness; and lethargy.

Ear mites

If your Bully is scratching his ears constantly, or rubbing his head along the carpet or a piece of furniture, make an appointment with your veterinarian, and have him check your dog's ears. Because ear mites can live on other areas of the body as well as the ears, you may need to dust your Bulldog with flea powder or have him sprayed or dipped for 3 to 4 weeks, which covers the 3-week life cycle of the mite. Ear mites are more common in cats than in dogs, so this problem may not occur for you and your Bully.

Mange

Two types of mange exist that can affect your Bully, and tiny mites cause both types. Sarcoptic mange is most noted by intense itching, and as the mange advances, skin lesions and hair loss occur. Sarcoptic mange is treated externally with sulfur dips and internally with ivermectin. Revolution, a monthly flea and tick preventive, is also an effective treatment. Treatment lasts 3 weeks, and your Bulldog's bedding should be thoroughly disinfected or thrown away.

Demodetic mange is passed from the mother to the puppies and affects puppies between the ages of 3 and 10 months. Demodetic mange is diagnosed by examining skin scrapings. This form of mange doesn't cause the intense itching that Sarcoptic mange does. With Demodetic mange, your dog may experience hair loss.

Your veterinarian uses ivermectin to treat Demodetic mange and may also recommend a special shampoo. If the mange isn't widespread, it may go away on its own, but if it spreads beyond small, localized areas, it may need up to a year of treatment. Bulldogs with compromised immune systems may be susceptible to Demodetic mange their entire lives.

Guarding Against Internal Parasites

You can't see an internal parasite by rubbing your dog's fur the wrong way. Your veterinarian wants to do a fecal check once or twice a year to check for whipworms, hookworms, tapeworms, and roundworms. Heartworms require a blood test, and tapeworm segments are usually evident with the naked eye.

Tapeworms

Tapeworms are the least harmful, but most common, of all the types of worms that may infest your Bulldog. One of the ways your dog can get tapeworms is by swallowing a flea, so controlling the flea population prevents tapeworms in your dog. Tapeworm segments look like tiny grains of rice in your dog's stool, so check periodically for this evidence of tapeworms. If you never treated for tapeworm, your dog would survive, but any parasite takes nourishment away from its host, so your dog would want more and more food.

Hookworms

Hookworm eggs pass through feces and can live in the soil. They also pass from a mother to her puppies. Instead of maturing, the larvae live in the female and then pass to the puppies through their mother's milk. Hookworms feed on the blood of their host and can cause fatal anemia in puppies. Untreated adult dogs will become anemic, and the constant irritation from the worms can cause gastroenteritis, or inflammation of the bowel, which may cause diarrhea and lessens the amount of nourishment the dog can get from food.

Roundworms

Roundworms, like hookworms, can contaminate the soil, and the eggs are highly resistant to adverse conditions. Roundworms live in soil for years. Most puppies are born with these worms because the larvae live in the mother but don't infect her. Even if your female Bully tests negative for roundworms, her puppies can still have them. Roundworms in puppies can cause death from intestinal blockage, and if the worms migrate to the lungs, they may cause pneumonia. Adult dogs may have diarrhea and abdominal pain, and may suffer from dehydration.

Whipworms

Whipworms can cause a deep inflammation of the colon. If your Bulldog has periodic bouts of diarrhea, with blood and mucus present, whipworms may be the culprit. Left untreated, your Bully will become dehydrated, and the inflammation of the colon will become worse. He may suffer abdominal pain, become anemic, and lose weight. Once again, contaminated soil is to blame, and the bad news is that after you have whipworms in your soil, paving the entire yard is about the only way to solve the problem. Protect your Bully with periodic fecal checks.

Heartworms

Heartworm is a deadly parasite that doesn't show up in fecal checks but requires a blood test. This parasite can kill or incapacitate your dog, and the cure can be almost as bad as the disease, so preventing heartworm is better than having to cure it.

Heartworm larvae develop in mosquitoes and enter a dog's bloodstream when a mosquito bites the dog. These larvae then move to the chambers on the right side of the dog's heart. Once in the heart, the worms mature and produce microfilariae, which circulate in the blood until another mosquito picks them up after feeding on the dog. Adult heartworms can completely fill the heart chambers. An infected dog may tire easily and develop a cough.

The annual blood test by your vet detects the presence of microfilariae. Talk to your veterinarian about a monthly heartworm preventive for your dog. Some medications prevent only heartworm; some also include chemicals that kill other worms, such as hookworms. A shot is also available that is effective for up to 6 months.

If you live in an area with a short mosquito season or no mosqui-toes at all, you may opt not to give your Bully any medication, but just have him tested every 6 months to see if he's infected.

If your dog does contract heartworm, the first step in the cure is to get rid of the adult worms, which involves arsenamide injected intravenously twice a day for 2 or 3 days. Your vet can do this for you or show you what you need to do. The worms in the heart die slowly and travel to the lungs through the bloodstream. The worms gradually disintegrate in the lungs. The worms must be poisoned slowly, because if all the worms were killed immediately, simultaneous embolism can prove fatal to your dog. Even killing the worms slowly stresses your Bulldog's lungs and may cause per-manent damage. Enforced rest for 4 to 6 weeks following treatment is usual to help your Bully recover.

Recognizing Skin Problems

Bulldogs are very susceptible to skin problems, so if you notice your dog scratching or licking, or if you observe any hair loss, red-ness of skin, or a rash, have your veterinarian check your dog before the problem gets worse. Most skin problems can be cured or kept under control with medications, especially if they are not allowed to spread. Check with your vet to make sure your dog's skin problems aren't being caused by parasites or allergies, dis-cussed earlier in the chapter.

Hot spots are raw, oozy round patches of skin and are created when your dog bites and licks a bug bite or an itchy spot. These spots need to be treated before they become infected. Hot spots are not limited to Bulldogs but are common enough to cause problems.

Use a dab of triple antibiotic cream, available at any drugstore, on hot spots. If the spot doesn't clear up in three or four days, see your veterinarian, who may want to prescribe an oral antibiotic. For more information, also see Chapter 8.

Taking Care of Interdigital Cysts

Interdigital cysts may be caused by almost anything that gets caught between a dog's toes and starts to work its way into the skin, but Bulldogs are quite likely to get interdigital cysts because of the short hairs between their toes. These short hairs can get bent backward into their roots, and the irritation to the skin results in a cyst, frequently filled with pus. The cysts can be painful, and you may notice your Bulldog limping, or constantly licking or biting his toes. There is a danger of bacterial infection if the cyst is left untreated.

Check with your veterinarian if your Bully gets a cyst. With time, your veterinarian may recommend ways to treat the cyst at home, and once you've dealt with a few of the cysts, you'll get to know how to deal with them yourself and when you need to have your dog looked at by a professional:

✔ Many Bulldog breeders soak the infected paw in warm water with Epsom salts or with an antibiotic solution added.

✔ Soak the paw for about 10 minutes. If your Bulldog won't agree to have one paw in a pan of water, use the bathtub. The treatment won't do any harm to the other paws.

✔ After drying the paw, apply an antibiotic ointment to the cyst. Some people use Preparation H, which seems to help.

Some breeders pop small cysts before they have time to grow to a size that irritates the dog, but if you think that's what you want to do, make sure the area is clean, and watch closely for infection.

Knowing the Truth about Bulldog Breathing Problems

Bulldogs have the unfortunate reputation for having breathing problems, associated with small tracheas, elongated soft palates, or stenotic nares. Not all Bulldogs have breathing problems. Conscientious breeders are working hard to correct these problems. However, your Bully may be affected by one or more of these problems, and it's a good idea to understand them and to know what you can do to help your dog breathe easier.

Elongated soft palate

The soft palate is the soft extension of the roof of the mouth that forms a flexible barrier and prevents food and water from going up the nose when your Bulldog swallows. (See Figure 14-1.) Fold your tongue back in your own mouth, and you can feel your soft palate. In many Bulldogs, this soft flap extends back into the throat and can fall into the larynx when the dog breathes in. If your Bully becomes excited or stressed and is breathing hard, the soft palate gets longer and swells. Then your Bully is faced with the vicious cycle of trying harder and harder to get air, and the airway becoming more and more blocked.

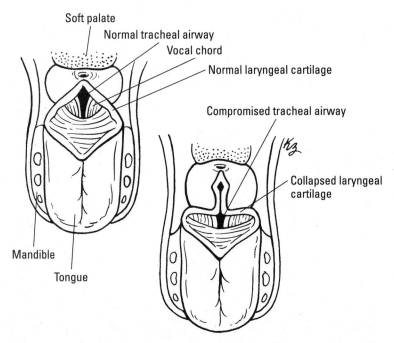

Soft palate
Normal tracheal airway
Vocal chord
Normal laryngeal cartilage
Compromised tracheal airway
Collapsed laryngeal cartilage
Mandible
Tongue

Figure 14-1: An elongated palate makes it harder for your Bulldog to breathe.

This phenomenon is why heatstroke is such a danger (and I mention it so much), even when you may not think the weather is hot. The soft-palate problem is also why you shouldn't get into battles of will with your Bulldog. Bulldogs are bred to be tenacious and determined, but that can work against them because they won't give up and continue to fight. If you are trying to work with your Bully to get him to do something, like let you cut his nails, don't keep struggling. The struggle can cause greater problems.

The elongated soft palate can be surgically corrected. Laser surgery makes the process quick, and less bleeding and swelling occurs with laser surgery than with other methods. Talk to your veterinarian about whether she recommends this surgery for your Bulldog.

Elongated-soft-palate surgery sounds simple but is actually quite an art form, and complications can be dangerous. Owners should seek out a veterinarian with a history of performing the surgery successfully and with the desired results.

Small trachea

Besides the breathing problems caused by an elongated palate, Bulldogs may have extremely small tracheas, sometimes only the size of a pencil in diameter. Breeders are working to correct this problem, so your Bully may have a trachea that is normal for his size and weight, but you should be aware that it may be a problem.

Carry a little squirt bottle filled with lemon juice and water. Lemon juice cuts the phlegm that can build up in your dog's throat as a result of the elongated soft palate and the small trachea.

Stenotic nares

Stenotic nares is the technical term for pinched nostrils, and most Bulldogs are born with this condition. The opening of their nostrils is narrow, and the separating cartilage is soft. So when the dog breathes, the cartilage closes in, further decreasing the size of the opening for air. Your veterinarian can easily remove a small piece of the wall of each nostril so your Bully can breathe easier.

Being overweight

Breathing problems increase the heavier your dog is. Don't let your Bully get overweight. Bulldogs are no more prone to being overweight than another dog, but because Bulldogs are more laid back than many breeds, they may not get the exercise they need to burn the food they are given. Extra pounds aren't good for any dog. You should be able to feel your Bully's ribs when you run your hands down his sides. If you can't feel them, it's time to cut back on a snack or two.

Handling Heatstroke

I mention heatstroke in Chapter 15, on first aid, but it's here (and throughout the book) too because various situations can lead to your dog's overheating, and heat can kill your Bully.

All dogs cool off by panting. By breathing quickly, Bulldogs exchange the hotter air in their lungs for the cooler outside air. The air moving over the tongue also helps in the cooling process, and this process allows for some heat exchange. The tongue is full of blood vessels close to the surface, and the cooler air hits the blood vessels and cools the blood that is then sent to the rest of the body. This process of panting eventually cools the entire body.

Some Bulldogs cannot exchange air as fast as other dogs because of their narrow tracheas and the shape of their noses. When heatstroke occurs, they begin to pant more rapidly. This panting may add stress, which can cause swelling of the throat, making panting less and less effective as a way for your Bully to cool off.

Bulldogs are cute puppies, and the attention you get when you take your Bully out in public may be nice, but use common sense when you care for and travel with your Bully:

- ✔ Put some ice cubes in your Bully's water dish. He'll enjoy fishing them out, and the ice keeps him cool.

- ✔ Give your Bully frozen treats instead of regular dog treats from time to time. Freeze meat-based broth in ice cube trays, and pop one out for a treat a couple times a day.

- ✔ Never leave your dog outside unattended on a hot day. Your dog may love to go with you in the car, but if it's a hot day, leave him at home. Even with the windows down, a car in summer can be too hot for a Bulldog.

- ✔ During the summer months, carry a squirt bottle of water with you.

- ✔ Invest in a cooling jacket for your Bully.

- ✔ Don't take your Bully to the beach. (You can return his water wings now.)

- ✔ Don't go jogging with your Bully. You can take your Bully for walks, and I hope you do, but be aware of his panting and level of energy.

- ✔ Monitor his activity. For instance, if he has a favorite toy, take it away from him before he gets too warm playing.

If your Bulldog is panting or slobbering excessively, has diarrhea or is vomiting, or if he's collapsed, heatstroke can be the cause. Move your dog to the shade, and soak him with cold water. Give him small amounts of water to drink. If your dog is unconscious, get him to the veterinarian immediately.

Eyeballing Eye Problems

Your Bulldog may live his life and never have an eye problem, or he may have one or more of the following. Knowing what to look for and taking prompt action with a veterinary visit will help protect your Bully's vision and prevent discomfort.

Eyelid issues

Eyelid problems are the most common eye problems in almost every breed, and fortunately, they are the easiest to correct if caught early. They can be very painful, though, so prompt attention is necessary.

All those lovely wrinkles that give a Bulldog his special look may also be the cause of two types of eyelid problems: *entropion* (the inward turning of the lower eyelid) and *ectropion* (the outward turning of the lower eyelid). Fortunately, both of these conditions are easily corrected with surgery.

Entropion eyelids

With entropion, the eyelashes rub against the cornea. The cornea becomes severely irritated or damaged as the chronic abrasion wears away the corneal surface. In some cases, deep ulcers form in the cornea, even to the point of rupturing its surface. This damage quickly leads to inner eye infections and potential blindness. After diagnosis, surgery is the only treatment.

Several different surgery techniques are available, but typically, a small incision is made below the lid and a small portion of skin is removed, and when the two sides of the incision are sutured, the incision pulls the border of the lid downward into a normal position. Antibiotic ointments may be applied if infections are present.

In rare cases, the upper lid can also be affected to some extent. One or both eyes may be involved. Most dogs with entropion squint and have a reddened, inflamed eye. Because of the pain involved, dogs tend to scratch the eye, possibly doing further damage. Left untreated, severe eye infections may develop.

Ectropion eyelids

Ectropion describes a condition where the lower lids are loose, causing a drooping of the eyelid's margins. The lower lids actually turn outward. With ectropion, part of the inner eyelid is exposed and can become inflamed. Also, ectropion, if not corrected, can reduce the amount of tears produced. As the lower lid sags downward, the underlying conjunctiva is exposed. An eyelid pouch forms, allowing pollens, grasses, dust, and so on to accumulate and rub against the sensitive conjunctiva — a consistent source of irritation for your Bully — leading to increased redness of the conjunctiva and occasional watering of the eye, which then spills out over the lower lid and face.

Many Bulldogs live normal lives with ectropion. However, some develop repeated eye infections due to the collection of air particles. The risks are minor except in severe cases, where secondary eye infections may develop. Some Bullies require no treatment; however, if eye irritations develop, medical attention is advisable. Mild cases can be treated with eye drops or salves to alleviate irritations and/or infections when they occur. In severe cases, a surgical procedure is preferred, which removes excess tissue, thereby tightening the lids and removing the abnormal pocket.

Cherry eye

Cherry eye is a condition in which a gland attached to the third eyelid — the membrane that covers the eye sideways — gets inflamed and becomes a red, swollen mass in the inside corner of the eye. The cure used to be removing the third eyelid, but removal frequently led to dry eye, so now, the membrane is tacked back into its correct position.

Because of the shape of a Bulldog's head, only a board-certified ophthalmologist should perform this surgery.

Dry eye

Dry eye is just what it sounds like. The eye, for whatever reason, doesn't produce tears. The condition can lead to blindness if not treated, and the treatment is usually eye drops and either Cyclosporin or Tacrolimus. Some dogs will need eye drops for the rest of their lives; some will begin producing their own tears again, and the drops can be stopped. See Chapter 16 for more information.

Getting Hip to Hip Dysplasia

Hip dysplasia is the abnormal development of the head of the femur. Instead of fitting properly in the socket of the hip joint, the femur fits loosely and may come out of the socket altogether. Considerable swelling and ruptured ligaments may occur. A dog with hip dysplasia may develop arthritis in the joints and may also be lame and in pain.

Hip-replacement surgery is an option. In many breeds, breeders have their dogs x-rayed to determine the quality of the hips. The x-rays are studied and given a rating by either the Orthopedic Foundation for Animals (OFA) or by the University of Pennsylvania Hip Improvement Program (PennHip).

Most Bulldog breeders do not x-ray hips, and it is likely that your Bulldog will have hip dysplasia. Bulldogs hips are generally dysplastic on x-rays, but this rarely causes clinical problems for the dog. The Bulldog's unique musculature supports the hip in a way that is not seen in most other breeds. Most rear-leg lameness in Bulldogs will originate in the knee or stifle, and owners and vets should not be led astray by the hips' appearance on x-rays.

Because one of the signs of hip dysplasia can be a rolling gait, many people believe that this is what gives the Bulldog his distinctive gait. In fact, Bulldogs have such a gait because of their general build. The wide, heavy front and the narrower, lighter hindquarters give the Bully his distinctive gait, not badly formed hip joints.

It Hurts When I Sit! Ingrown Tails

If your dog has an ingrown tail, the tail grows backward and down. This awkward growth creates a deep pocket and can be painful and infected. If your dog has an ingrown tail, you'll need to pay special attention to keeping the area clean and dry. In severe cases, the tail is amputated.

The tail end of the discussion: The standard for the Bulldog says that the tail may be either straight or screwed, but breeders disagree and say that the tail should be straight. The reasoning is that the tail is an extension of the spine. Says one breeder–veterinarian, "If the tail isn't wagging, the spine isn't normal."

Speaking of Spines: Hemi-vertebrae

Hemi-vertebrae are vertebrae that are malformed, looking more like triangles than blocks. A Bulldog may have malformed vertebrae and be just fine, but some will start to have trouble walking at around 5 months old and will eventually not be able to walk at all.

Patellar Luxation

Patellar luxation is the partial or complete dislocation of the patella, or kneecap. The kneecap normally fits into a groove in the thigh bone. The kneecap may slip out of the groove because the groove is malformed, which can be hereditary, or the kneecap may slip as the result of a fall or a blow to the leg. When the kneecap is out of the groove, your dog will limp. The kneecap may pop back into the groove on its own, or your veterinarian may be able to push it back. Severe cases will require surgery. Left untreated, your dog can develop osteoarthritis in the joint.

Chapter 15

Familiarizing Yourself with Fido First Aid

*A*ccidents happen, and you should always be prepared to help your Bulldog if he needs it. The odds are good that you won't need most of the information in this chapter, but think of the facts as a safety net. (It's nice to know that the net is there, even if you never need it, rather than not have it at all.) Discover common first-aid issues and what supplies you should keep on hand in case of an emergency.

Your dog may generally be healthy, but any dog can get ill or be hurt. With time and practice, you'll soon be able to tell what is a minor problem that can wait or that you can treat yourself, and what needs an emergency run to the veterinarian or the nearest pet hospital. I personally am a member of the better-safe-than-sorry club, and if there's any doubt at all, we see our veterinarian. I'd rather pay for an unnecessary trip to the veterinarian than make the wrong decision and be sorry.

Your veterinarian isn't always just treating your dog. With my first dog, I called the veterinarian much more than I do now. Once, when I had called after hours, my veterinarian said, "The dog can wait until morning, but can you?" He understood my concern and was willing to make the trip to his office to meet me if it would help me.

I'm better about emergency calls, but I'd rather err on the side of caution. For instance, if one of my dogs has a touch of diarrhea or has thrown up once or twice, I may just stop all food for a day and then feed cooked ground meat and rice for a day or two. The starch in the rice helps "dry up" the diarrhea, and the diet is bland, so it doesn't further irritate the colon. This mixture usually does the trick, but if the diarrhea continues or vomiting lasts for more than 24 hours, I head to the veterinarian.

Keeping Your Kit Stocked: First-Aid Supplies

Many dog first-aid supplies are the same as human first-aid items, so one first-aid kit can work for both you and your Bulldog. Whether you have a separate first-aid kit for your dog or just keep supplies in a bathroom drawer, you should have some basic items available for emergencies. If you travel frequently with your dog, keep a few supplies in your car as well. At first glance, the following list looks daunting, but you probably have many of these items already. They just may not all be in one location. Centralize these items for your emergency kit:

- **Activated charcoal.** Give orally if your dog has eaten something poisonous. The charcoal helps neutralize poison. Don't mash up charcoal briquettes — they're not the same thing. Check with your pharmacist for the proper kind of charcoal.

- **Adhesive tape and vet wrap.** Vet wrap is sold in pet-supply catalogs, or your veterinarian can sell you a roll. The wrap holds bandages or splints in place and doesn't stick to your Bully's coat.

- **Antibiotic ointment.** Use for scrapes or cuts.

- **Artificial tears.** Apply to eyes for eye irritations.

- **Benadryl.** This drug works for allergic reactions. Give 1 milligram per pound of body weight of your dog.

- **Children's aspirin.** Use for fever or pain. Give 1 tablet per 10 to 15 pounds of body weight.

    Use only aspirin for your dog. Do not use ibuprofen or acetaminophen. Ibuprofen causes kidney damage and gastric ulcers.

- **Cotton balls.**

- **Gauze.** Roll of gauze and various sizes of gauze pads.

✔ **Hemostats and/or tweezers.**

✔ **Hydrocortisone ointment.** Apply to bug bites or rashes.

✔ **Hydrogen peroxide.** Use it to clean and disinfect wounds. It may also be used to induce vomiting, so if you've got a large bottle of hydrogen peroxide, you can eliminate the syrup of ipecac.

✔ **Kaopectate.** Helps control diarrhea. Give 1 teaspoon per 5 pounds of body weight every 1 to 3 hours.

✔ **Pepto-Bismol.** Have your dog ingest to alleviate both vomiting and diarrhea. Give 1 teaspoon per 20 pounds of body weight every 4 hours.

✔ **Rubber gloves.** Do I need to explain why?

✔ **Scissors.**

✔ **Syringes.** Stock 3-, 6-, and 12-centimeter syringes for administering medication. They come in cubic centimeters or milliliters.

✔ **Syrup of ipecac.** Give by mouth to induce vomiting.

✔ **Thermometer.**

✔ **Vet's phone number.** An index card with your veterinarian's phone number and the number of your local emergency clinic.

✔ **Veterinary first-aid manual.**

If you prefer holistic medications, consider adding these items to your first-aid kit:

✔ **Aloe vera.** Helps relieve pain and itching from hot spots, insect bites, and other skin irritations. Besides being nontoxic, should your dog try to lick the aloe off, it also has a bitter taste, so licking may be discouraged. Licking can slow healing.

✔ **Arnica gel.** Use for sprains and bruises.

✔ **Calendula gel.** Apply to scrapes and wounds. Promotes healing.

✔ **Cayenne pepper.** Apply to the site of bleeding to stop blood flow.

✔ **Comfrey ointment.** Use for minor scrapes and wounds.

Knowing the First-Aid Basics

Whether your Bulldog gets sick or injured, you should know some first-aid basics so you are prepared to deal with emergencies as they arise. Knowing how to take your dog's temperature, for example, and knowing what is a normal temperature can help you determine whether your dog is ill. Here are some aspects of first aid that every Bulldog owner should know:

- ✔ Your Bully's normal temperature should range from 100 to 102 degrees. If the temperature goes above 104 or below 100, call your veterinarian. Buy a rectal thermometer, and take your Bulldog's temperature sometime when you don't need to. Don't be afraid to insert the thermometer; you can't hurt anything. Your dog may not like it, but the process won't hurt him.

- ✔ Practice taking your dog's pulse. If you know how, if there's an emergency, you'll know just what to do and will be less apt to panic. Use the femoral artery on the upper rear leg, where the leg joins the body. Find the top bone — the femur — of your dog's leg. Move your fingers forward, and you should be able to feel the artery. If you're not sure or have trouble on your own, ask your veterinarian to show you during a regular exam. If your veterinarian helps you, make a note of what is normal for your dog so you'll have a number for comparison in an emergency. The normal pulse rate for a dog is between 80 and 140, and the smaller the dog, the higher the number.

- ✔ When a Bulldog is hurt or frightened, he may snap blindly at any touch, even yours. With many dogs, a simple muzzle keeps you safe and makes treating your dog easier, but with Bulldogs, muzzles are not an option. Even if you can put one on a Bulldog, muzzles restrict breathing (especially if your Bully is injured).

    The best alternative to the muzzle is a common blanket or newspaper wrapped around your dog. Have the wrapping extend beyond the dog's head. This extension keeps your dog's jaws away from you but won't interfere with his breathing.

- ✔ If your dog's injuries are severe, transport him on a blanket or a board, especially if you suspect damage to the spinal cord. Get help if you can, and try to shift the dog all at once onto the blanket or board. Call your veterinarian, and give her a brief description of your dog's injuries.

✓ Any injury is scary, and you may want to get to the vet as fast as you can, but take the time to call the office and let them know that you're on the way. You may think that calling the doctor's office is a waste of time, but in fact, the phone call can save time. Your call gives the staff the lead time they may need to prepare for the emergency, and it lets them know just what type of problem they may be facing.

Consider taking a course in animal first aid. Many Red Cross branches offer such courses. Having some basic knowledge can help you aid your dog until you can get to your veterinarian's office. Basic knowledge also helps keep you calm.

In an emergency, panic is a natural response, but you need to stay calm for the sake of your dog. The voices in your head may be screaming and telling you to hurry, but resist. Slow down. Take a moment to think about the best course of action. Improper handling and reactions can result in further injury to your dog. A vet once told me that the first thing to do in an emergency is take a deep breath. It's good advice.

What To Do if Your Bulldog Gets Hurt

We don't always act rationally or competently in an emergency. Knowing what may happen and the proper way to react can improve the odds on doing the right thing when our dog gets hurt. A head wound produces a lot of blood, but the wound itself may be superficial, is not the first thing to worry about. A broken bone can be ugly but won't necessarily be life threatening. This section deals with possible problems from the most serious down to "not so bad."

Handling injuries from auto accidents

Your Bully is not the fastest runner of all the breeds, but occasionally he may get out the front door or get loose from his leash, and the risk of getting hit by a car exists. You must remain calm in this emergency situation. Cuts and lacerations can look awful and produce a lot of blood, but they are likely to be the least life threatening. Ignore the blood, and focus on what is important.

Artificial respiration

First, check to make sure that your dog is breathing. If your Bully is not breathing, you need to start artificial respiration:

1. **Extend your dog's neck.**

2. **Clear any mucus from his mouth.**

3. **Pull his tongue forward.**

4. **Breathe into his nose, closing your mouth tightly over his nose.**

5. **Breathe for 3 seconds; rest for two.**

6. **Continue until your Bully is breathing on his own or until you get to the hospital.**

You can also use the compression method of respiration, but beware of internal injuries. Place both your hands on your dog's side, near the last ribs, and press down. Release quickly. Plan on 12 compressions per minute. If you have help, someone can drive you to the veterinarian's office while you continue artificial respiration. Don't want to use the compression method of artificial respiration. Stick with breathing through your dog's nose.

Circulation

After respiration, consider circulation. Your dog may be in shock. Shock is usually characterized by loss of blood pressure, diminished blood circulation, and inadequate blood flow to the tissues. Your Bully's breathing can be shallow and irregular, and his pulse may be fast and faint. Pale gums, lips, and eyelids are signs of shock.

Your dog may also feel cool to the touch. Check his temperature. Wrap your Bully carefully in a blanket, jacket, coat, or even newspapers — anything to keep him warm.

Never use a heat pad or heat lamp to warm your dog, because if your dog is unconscious, he won't be able to move away from the heat if he is too hot. Even if he's not unconscious, if he's in shock, his circulation is poor, and in both cases, the exterior heat source can cause burns.

Pale lips and gums may also be signs of major blood loss. Look for external wounds that may need a pressure bandage. If you don't have a bandage, use a towel or, if necessary, your hand. Keep your dog in a horizontal position or elevate the hindquarters slightly.

A tourniquet stops blood flow, but because it does, the tissue below the tourniquet starts to die. Never use a tourniquet unless you are certain that without it, your pet will die. Tighten the tourniquet only enough to stop the bleeding, and get to the veterinarian immediately.

If you suspect that your Bulldog has sustained injury to his head, neck, or back, you must try to stabilize him:

✔ Try not to move him any more than is absolutely necessary.

✔ Slide him onto a board, a piece of cardboard, or a blanket.

✔ Try to move him all at once.

✔ Use gauze strips to secure your Bully to the board for the trip to the veterinarian.

Pantyhose work really well if you don't have a roll of gauze.

Broken bones

Broken bones are likely if your Bully's been hit by a car. If you think that your dog has a broken leg, try to splint it to hold it in place. There are several materials that work well as a splint:

1. **Protect the leg with some kind of padding.**

2. **Use sticks or pieces of wood as your splint.**

   If wood is not available, roll a newspaper or a magazine around your dog's leg.

3. **Tie the splint in place with strips of gauze, vet wrap (if you have it), nylons, or a kneesock.**

4. **Extend the splint beyond the joints on either side of the break.**

5. **If the bone is protruding, don't try to push it back into place.**

   a. Cover the protrusion with gauze.

   b. Stabilize the area as well as you can.

6. **Get your Bully to the hospital or vet.**

If you think that your dog has broken or cracked ribs, bandage gently to help hold the ribs in place. The operative word is *gently*. You don't want to restrict your dog's breathing, which may already be labored.

Puncture wounds

If there's a puncture wound or any kind of wound that penetrates the chest cavity, try to make it airtight. Plastic wrap or even a plastic bag is a good way to seal the area.

If whatever made the wound is still protruding from your Bulldog's body, *do not remove the object.* Leave the foreign body in place, and let your veterinarian remove it. Pulling the object out can cause more damage and bleeding. Stabilize the object if you can so it doesn't continue to injure your dog.

Eye injuries

Check your Bulldog's eyes for signs of injury. Are there surface cuts or lacerations? If the eyelid is bleeding, use a gauze pad to gently hold the lid in place, but again, remember to be gentle. Too much pressure can cause more damage. If you see blood inside your Bully's eyeball, proceed directly to a pet hospital or your vet's office.

If your dog's eye has actually come out of the socket, keep the eye moist during your trip to the vet. Use artificial tears, contact-lens fluid, plain water, or cod-liver or olive oil. Apply the liquid every 15 minutes.

Outward signs of injury may not be evident if your Bully gets hit by a car, but severe internal damage may be a problem. Even if your dog looks just fine, get to your veterinarian immediately!

Fighting doesn't solve anything, boys!

A dog fight is generally more frightening than dangerous. Everything you read about fights tells you never to try to get between the dogs who are fighting, but in real life, people try to stop dog fights all the time. You can reach in and try to pull the dogs apart, but the odds are good that you'll be bitten. In the heat of battle, even your dear, sweet pet can bite you. Try using different items to break up the fight:

- ✔ **A broom or broom handle.** Use it to pry the dogs apart rather than hit them.

- ✔ **A chair.** Again, use it to pry the dogs apart, and try to avoid hitting them.

- ✔ **A hose.** Squirt the dogs with water.

If the dogs continue to go after each other, if you have help, you and the other person can each grab the hind legs of a dog and pull the dogs apart. You're less apt to get bitten with this technique.

Puncture wounds are the most typical wounds you'll see from a dog fight. Clean the wounds with hydrogen peroxide, but don't bandage. Check with your veterinarian about getting an antibiotic. She may want to see your dog, or she may just give you the medicine. Either way, keep an eye on the wounds to make sure that they don't get infected.

Dog fights can kill long after the fight is over. Sometimes the fight that leaves little bleeding is the most dangerous. A dog can suffer severe bruising and muscle damage without any real lacerations. Dogs sometimes die of shock or organ failure due to the damaged tissue's breaking down and overwhelming the kidneys. Dogs can become critically ill hours later or even the next day. If the dog seems ill, depressed, or in pain, go to a vet immediately, or in the middle of the night, find a pet hospital.

Poisoning

Getting hit by a car is not the only way your Bully can become injured. Your puppy may like to stick his nose in every corner he finds, and eventually he may find the wrong corner and eat something he shouldn't eat. You need to be ready to act to protect your Bulldog. The Cheat Sheet in this book contains information on stuff around the house that can poison your Bulldog, and removing these things from your home goes a long way toward keeping your Bully safe.

If you suspect that your Bulldog has been poisoned, don't wait! Call your veterinarian, and tell her you're on the way. If you know what your Bully ate, take some of it with you.

Signs of poisoning can be single or multiple. Watch for these symptoms that may indicate that your dog has been poisoned:

- ✔ Abdominal pain
- ✔ Diarrhea
- ✔ Excessive drool
- ✔ Slow breathing
- ✔ Vomiting
- ✔ Weakness

Preparing yourself for natural disasters

Depending on where you live, you can experience many different natural disasters: hurricanes, tornadoes, floods, fires, or mudslides. Be prepared to leave your home for a few days. Follow these tips for preparing for and evacuation your house:

✔ Keep your dog's crate fully assembled and ready to go. If you don't keep a crate in the car, store your crate where you can easily get it in an emergency. Keep it by the door or in the carport or garage. Stuff a blanket in it or a few old towels.

✔ Make sure that your dog has identification on his collar and/or is microchipped. (See Chapter 6.)

✔ Keep your dog's lead handy, or carry a spare in the car. If you're trying to get out fast, and you forget the lead by the door, the spare will be important.

✔ Have a supply of water. Two or three gallon jugs will keep you and your dog for a day or two.

✔ Have at least a 3-day supply of your dog's food in a travel container. Rotate this food every month, or according to any expiration date on the packaging, so that it doesn't spoil.

✔ Keep a copy of your dog's vaccination records in the glove box of your car, including his rabies certificate.

✔ If your dog is on medication, make sure that you take it with you.

✔ Make a list of the things that your dog will need should you have to leave your home quickly. You may not be able to stock everything in the car or near the door, but a checklist reminds you of the necessities and helps you when you may be in a panic.

✔ Think about where your dog can stay if he can't stay with you. If you have more dogs than your car holds, or you need to stay in a shelter that won't allow you to have your dog with you, where can your dogs go? Make arrangements ahead of time with a friend or with a boarding kennel. Maybe your breeder will be able to take care of your Bully. If your local animal shelter is not threatened by the disaster, you may be able to leave your dogs there.

If the unthinkable happens and you must leave your dog behind, turn him loose. Don't shut him in the house with no escape.

If you don't know what your dog ingested, and your pup has vomited, take a sample of the vomit with you to the vet. If what your dog ate is a plant or a specific food, you can use hydrogen peroxide to make him vomit. Give 1 to 2 teaspoons of hydrogen peroxide every 5 minutes until your dog vomits.

Don't try to make your Bulldog vomit if you don't know what poisoned him or the poison is a caustic product. Many household cleaners contain ingredients that cause more harm when vomited. If you find your dog lapping up something he found under the sink, give him lots of milk or vegetable oil to drink. These products help dilute caustic substances and also coat the digestive tract until you can get to the vet's.

If you're unable to reach your veterinarian, there are places you can call for help. The National Poison Control Center of the ASPCA has two phone numbers in case your Bulldog has been poisoned. Have your credit card ready. Charges are assessed:

- Call (800) 548-2423. $30 charge.

- Call (900) 680-0000. $20 for the first 5 minutes and $2.95 for every minute over the first 5.

  Charges are not assessed on follow-up calls for the same case.

Another number is the Pet Poison Helpline at (800) 213-6680. It charges $35.

Insect stings

We tend to think of poison as something that has been eaten, but insect and reptile bites and stings are also a type of poison. If you notice a lump that seems tender or looks like an insect bite, and your dog is showing any signs of illness, get to your veterinarian's office immediately. If your dog's breathing is affected, give an antihistamine, like Benadryl.

Electrocution

This injury poses the most threat when your Bulldog is a puppy and is always looking for something interesting to chew. If your dog, at any age, chews through an electrical wire, the possibility of electrocution exists.

Follow certain steps to protect your Bully and yourself from further harm if your dog has been electrocuted:

1. **First, turn off the power, if that's possible.**

2. **Use a wooden stick, like a broom or mop handle, to move your dog away from the source of electricity.**

Do not, under any circumstances, touch the dog while he is still in contact with the wire. You risk getting electrocuted yourself.

3. **Check for breathing.**

4. **If your Bully is breathing on his own, get him to your veterinarian quickly.**

   He may need to be treated for burns around his mouth and for shock, but one of the biggest threats is fluid buildup in the lungs, which needs immediate attention.

5. **If your dog isn't breathing, start artificial respiration, as described earlier in the chapter.**

Drowning

Bulldogs may enjoy water for cooling off, but most of them swim like rocks. If your Bully sinks, get him out of the water, hold him by the hind legs for about 30 seconds to drain water from his lungs, and then start artificial respiration.

Keep your Bully on a lead when you're around bodies of water. If you have a pool, and it's fenced, make sure your dog stays on the side of the fence without the water. If your Bully does have access to the pool, make sure there are steps or a ramp so that if your Bully falls in, he can get out on his own. Practice the escape route with him. If your dog likes the water, get in the water with him, and gently guide him to the steps or the ramp. Never leave your Bulldog in the pool area unattended. It takes only a minute for your dog to drown.

Choking

If your dog is choking, use the handle of a screwdriver between his back teeth to keep his mouth open and to prevent his biting you as you check his mouth and throat. He will not take kindly to your efforts, so if you've got someone who can hold the dog for you, have him do so. If you can reach the obstruction, use your fingers or a pair of needle-nosed pliers to grab and remove it. If you can't reach the problem, try holding your dog by the hind legs and shaking. If that doesn't work, use the Heimlich maneuver.

1. **Make a fist.**

2. **Apply sudden, forceful pressure to the abdomen at the edge of the breastbone.**

If this doesn't dislodge the object after two or three tries, get to your veterinarian immediately. How much time you have depends on how large the object is and how much air it is cutting off.

If you do manage to remove the object, your dog may have a sore throat for a couple of days, so switch to a soft food during that time.

Suffering from heatstroke

Yes, heatstroke is discussed in Chapter 14 and throughout other parts of the book. You are not hallucinating, and that sentence was not a typographical error. Heatstroke is a real threat to Bulldogs, and if you're not reading this book straight through, I don't want you to miss this information. Signs of heatstroke include

- ✔ Temperature over 106 degrees
- ✔ Panting and slobbering excessively
- ✔ Vomiting
- ✔ Diarrhea
- ✔ Collapsing
- ✔ Hot and dry skin
- ✔ Pale lips

Try to cool down your Bulldog. Move him to a cool, shady area, and soak him with cold water. Move his legs gently to increase circulation. If he is alert and can drink, give him small amounts of water. Take his temperature every 15 minutes until it is below 103 degrees and stays there. In advanced stages, get your Bully to your veterinarian as soon as possible.

Chapter 16

Caring for Your Senior Bulldog

. . . .

In This Chapter

▶ Battling old age

▶ Feeding sensibly for seniors

▶ Revising the exercise schedule

▶ Saying goodbye to your Bully

. . . .

Gandhi said, "The greatness of a nation and its moral progress can be judged by the way that its animals are treated." I think those are valuable words to live by. Think about how you may take care of your Bulldog as she grows up. Now think about the time, much farther down the road, when she becomes a senior dog. The methods of care are completely different.

How do you take care of your Bully when he becomes an elder of the dog world? Just like people, a senior dog can be active and happy, but adjustments may need to be made. This chapter covers all your needs for making your Bulldog's senior years enjoyable.

Easing Your Bully into the Autumn Years

As your Bulldog ages, he may experience some of the same problems that aging humans face. When your dog reaches his seventh birthday, add a chemical blood screen test to his annual checkup. A geriatric profile done early may alert you and your veterinarian to a problem, and early detection means early treatment and a better chance to stop, or at least control, a problem.

An older dog may show signs of senility or *cognitive dysfunction*. Cognitive dysfunction is a degeneration of the brain and nervous system and is the equivalent of Alzheimer's in people. Symptoms include

- Withdrawing from interaction, and wanting less petting and attention
- Not recognizing family members
- Sleeping more during the day and less at night
- Staring at walls or into space
- Difficulty learning new commands, and ignoring known commands
- Pacing or wandering aimlessly
- Becoming lost in familiar places
- Standing at the hinge side of the door

Talk to your veterinarian about drugs that can help your Bully be more aware and able to enjoy life more.

Dealing with hearing problems

Your Bulldog's hearing may not be as acute as it once was. He may not hear you enter the house when you come home from work, or he may miss the rattle of his food bowl at dinner. The fact is that dogs of any breed can have deafness from a variety of causes:

- **Drug toxicity:** The administration or application of a drug or chemical that either directly or indirectly destroys cochlear hair cells, resulting in hearing loss or even total deafness.

- **General anesthesia:** May cause bilateral deafness from unknown causes. The body may push blood away from the cochlea during anesthesia to protect other critical organs, or pressure or jaw positioning may compress the arterial supply to the cochlea.

- **Noise trauma:** Depending on the loudness, noise can produce temporary or permanent hearing loss. This type of hearing loss can be prevented in minor ways.

  In response to loud sounds, tiny muscles in the middle ear contract to reduce sound transmission into the inner ear. However, percussive noise, such as occurs with gunfire and explosions, occurs too rapidly for the reflex to provide protection. The noise actually disrupts the hair cells and their support cells. If a ringing sensation occurs in your ears while you are with your Bulldog, damage is occurring in the ears of both you and your dog.

✔ **Otitis:** Infections of the middle ear *(otitis media)* or inner ear *(otitis interna)*. These infections can produce temporary or permanent deafness. After the infection ends, the otitis media may leave behind crud that blocks sound transmission to the inner ear. Your Bully's body eventually clears the crud out, and hearing gradually improves. Otitis interna, if not quickly treated, produces permanent nerve deafness.

✔ **Presbycusis:** Age-related hearing loss that is progressive and cannot be reversed. Your Bully's hearing may in fact have been diminishing over time, but you may have been unaware because she compensated until she could no longer hear adequately to get by. The onset appears sudden, but the hearing loss has been progressive.

No matter what the cause of hearing loss in your senior Bully, make allowances for her diminished hearing. Don't sneak up on her and startle her. Some suggestions for compensating for the loss include

✔ Stamping on the floor as you approach your dog; the vibrations alert her to your presence.

✔ Incorporate hand signals into your obedience commands (if you haven't already done so). Hand signals help your Bulldog understand what you want her to do.

✔ Use a small flashlight, instead of a clicker, to act as a marker when teaching a new behavior. Use a flashlight that will light with a push of a button. Flashlights that require moving a switch will be too slow for training.

✔ Invest in a vibrator collar. You can use this to train your dog by making it vibrate when he does something right. Combine it with hand signals and treats. Or use it to mean "Someone is calling me."

Always keep your dog on lead when you're not in your fenced yard. Your deaf Bully won't be able to hear cars or other dogs coming.

Your Bulldog may be old, but you can teach an old dog new tricks. (That adage just isn't true.)

Keeping an eye on failing eyesight

Several diseases may cause blindness in a dog. If you suspect your Bulldog is having sight problems, take him to the vet to see what treatments are available. Some conditions are quite treatable, so it's worth it to investigate them to help save your Bully's eyesight. Here are the most common conditions:

- Dry eye, or Keratoconjunctivitis, is common in Bulldogs and is the result of inadequate tear production. It has the potential to blind, but it is easy to diagnose and responds favorably to treatment, which includes "artificial tears" and the drugs Cyclosporin and Tacrolimus.

- Corneal ulcers are caused by irritation to the eye, trauma to the eye, or inadequate tear production. Minor ulcers may heal without complication, but more serious ulcers can cause scarring of the cornea and can even lead to blindness. Signs of an ulcer including squinting, redness, discharge, and discoloration of the eye.

- A cataract is a clouding of the eye's lens. Cataracts give a cloudy, whitish-blue look to the eye. Your veterinarian will tell you whether your dog has a cataract or if the lens has a bluish look from normal aging, which does not affect vision.

- Glaucoma causes blindness when it produces elevated pressure within the eye. The amount of pressure will determine how quickly a dog will lose his sight. If the pressure change is caught early, medication can lower the pressure temporarily. Long term, only surgery can help, and even the surgery doesn't always work.

- Progressive retinal atrophy is an inherited disease, but there is also a noninherited form called Sudden Acquired Retinal Degeneration. Both of these cause irreversible blindness and generally affects dogs between 6 and 8 years of age. Night vision goes first, and finally, the dog becomes totally blind.

Your Bully's hearing may remain just fine, but if his eyesight fails, remember that he still has his nose and his old habits and patterns. If you have lived in the same house for several years, your Bully knows his way around. Make sure to keep his surroundings familiar to him:

- Keep the food and water bowls in the same place.

- Try not to wash the dog toys that have your Bully's scent on them. (If the plush toys are filthy, you can make an exception.)

- Don't rearrange the furniture.

- ✔ Don't decide that this is the time to move his bed from one side of the room to the other.

- ✔ Keep the door to the basement shut so your Bully doesn't accidentally tumble down the stairs.

- ✔ Use squeaky toys or balls with bells in them so your dog can find them.

- ✔ Add textures to the floor. Place a looped throw rug near the stairs or a sisal mat to mark the door to outside.

- ✔ Use scent as a marker. Put a drop of vanilla extract near food and water bowls. Spritz lavender essential oil at the top of stairs. Use another scent to mark a door.

Avoid lemon scent unless you want to keep your dog away, because most dogs don't like the smell.

You can still take your Bully for walks on a lead along his regular route, but be alert for anything in your path, like a fallen branch or a child's toy, that may cause your dog a problem.

Talk to your dog when you approach him, and remind others to do the same. Even the gentlest, most loving dog may snap if he's frightened by an unexpected touch.

Treating arthritis

Dogs can get arthritis as they age, just as people can. A dose of aspirin may be all your dog needs to be comfortable, but sometimes he needs more. Rimadyl is the drug most often prescribed for arthritis and can give wonderful relief to your dog. But Rimadyl has its drawbacks. If your Bully has current liver problems, he should not take Rimadyl. Ask your veterinarian to run blood tests regularly to detect any liver problems as a result of the drug.

Keep your senior dog comfortable. Always keep your Bully cool, but now, in his older years, take a closer look at where he sleeps. Drafts may aggravate stiff muscles and arthritis, so your dog may feel the cold more. Give him the option of being able to warm up a bit. A bed made of layers gives your Bulldog the opportunity to shove aside bedding when he's hot or to burrow under a towel or two if he's cold.

Protect your Bully's aged joints by adding some padding to his bed. If he's always slept on three or four folded towels, put a foam pad on the bottom.

Adjusting the potty schedule

Sometimes older dogs may have a problem with incontinence, especially when they're sleeping. If your dog is incontinent, make sure that the leaking is not a symptom of something more than just weakening muscles. A low-grade bladder infection may be the cause, in which case your veterinarian will prescribe an antibiotic. Your vet may run blood tests or take x-rays to rule out a tumor. If incontinence is a result of weakening muscles, your veterinarian can prescribe medications to stop or lessen the problem.

If your dog leaks urine in his sleep, make sure to:

- ✔ Add a plastic cover to the foam pad.
- ✔ Add a layer of fleece to the bedding. Liquids tend to go through fleece and keep your Bully dryer.
- ✔ Make sure that you wash your dog's bedding whenever necessary to keep his resting place sanitary.

One way to help alleviate accidents is to make sure that your Bully goes outside regularly. A schedule of potty breaks three or four times a day when your dog was younger may not be enough now that he's older. If you can, try to let your senior dog out every 4 hours. Everyone benefits from this increased schedule.

Keeping a beautiful smile

Continue to take good care of your dog's teeth. If there's an infection, an older dog may not be able to fight off the disease as easily as a younger dog. See Chapter 8 for information on Bulldog dental care.

Feeding a Sensible Senior Diet

As your Bulldog ages, he may slow physically. Even if he seems just as active, his metabolism may be slowing. As your Bully ages, his body may not be able to process the food he consumes efficiently. If you are feeding the regular quantity of food, pay attention to weight gain or loss. If either drastically occurs, schedule an appointment with your veterinarian to rule out any major health problems.

Talk to your veterinarian about the idea of senior food. Senior foods are formulated to provide fewer calories but still provide your dog the nutrients he needs.

Some veterinarians recommend specialty foods, such as Canine k/d by Hills Science Diet and Purina Veterinary Diets NF formula for the nutritional management of dogs with kidney disease because these foods are easier on the kidneys. A veterinarian may also recommend the addition of B vitamins, especially if your dog is urinating and drinking excessively. The B vitamins are known as *energy vitamins* because of their energy-creating traits. B vitamins are cofactors for a number of important biological processes:

- ✔ The breakdown of carbohydrates into glucose, which provides dogs energy

- ✔ The breakdown of fats and proteins, which aids the normal functioning of the nervous system; muscle tone in the stomach and intestinal tract; and healthy hair, skin, and eyes

- ✔ Maintaining a positive environment for neural regenerative efforts

- ✔ Water solubility so excess Vitamin B is eliminated in the urine

If you decide to leave your Bully on his regular food, you may choose to cut back the amount to bring his weight down or to maintain your Bully's current weight. Your Bulldog may notice a significant cut in his food and wonder where the rest is.

Add canned pumpkin to your Bulldog's food dish. He'll love it, and the fiber makes him feel fuller without adding many calories. Just remember to use regular canned pumpkin and not canned pumpkin pie filling.

Exercising Your Older Bully

Bulldogs are not high on the list of canine athletes, but maybe you practice agility, show your dog, or compete in obedience. Your Bully may have a touch of arthritis setting in, and moving takes more effort. Pay attention to your dog's reactions to various activities. If he seems stressed or gets tired faster than he used to, cut back.

You may need to slow down on agility with a senior dog, but you can continue to attend shows and competitions. Even these events can put a strain on your senior Bully, so look for signs of fatigue and stress in your dog. Just the stress of traveling to a show can take its toll on an older dog. People retire when they get older; it may be time to retire your Bulldog too.

Retirement shouldn't mean the end of all physical activity, but taking a step back may mean that you need to shorten those times when your Bully is active. Here are some tips to keep your aging Bully happy:

- **Don't skip dog shows.** If your Bulldog loved to travel to dog shows and competitions, he may miss the traveling, even if he doesn't have the stamina for a day at a show. Take him for shorter trips or to a show close to home. He can compete in smaller shows or just go to watch.

- **Continue to play games.** If your dog has always enjoyed a game of fetch, don't eliminate the game; just make it shorter.

- **Keep moving.** Even if your dog has arthritis, moving is important. The movement keeps the muscles in shape and alleviates pain in the long run. If your daily walks have always been three times around the block, once around may now be all your Bully can comfortably manage. But at least you and your dog are still taking the time to walk together.

- **Experiment a little.** If you have the time, and your normal routine used to be two walks a day, maybe you can now do three shorter walks each day.

Exercise doesn't have a hard-and-fast rule. You need to understand your own dog and adjust to his needs.

Include your dog in as many activities as possible. Just because he slows down doesn't mean he should be isolated. He may need your love and attention more than ever.

When It's Time to Say Goodbye

No matter how well you care for your aging Bully, a day comes when you have to say goodbye. We may wish that when the time comes for our dog to pass that he would just go quietly in his sleep to keep him from suffering even more, but unfortunately, that's not usually the case.

Most dogs' lives are ended by _euthanasia_ — that is, the painless putting to death of your dog by your veterinarian. Deciding when that should happen is the hardest decision you'll ever make as a dog owner. As hard as that decision is, euthanasia may also be the kindest thing you ever do for your dog. You have the power to end suffering and pain when there's no longer any hope. The hard part is finding the line where no hope exists. You don't want to wait too long but always wonder if it is too soon. It is a fine like to walk.

Handling grief

Grief is natural, and grieving over the loss of your Bully is natural too, so stay away from people who are likely to say, "It was only a dog." Spend time with people who understand your loss and sympathize with you.

Grief is an individual emotion and is expressed many ways. Some people heal faster when they immediately get another dog; others need some time before they can welcome another canine pal. Some people stick with the same breed of dog; others want another dog but can't bear the thought of having the same breed. Don't let anyone talk you into anything you're not ready for. You are the only one who knows what's best for you.

Fortunately, in many communities support groups exist that can help you deal with the loss of a pet and the grief that accompanies that loss. Check with your local shelter or kennel club. Your YMCA or YWCA may offer sessions too. You may also talk to a clergyman or a counselor.

Sometimes, writing a letter to the deceased pet helps. The letter can be as short as "I loved you" or as long as needed. You may want to explain to your pet how you felt throughout his life or what it was like during the final stages of his illness. Whatever you write, the words help you deal with your loss.

Other avenues to memorialize your pet include ways to remember and celebrate your years together:

Memorials

✔ **Memorial marker.** This marker can be as plain or as elaborate as you want. Even if you've had your pet cremated or buried elsewhere, a marker in the back-yard can be a tribute to your dog.

✔ **Plant a tree or flowering shrub.** Watching it grow helps you remember the life of your Bully.

✔ **Make a donation.** A friend of mine has donated to the local humane society whenever I've lost a dog, and I like knowing that my friend cares. Most veteri-nary schools also accept memorial donations.

✔ **Check the Internet.** You'll find memorial sites where you can post your dog's picture, along with information about him. A recommended site is The Senior Dogs Project at `www.srdogs.com/Pages/loss.html`.

(continued)

(continued)

Containers for ashes

✔ **Urns, boxes, and glass pendants.** A variety of items exist to preserve your Bully's ashes.

✔ **Synthetic gemstones.** This jewelry item can be made from your pet's ashes, and you can wear the item to remember your Bully every day.

✔ **Stored ashes.** Depending on the regulations in your area, you may want your dog's ashes buried with you. A friend of mine has left her dog's ashes with a funeral home. When she dies, the ashes will be placed in her casket with her.

Other options include lockets with snips of your dog's hair and the most expensive option of having your pet freeze-dried. In this process, the dog is posed in whatever position you have chosen and then is frozen, and the moisture is drawn out in a climate-controlled machine. This differs from taxidermy, in which the hide is stretched over an artificial form. For a Bulldog, the cost will run $3,000 to $5,000.

For euthanasia, most veterinarians use an overdose of the anesthetic pentobarbital. It is fast and painless.

Other dog owners may tell you that you know when it's time to let your dog go — your dog "tells you" when it's time. Maybe. Maybe not. I don't think you always know or that your dog always tells you, or, if he is telling you, that you always understand. Your Bully's life is so short in comparison and we love our dogs so much that the final goodbye is not always easy to say.

Making preparations in case your Bulldog outlives you

A Bulldog's life is so much shorter than a human's that you may never even consider that your Bully could outlive you. Even if you have thought about dog care, you may just think that your family or friends will take care of your dog, but it's best to make sure and to update your plans every year or two. Your best friend may have agreed to take your dog when she was single, but now that she's married with two children, plus a job, the responsibility may not be as practical for her or her household as it once was. It's not a bad idea to also have a backup plan.

Several years ago, I had a casual agreement with two other women that if anything happened to any one of us, the other two would take the dogs and either keep them or find good second homes for the dogs. Because we all had multiple dogs and homes and yards that would accommodate these animals, we thought the arrangement was perfect. Then one summer, we had a car accident, and all three of us were in the car.

We all survived but realized that our casual plan wasn't enough. More recently, two of us have moved to smaller places and wouldn't be able to keep extra dogs.

My new plan includes a breeder friend who can easily take my two dogs, and I trust her to do what's best for my dogs. As a backup, if an emergency occurred, I have another friend who would take my dogs. She has a different breed, but again, I trust her to do what's best.

What's best depends on the age of the Bulldog and his disposition. A young dog may go easily to another home, either directly or through a rescue agency. An older dog with health problems may not be so easy to deal with. If my older male can't go back to his breeder to live out his life, I'd want him to be euthanized. No matter how much we like to think that our older dog will be adopted from a shelter, the cruel truth is that people want puppies. Take an older dog to a shelter, and he'll spend his last days in a shelter run and not in a loving home.

Think about the cost of caring for your dog. Make provisions in your will so that the friend who gladly takes your dog has the resources to care for your dog as he ages. Sometimes, our dog is such a part of our life that we forget just how much work is involved. Make a list of all the special information that pertains to your Bully:

✔ Allergies.

✔ Feeding time, including quantity and brand of food.

✔ Habits. If your Bulldog always curls up with you when you nap, write it down.

✔ Information about the dog's general health.

✔ Likes and dislikes.

✔ Medications, including vitamins and supplements.

✔ Rapport with other dogs, cats, or children. If your dog wants to kill the neighbor's cat, you should include that in your list.

✔ Veterinarian's phone number.

This list also comes in handy during temporary emergencies or as a guide for pet sitters, and if you write everything down when you're calm and have the time, you won't forget something important in the case of an emergency. See Chapter 17 for more information on resources for caring for your Bully when you can't.

Talk to your veterinarian about your dog's condition, and pay attention to physical signs and to your dog's quality of life. If you start to notice the following warning signs, the time has come to give your Bully the last gift you can give:

✔ If he no longer enjoys his food

✔ If he's in constant pain

✔ If the bad days outweigh the good

> ✔ If he doesn't always recognize his friends
>
> ✔ If there's no way to reverse any of the above

Talk to your veterinarian ahead of time about the procedures of euthanasia. Your veterinarian may give you the option to stay with your dog in his last moments. This decision is personal, and don't let anyone tell you that one way is better than another. Some people simply can't bear to be with their dog at the time of death. Others are by their Bully's side until the final breath. I had a friend who loved and cared for her dogs for generation after generation, but she just couldn't be there at the end. I stay with my dogs, offering whatever comfort I can. If illness hasn't robbed my dog of his appetite, I feed him hot dogs just before the needle finds the vein. I am comforted to have, as a last memory, the image of my dog gulping down the delicious treats.

Ask about how they dispose of the body. Many veterinarians offer individual cremation and return the ashes to you if you want. Some offices have their own crematory; other locations send the bodies away. If you decide to bury your dog yourself, check your local health regulations to make sure that you can legally bury your Bully under his favorite tree.

In the end, where and how your dog is buried is less important than what you shared while the dog was alive.

> "... For if the dog be well remembered, if sometimes she leaps through your dreams actual as in life, eyes kindling, laughing, begging, it matters not where that dog sleeps. On a hill where the wind is unrebuked and the trees are roaring, or beside a stream she knew in puppyhood, or somewhere in the flatness of a pastureland where most exhilarating cattle graze. It is one to a dog, and all one to you, and nothing is gained and nothing lost — if memory lives. But there is one best place to bury a dog.
>
> "If you bury her in this spot, she will come to you when you call — come to you over the grim, dim frontiers of death, and down the well-remembered path and to your side again. And though you may call a dozen living dogs to heel, they shall not growl at her nor resent her coming, for she belongs there.
>
> "People may scoff at you, who see no lightest blade of grass bend by her footfall, who hear no whimper, people who have never really had a dog. Smile at them, for you shall know something that is hidden from them.
>
> "The one best place to bury a good dog is in the heart of her master. ..."

Ben Hur Lampman in *The Oregonian,* 1925

Part V
The Part of Tens

The 5th Wave   By Rich Tennant

"What makes you think the neighbors
are getting an English Bulldog?"

In this part . . .

The Part of Tens is the way all For Dummies books end, and this part just happens to be my favorite (and not just because it's easier to write!). This part arranges neatly into lists of ten (or so) items that you may find useful in your quest with your Bulldog. Here you find ten great resources for more information about your Bully, ten reasons not to breed your Bully, and ten important things you can do for your new household addition. So hug your Bulldog, if you already have one, give him a dog biscuit, and curl up on the couch and enjoy The Part of Tens.

Chapter 17

Nine Great Resources for Bulldog Owners

In This Chapter
- Utilizing Bulldog resources
- Joining kennel clubs
- Planning for your Bully's future

The resources included in this chapter offer a lot of extra information that you can look up on all aspects of Bulldogs, from the history of the breed, healthcare, information on Bulldog rescue, shopping opportunities, and books to read just for fun. And if you'd like to join a club just for Bulldog lovers, find out how in this chapter!

Finding Bulldog Information on the Internet

If you search the Internet by typing **Bulldogs**, you will literally get thousands of hits for sites to search for information. One good site, supported by the American Kennel Club, is The Bulldog Club of America's site. Visit www.thebca.org for a variety of general information about Bulldogs. Discover the annual specialty show; find breeders; subscribe to *The Bulldogger*, the club newsletter; get information about joining the Bulldog Club of America; and learn about rescue.

For more Bulldog info, visit some of the following sites:

- Bark Bytes Canine Cyber-Magazine, www.barkbytes.com/clubs/bulldog.htm
- Bulldog Club of Greater Tulsa, www.bulldogclubofgreatertulsa.com

- Bulldog Club of Northern California, www.thebcnc.org
- Chaparral Bulldog Club, www.chaparralbulldogclub.org
- Heart of America Bulldog Club, www.heartofamerica bulldogclub.org
- The Lone Star Bulldog Club, www.lonestarbulldogs.com/rescue.html

Contacting the Kennel Clubs

Kennel Clubs provide many resources and connections within the Bulldog world. For that reason, getting registered with a recognized club has many benefits, even if you choose not to show your Bully.

The American Kennel Club

The AKC's Web site, www.akc.org, gives you information on all the AKC events, as well as general articles on dogs and their care. You can even shop at the online store. Contact the AKC by mail at 5580 Centerview Drive, Raleigh, NC 27606. For registration information, call 919-233-9767 or e-mail info@akc.org.

The United Kennel Club

The United Kennel Club is the second oldest and second largest all-breed dog registry in the United States. Its Web site, www.ukcdogs.com, has information on registering your Bulldog, as well as UKC-sponsored events, and a store. Its address is United Kennel Club, 100 E. Kilgore Road, Kalamazoo, MI 49002-5584. The phone number is 269-343-9020. Fax: 269-343-7037.

The Kennel Club

The Web site for The Kennel Club (United Kingdom) is www.the-kennel-club.org.uk/. The club has registration forms online, as well as an e-mail form. The address is 1 Clarges Street, London W1J 8AB. The telephone number is 0870 606 6750. Fax: 020 7518 1058.

Checking with the Local Breed Clubs

Local Bulldog clubs can provide you and your Bulldog lots of hands-on help, great new friends, and practical advice. Bulldog breed clubs also give shows and matches for Bulldog fanciers, and they also often give conformation and obedience classes. The Web sites of some clubs are listed in other sections of this chapter, and you can find more through The Bulldog Club of America: www. thebca.org.

Browsing for Books

For more information of the Bulldog breed, consider reading *The New Complete Bulldog,* by Bailey C. Hanes (Howell).

Also recommended are health books for dog owners. These books are not intended to replace your veterinarian, but to guide you in understanding canine healthcare and what you can do, with your veterinarian, to ensure your Bulldog's good health:

- ✔ *Pet Care in the New Century: Cutting-Edge Medicine for Dogs and Cats,* by Amy D. Shojai (New American Library)

- ✔ *The Angell Memorial Animal Hospital Book of Wellness and Preventive Care for Dogs,* by Darlene Arden (McGraw-Hill)

- ✔ *Pills for Pets: The A to Z Guide to Drugs and Medications for Your Animal Companion,* by Debra Eldredge, DVM (Citadel Press)

For training your Bulldog, *Dog Training For Dummies* (Wiley), by Jack and Wendy Volhard, is a good basic book that will get you and your Bully off to a good start.

If you're interested specifically in clicker-training your Bulldog, read anything by Karen Pryor. Also, visit her Web site at www. clickertraining.com/home. This site provides a wealth of information, from the basics of training to conferences and events you can attend.

Flipping through fabulous dog fiction

There may be a reference or two about Bulldogs in the following books, but they make great reading no matter what breed is featured. Dog lovers love to read about dogs, and it doesn't matter what breed the dogs are. These are some of my favorites:

✔ Any book by Albert Payson Terhune. Stories about his Sunnybank Collies make great reading.

✔ Any book by Susan Conant. Conant writes mysteries featuring a dog writer named Holly Winter and her two Alaskan Malamutes, Rowdy and Kimi.

✔ Any book by Carol Benjamin. Her detective, Rachel Alexander, has a pit bull named Dashiell, as well as various other breeds in each novel, from a Dachshund in *The Long Good Boy* to a Puli in *Lady Vanishes*.

✔ Virginia Lanier wrote a book series based on trailing with Bloodhounds. Besides being gripping stories, you can learn about trailing.

✔ Rita Mae Brown's mysteries feature a Corgi and a cat.

Acquainting Yourself with Agility Sources

Do you want your Bulldog to be quick and clever? Well, he's not going to be the fastest of all the breeds, but to help with his agility, check out these helpful resources:

✔ The United States Dog Agility Association (USDAA) promotes the international standards in dog agility. For the complete text of the official rules and regulations, visit www.usdaa. com/rulesReg_eBook.cfm.

✔ The North American Dog Agility Council (NADAC) lists its information at www.nadac.com/rules.htm.

✔ If you're not particularly competitive, but you'd like to enjoy agility anyway, consider *Just for Fun: Dog Agility For the Rest of Us*. Check out the Web site, www.dogwoodagility.com/ JustForFun.html.

✔ For advice on training for agility, try the book *Having Fun with Agility*, by Margaret Bonham. The guide is easy to read and understand, and may be just what you need to get you and your Bully started in agility. For more information on Bonham's book or agility according to Bonham, visit www.havingfun withagility.com.

Pursuing Holistic Medicine

You may pursue holistic medicine for your Bulldog for personal reasons or for general relief from chronic disease. With holistic medicine, the possibility exists to reduce medications, which in turn reduces side effects and improves your pet's health.

Acupuncture is one component of holistic medicine. The International Veterinary Acupuncture Society is a nonprofit organization with a Web site that can help you find a certified veterinary acupuncturist in your area. Visit www.ivas.org for an acupuncturist directory.

Homeopathy, another part of holistic medicine, is a system of treating disease based on the administration of small doses of a drug that in massive amounts would produce symptoms in healthy individuals similar to those of the disease itself. For further information, you can visit www.holisticdog.org or www.alternativesfor animals.com, or contact your local veterinarian's office.

Rescuing Bulldogs

Hundreds of sources exist in print and on the Internet as references for rescuing Bulldogs. Every year many Bulldogs are placed in rescue organizations' care because their owners have mistreated, abandoned, or forfeited their right to their pets. If you want to be part of these kind of organizations or wish to receive your Bulldog through rescue, try perusing the following Web sites to get the process started:

- Cascade Bulldog Rescue, www.cascadebulldogrescue.org
- Long Island Bulldog Club, libcrescue.tripod.com
- On the Rebound Bulldog Rescue Foundation, www.onthe rebound.org
- Smoky Mountains Bulldog Rescue, www.discoveret.org/ smbc/rescue.htm
- The Bulldog Club of America, www.rescuebulldogs.org

Recovering Lost Bulldogs

AKC Companion Animal Recovery (AKC CAR), at www.akccar.org, gives you information to enroll your Bulldog in its program. AKC CAR keeps track of your dog's microchip number, as well as information on how to reach you should someone find your dog. All animals are eligible for enrollment in AKC CAR regardless of identification brand or type, or microchip, tattoo, or AKC CAR collar tag. The AKC CAR database stores close to 3 million enrollment records and has been used to perform nearly 300,000 recoveries If you have questions about the program or need to update your records, e-mail Found@akc.org.

Providing for Your Bulldog When You Can't

A time may come when you are no longer able to care for your Bully. As sad as that day may be, you owe it to your dog to plan ahead. Who will take care of your Bulldog in the case of your death? What will you do if you are physically unable to meet the daily needs of your dog? Death or losing our capability to take care of our dogs is not something any of us likes to think about, but thinking about your future and the future of your Bully is the responsible method of long-term care.

Many sources are now offering information and help to pet owners facing this dilemma, offering information about shelters and sanctuaries, as well as explanations of trusts and wills. The Washington State University Office of Veterinary Medicine and the Kansas State University College of Veterinary Medicine are only two examples of places you can contact for more information. Their Web sites can be found at:

> Washington State University Office of Veterinary Medicine, www.vetmed.wsu.edu/depts-prd/pc.asp

> Kansas State University College of Veterinary Medicine, www.vet.ksu.edu/depts/development/perpet/program.htm

Lisa Rogak's book *PerPETual Care: Who Will Look After Your Pets If You're Not Around?* (Williams Hill) also provides useful information on this subject.

Chapter 18

Ten Good Reasons for Not Breeding Your Bulldog

*Y*our Bulldog's biological clock is not ticking. Having puppies does not "fulfill" your bitch or "complete" your male. Breeding may make you feel good and instill a sense of pride in your dog, but that's a selfish reason to breed your Bully. And because Bulldogs are bred artificially, "What's love got to do with it?" (to quote Tina Turner). Absolutely nothing! For Bulldogs especially, breeding comes with a huge set of complications, which are covered in this chapter. Before you get your heart set on breeding your Bulldog, please read this chapter.

Assessing the Health Risks to Your Bulldog

Male Bulldogs who have not been neutered have a greater chance for testicular tumors and prostate cancer. Risks of mammary tumors and ovarian cancer increase in females who remain unspayed. Females frequently get bladder infections following a heat cycle. *Pyometra,* which can be a fatal ailment for female Bulldogs, is an infection of the uterus, more specifically an accumulation of pus in the uterine cavity. Medical treatment can be lengthy, expensive, and often unsuccessful. Spaying a bitch with Pyometra can cost over $1,000. Spaying your puppy, on the other hand, is closer to $200. Spaying your puppy is an important step in prevention and will also save you money.

Dealing with Behavior Problems

An intact male may want to mark his territory, which can include the corner of your sofa or the brand-new pair of shoes you bought last week. Intact males can be more aggressive when defending their right to a female in heat. Females in season may be a bit cranky as well, aggressively attacking other females.

Having to Separate Your Love Birds (1 Mean Bulldogs)

If you have Bulldogs of both sexes, you may want to board one or the other of the dogs while the bitch is in season, adding another price between $200 and $1,000 for at least 3 weeks of boarding each year.

Tackling the Messier Details

If your bitch is in season, you may want to confine her to one area with a washable floor instead of letting her have access to the imported oriental rug. Otherwise, you may be following your Bully around with a bucket of soap and water to clean up after her. Who has that much time? One alternative to doggy solitary confinement include using doggy diapers. Washable diapers run about $20 apiece. Sanitary panties have a place to insert a sanitary pad. These panties cost between $15 and $20. Pads cost around $5 for 10 or 15, depending on where you shop. Not cheap!

Because of the way Bulldogs are built, they can't reach to clean themselves. You have to keep your dog clean. Also keep in mind that some females can develop an intense hormonal smell (frankly, they can really reek!). Regular attention to your dog's hygiene will help her stench go away.

Testing, Testing, and More Testing

Make sure that your bitch is ready to be bred. Tests need to be run, above and beyond any health checks that you decide to do, before breeding. Don't forget the cost of the actual insemination:

✔ Progesterone testing and vaginal smears usually run $80 to $100 each, with four to six tests needed per breeding.

✔ Artificial insemination usually costs $100 to $300. This includes only the insemination process, not the cost of the actual semen!

It's the Human Who Becomes the "Mommy," Not the Bulldog!

Bulldog puppies are hand raised. Having a bitch with puppies is a time-consuming process with any breed, but with Bulldogs, the amount of time is even greater. Say goodbye to your vacation on a tropical island, because the time off is essential for you to raise your new puppies. If the bitch has milk, she needs to nurse her litter, but you need to get up every 2 or 3 hours to put the puppies on the nipples. Make sure that all the puppies suck properly. Hold each one, and let the mother clean them after they've eaten. If you're thinking that you already don't have enough time for the process, let alone vacation time, think about hiring someone to take care of the puppies (add a sitter to your list of costs).

The puppies need to be in a separate box to prevent the mother from accidentally lying on them. If the mother doesn't accept them for nursing and cleaning, you need to do the entire job, from bottle or tube feeding to using a cotton ball to stimulate them to defecate and urinate.

Three (Or More) Is a Crowd

Before the puppies were born, you may have thought you had homes for those puppies, but things can change. Remember, those puppies are your responsibility. If you can't find homes for two or three . . . or four puppies, you must care for them until you do. That means separate crates, vaccinations, beginning to housetrain them, and the work of socializing those puppies, not to mention food and cleanup.

If you breed your Bulldog, you must be prepared to care for the puppies you produce!

Bulldog Breeding Is More Technical than Natural

Bulldogs are rarely ever bred naturally. Breeding occurs completely through artificial insemination, which is a costly fee. You also pay to have the semen (fresh, chilled, or frozen) shipped. Collecting and shipping fees are in addition to whatever stud fees you've agreed upon.

Subjecting Your Dog to Cesarean Section

Bulldog puppies are delivered by Cesarean section (C-section) — another veterinary bill for your files, this time, anywhere from $600 to $2,500, depending on where you live and how complicated the operation becomes. Also, vets don't guarantee any live puppies from a Cesarean section. Either way, you pay.

Adding Up the Bill

This chapter covers a lot about Bulldog breeding that costs a lot of money, but have you considered how big the bill is when you add up these costs? These costs can have a real financial impact! Consider the list, and add away:

- **Common health ailments from breeding (including cost for treatment and removal of tumors):**
  - Mammary tumors: $300 and up
  - Testicular tumors: $350 and up
  - Prostate problems: $300 and up
- **Spaying** ($100 to $200) **or neutering** ($75 to $150)
- **Boarding:** $200 to $1,000 twice a year
- **Dog supplies (Doggie diapers, milk, cotton balls; the hidden extras):**
  - Diapers: $20
  - Sanitary pads per season: $25
  - Whelping box: $30 to $75, depending on whether you make it or buy it

- Hard-sided kiddy wading pool: $5 to $10

- Supplemental puppy formula: $30 for 28-ounce size dry

- Small nursing bottle with four nipples: $3.50. (Extra nipples: $3.)

- Heating pad or heat lamp: $20 to $30

✔ **Artificial insemination, including office visit, vaginal smear, progesterone testing:** Anywhere from $145 to $250. You usually do this at least twice, so double those figures.

✔ **Collecting and shipping chilled semen:** $180 to $250.

✔ **Surgical implantation, if using frozen semen:** $300

✔ **Stud fees:** $500 to $1,000 (generally nonrefundable)

✔ **Health checks for breeding:**

- Vaginal smears and progesterone testing: $80 to $100 up to six times

- Physical, including blood work: $65 to $150

✔ **C-section:** $600 to $2,500.

Facing the Likelihood of Heartbreak

Breeding is not for the faint of heart. You may lose puppies — some before you get to know them. You work and worry and fuss over a puppy, and she may die anyway. Sometimes it's not the puppy who dies, but the mother. Are you willing to risk losing the girl you've had since she was a puppy? Are you prepared to give up sloppy kisses and cuddling on the couch? As expensive as purchasing a Bulldog puppy may be, it's much easier to write checks for purchase and spaying or neutering than to breed a litter.

As bad as it is to lose a puppy, losing the mother is heartbreaking, and that is a danger every time you breed. One breeder, after a particularly hard whelping, said if she could find the person who told her breeding was fun, she'd "nail him to a tree." Another friend, with a different breed, had a bitch who was just huge with puppies. As she was talking to her veterinarian on the phone, discussing having a C-section, because of the size of the coming litter, she heard a thud. The bitch had dropped dead; the mass of puppies pressing on her heart had been too much for her.

An intact male that is used at stud is more apt to mark his territory in the house and more likely to be aggressive toward other males. There is the risk of testicular tumors and prostate problems. Using a dog at stud is not like an anonymous sperm bank. Breeders want a dog that fits the standard, and generally, they want to breed to a champion. That means spending the time and money to go to enough shows to earn the points needed to win that title. And there are still the time and effort needed to collect the semen and have it chilled or frozen and shipped.

Good breeders know the danger signs of a bitch in whelp not doing well. It is very hard-won knowledge. Reputable breeders try to discourage people who just want a pet from breeding for all the above reasons.

Chapter 19

Ten Important Things to Do for Your Bulldog

*O*f course, there are many things you should do for your Bulldog to keep him (and you!) healthy and happy, but sometimes it's easy to fall into habits and forget about some of these things. This chapter covers ten important things that you should always remember to do in order to get the best out of your relationship with your Bulldog.

Cleaning Your Bully's Collar

It's not something people think of much, but daily wear can really dirty a collar, and pet owners tend to forget that fact. Imagine wearing a shirt or blouse day after day without washing it. Then imagine the collar. (They don't call it "ring around the collar" for nothing.)

Scrub and clean leather collars with saddle soap, which is usually sold with shoe-polish products, and nylon collars with hand soap. A bit of shampoo also works well at cutting the grease, and an old toothbrush makes a good brush (but don't put it back in the bathroom when you're finished).

Washing the Food and Water Dishes

Sometimes food and water dishes get neglected because the food dish, especially, is licked clean. Put yourself at the dining-room table, stuffed from the great home cooking. Now imagine each family member licking his or her plate after dinner and placing the dish back in the cabinet. Would the plates really be clean? Your Bulldog doesn't ask for much. Give him clean dishes. Stainless steel is the best choice, because ceramic dishes may have lead-based glaze or paint and plastic dishes may become chew toys.

Freshening Your Bulldog's Bed

Just like your own bedsheets, dog beds need to be washed. Aside from dirt from paws and tummy, a bed can harbor fleas and flea eggs. Remember, don't overdo the soap because excess soap can make your Bully itch. A splash of bleach in the wash water helps kill germs and freshen the bedding.

Vaccinating Your Bulldog

Even if you don't legally need the shot, as with a rabies shot, there are preventive vaccines that can help your Bulldog live a longer life. Talk to your veterinarian about the proper shots for your dog. For more vaccination information, refer to Chapter 13.

Grooming Your Bulldog

Grooming is fairly easy with a Bulldog. You can even groom while watching television (you can watch dog shows together). At least once a week, cleanse all your dog's wrinkles, and rinse out her ears. Don't forget your Bully's tail, especially if it has a pocket of skin around the base. A bit of Vaseline in the pocket can help prevent irritation. Refer to Chapter 8 for advice on how to groom your Bully properly.

Every year, Bulldog rescue groups receive many dogs with severe infections under the tail. Gently wiping this area helps but doesn't prevent all problems. Once again, Vaseline is very good at helping prevent trouble. It should be applied once or twice a week, more often if needed, and after every bath.

Get your vet to recommend a good ear cleaner. Wrinkles can be kept clean by gently wiping and then immediately applying some Vaseline. It acts as a moisture barrier and is very safe. Nail trimming is important too!

Exercising Together

You may not run marathons with your Bully (and you have to be careful she doesn't overheat), but she does benefit (as will you) from a brisk walk around the block. Play a game of fetch with her favorite toy, and think about mental exercise too. Play hide-and-seek or tag. Hide a toy, and have her find it. Exercising and games also increase the bond between you and your Bully because it is valuable time spent one on one.

Balancing Your Bulldog's Diet

Does your Bulldog need to go on a diet? Is a balanced diet part of your bully's routine? Your Bulldog can't choose his own diet; he depends on you to feed him what he needs. Table scraps — people food — may be the worst thing you can give him, even if it's what he likes best (which it wouldn't be if you never started in the first place). Ask your veterinarian about the ideal weight for your dog. Pay attention to your Bulldog's coat and overall condition. The food you're feeding him may be perfect, or he may need a change.

Keeping Up to Date on Bully Information

If you don't have a Bulldog, but you're thinking of getting one, consider the lifestyles of both you and a Bulldog before you get your Bully. If you already have a Bulldog, read all that you can about the breed. The more you know, the more you understand about Bulldog health and about how your pet behaves. If there's a local Bulldog club in your area, join. Research is another step to falling in love with your Bulldog.

Forgiving His Behavior

Forgiveness doesn't mean giving up on training or not petproofing your house, but don't lose your temper if an accident (or two) happens. Dogs shed. Puppies chew. How important is the dining-room table leg, really? How much love do you get from the table? Now think about how much love you receive from your puppy. You may regard the tooth marks fondly when your Bully is old and gray. You can have a perfect house, or you can have a Bulldog. I vote for the Bulldog.

Simply Enjoying Your Bully

Set aside time every day to play with your Bully. Watch the way she entertains herself, and supply a safe environment and appropriate toys. Take your Bulldog (on a leash, of course) to the pet store with you. Let her explore and pick out a new toy. Remember why you decided to get her and what a short time you may have her. With few exceptions, most of us outlive our dogs. Give your Bully your best, every day.

Index

• C •

BUSINESS, CAREERS & PERSONAL FINANCE

0-7645-5307-0

0-7645-5331-3 *†

Also available:

- Accounting For Dummies †
0-7645-5314-3
- Business Plans Kit For Dummies †
0-7645-5365-8
- Cover Letters For Dummies
0-7645-5224-4
- Frugal Living For Dummies
0-7645-5403-4
- Leadership For Dummies
0-7645-5176-0
- Managing For Dummies
0-7645-1771-6

- Marketing For Dummies
0-7645-5600-2
- Personal Finance For Dummies *
0-7645-2590-5
- Project Management
For Dummies
0-7645-5283-X
- Resumes For Dummies †
0-7645-5471-9
- Selling For Dummies
0-7645-5363-1
- Small Business Kit For Dummies *†
0-7645-5093-4

HOME & BUSINESS COMPUTER BASICS

0-7645-4074-2

0-7645-3758-X

Also available:

- ACT! 6 For Dummies
0-7645-2645-6
- iLife '04 All-in-One Desk Reference
For Dummies
0-7645-7347-0
- iPAQ For Dummies
0-7645-6769-1
- Mac OS X Panther Timesaving
Techniques For Dummies
0-7645-5812-9
- Macs For Dummies
0-7645-5656-8
- Microsoft Money 2004 For Dummies
0-7645-4195-1

- Office 2003 All-in-One Desk
Reference For Dummies
0-7645-3883-7
- Outlook 2003 For Dummies
0-7645-3759-8
- PCs For Dummies
0-7645-4074-2
- TiVo For Dummies
0-7645-6923-6
- Upgrading and Fixing PCs
For Dummies
0-7645-1665-5
- Windows XP Timesaving
Techniques For Dummies
0-7645-3748-2

FOOD, HOME, GARDEN, HOBBIES, MUSIC & PETS

0-7645-5295-3

0-7645-5232-5

Also available:

- Bass Guitar For Dummies
0-7645-2487-9
- Diabetes Cookbook For Dummies
0-7645-5230-9
- Gardening For Dummies *
0-7645-5130-2
- Guitar For Dummies
0-7645-5106-X
- Holiday Decorating For Dummies
0-7645-2570-0
- Home Improvement All-in-One
For Dummies
0-7645-5680-0

- Knitting For Dummies
0-7645-5395-X
- Piano For Dummies
0-7645-5105-1
- Puppies For Dummies
0-7645-5255-4
- Scrapbooking For Dummies
0-7645-7208-3
- Senior Dogs For Dummies
0-7645-5818-8
- Singing For Dummies
0-7645-2475-5
- 30-Minute Meals For Dummies
0-7645-2589-1

INTERNET & DIGITAL MEDIA

0-7645-1664-7

0-7645-6924-4

Also available:

- 2005 Online Shopping Directory
For Dummies
0-7645-7495-7
- CD & DVD Recording For Dummies
0-7645-5956-7
- eBay For Dummies
0-7645-5654-1
- Fighting Spam For Dummies
0-7645-5965-6
- Genealogy Online For Dummies
0-7645-5964-8
- Google For Dummies
0-7645-4420-9

- Home Recording For Musicians
For Dummies
0-7645-1634-5
- The Internet For Dummies
0-7645-4173-0
- iPod & iTunes For Dummies
0-7645-7772-7
- Preventing Identity Theft
For Dummies
0-7645-7336-5
- Pro Tools All-in-One Desk
Reference For Dummies
0-7645-5714-9
- Roxio Easy Media Creator
For Dummies
0-7645-7131-1

SPORTS, FITNESS, PARENTING, RELIGION & SPIRITUALITY

0-7645-5146-9

0-7645-5418-2

Also available:
- Adoption For Dummies
  0-7645-5488-3
- Basketball For Dummies
  0-7645-5248-1
- The Bible For Dummies
  0-7645-5296-1
- Buddhism For Dummies
  0-7645-5359-3
- Catholicism For Dummies
  0-7645-5391-7
- Hockey For Dummies
  0-7645-5228-7

- Judaism For Dummies
  0-7645-5299-6
- Martial Arts For Dummies
  0-7645-5358-5
- Pilates For Dummies
  0-7645-5397-6
- Religion For Dummies
  0-7645-5264-3
- Teaching Kids to Read
  For Dummies
  0-7645-4043-2
- Weight Training For Dummies
  0-7645-5168-X
- Yoga For Dummies
  0-7645-5117-5

TRAVEL

0-7645-5438-7

0-7645-5453-0

Also available:
- Alaska For Dummies
  0-7645-1761-9
- Arizona For Dummies
  0-7645-6938-4
- Cancún and the Yucatán
  For Dummies
  0-7645-2437-2
- Cruise Vacations For Dummies
  0-7645-6941-4
- Europe For Dummies
  0-7645-5456-5
- Ireland For Dummies
  0-7645-5455-7

- Las Vegas For Dummies
  0-7645-5448-4
- London For Dummies
  0-7645-4277-X
- New York City For Dummies
  0-7645-6945-7
- Paris For Dummies
  0-7645-5494-8
- RV Vacations For Dummies
  0-7645-5443-3
- Walt Disney World & Orlando
  For Dummies
  0-7645-6943-0

GRAPHICS, DESIGN & WEB DEVELOPMENT

0-7645-4345-8

0-7645-5589-8

Also available:
- Adobe Acrobat 6 PDF
  For Dummies
  0-7645-3760-1
- Building a Web Site For Dummies
  0-7645-7144-3
- Dreamweaver MX 2004
  For Dummies
  0-7645-4342-3
- FrontPage 2003 For Dummies
  0-7645-3882-9
- HTML 4 For Dummies
  0-7645-1995-6
- Illustrator cs For Dummies
  0-7645-4084-X

- Macromedia Flash MX 2004
  For Dummies
  0-7645-4358-X
- Photoshop 7 All-in-One Desk
  Reference For Dummies
  0-7645-1667-1
- Photoshop cs Timesaving
  Techniques For Dummies
  0-7645-6782-9
- PHP 5 For Dummies
  0-7645-4166-8
- PowerPoint 2003 For Dummies
  0-7645-3908-6
- QuarkXPress 6 For Dummies
  0-7645-2593-X

NETWORKING, SECURITY, PROGRAMMING & DATABASES

0-7645-6852-3

0-7645-5784-X

Also available:
- A+ Certification For Dummies
  0-7645-4187-0
- Access 2003 All-in-One Desk
  Reference For Dummies
  0-7645-3988-4
- Beginning Programming
  For Dummies
  0-7645-4997-9
- C For Dummies
  0-7645-7068-4
- Firewalls For Dummies
  0-7645-4048-3
- Home Networking For Dummies
  0-7645-42796

- Network Security For Dummies
  0-7645-1679-5
- Networking For Dummies
  0-7645-1677-9
- TCP/IP For Dummies
  0-7645-1760-0
- VBA For Dummies
  0-7645-3989-2
- Wireless All In-One Desk Reference
  For Dummies
  0-7645-7496-5
- Wireless Home Networking
  For Dummies
  0-7645-3910-8

HEALTH & SELF-HELP

0-7645-6820-5 *†   0-7645-2566-2

Also available:

✔Alzheimer's For Dummies
0-7645-3899-3

✔Asthma For Dummies
0-7645-4233-8

✔Controlling Cholesterol For Dummies
0-7645-5440-9

✔Depression For Dummies
0-7645-3900-0

✔Dieting For Dummies
0-7645-4149-8

✔Fertility For Dummies
0-7645-2549-2

✔Fibromyalgia For Dummies
0-7645-5441-7

✔Improving Your Memory For Dummies
0-7645-5435-2

✔Pregnancy For Dummies †
0-7645-4483-7

✔Quitting Smoking For Dummies
0-7645-2629-4

✔Relationships For Dummies
0-7645-5384-4

✔Thyroid For Dummies
0-7645-5385-2

EDUCATION, HISTORY, REFERENCE & TEST PREPARATION

 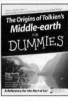

0-7645-5194-9   0-7645-4186-2

Also available:

✔Algebra For Dummies
0-7645-5325-9

✔British History For Dummies
0-7645-7021-8

✔Calculus For Dummies
0-7645-2498-4

✔English Grammar For Dummies
0-7645-5322-4

✔Forensics For Dummies
0-7645-5580-4

✔The GMAT For Dummies
0-7645-5251-1

✔Inglés Para Dummies
0-7645-5427-1

✔Italian For Dummies
0-7645-5196-5

✔Latin For Dummies
0-7645-5431-X

✔Lewis & Clark For Dummies
0-7645-2545-X

✔Research Papers For Dummies
0-7645-5426-3

✔The SAT I For Dummies
0-7645-7193-1

✔Science Fair Projects For Dummies
0-7645-5460-3

✔U.S. History For Dummies
0-7645-5249-X

Get smart @ dummies.com®

- **Find a full list of Dummies titles**
- **Look into loads of FREE on-site articles**
- **Sign up for FREE eTips e-mailed to you weekly**
- **See what other products carry the Dummies name**
- **Shop directly from the Dummies bookstore**
- **Enter to win new prizes every month!**

* Separate Canadian edition also available
† Separate U.K. edition also available

Available wherever books are sold. For more information or to order direct: U.S. customers visit www.dummies.com or call 1-877-762-2974.
U.K. customers visit www.wileyeurope.com or call 0800 243407. Canadian customers visit www.wiley.ca or call 1-800-567-4797.